The Trib

DEDICATION

To you, the reader. And to journalists everywhere, whose work one day reflects the thoughts of a nation … and the next is consigned to history's litter-tray. We salute you.

ACKNOWLEDGEMENTS

Thanks to Diarmuid Doyle for contacting and (gently) harrying the Trib staffers and reading the final proof. His calm advice and help in general were hugely appreciated. He sends his love to his wife, Elaine Edwards, and parents Joe and Kay.

Chenile and Robert at Y Books: this project wouldn't have worked without your vision, skill, patience and preternatural niceness.

To all those I chased and hassled: thank you for your time and generosity – in particular to John Boyne. Thanks also to my roadie, Gráinne Kenny, and family friend, Dr Richard Fitzpatrick.

Finally, and most importantly, my thanks and love go to my long-suffering wife Gillian Carroll. Your halo is in the post.

David Kenny

Highlights from
The Sunday Tribune

Edited by
NÓIRÍN HEGARTY

First published in 2011 by Y Books
Lucan, Co. Dublin
Ireland
Tel & fax: +353 1 621 7992
publishing@ybooks.ie
www.ybooks.ie
Follow us on Twitter @ybookstweets and join us on Facebook.

Text © by individual contributors
The Trib concept and compilation © David Kenny
Design and layout © 2011 Y Books
All photographs © Mark Condren

Paperback	ISBN: 978-1-908023-21-6
Ebook - mobi format	ISBN: 978-1-908023-22-3
Ebook - epub format	ISBN: 978-1-908023-23-0

A CIP catalogue record for this book is available from the British Library.

10 9 8 7 6 5 4 3 2 1

Typeset by Y Books
Cover design by Graham Thew Design
Front and back cover images courtesy of Mark Condren
Printed and bound in the UK by CPI Mackays, Chatham ME5 8TD

General Editor's note

An ink-veined editor once told me: 'Great journalism is no guarantee of success – or survival – in the newspaper business.' He then claimed it was my round, told me I was fired (although I didn't work for him) and ordered me to phone him a cab home. Whatever about the round, he was right about journalism. We had been talking about the *Irish Press* and the conversation had, inevitably, turned to the perpetually struggling *Sunday Tribune*, where I worked at the time.

When the Press Group closed in 1995, some of the finest journalism ever produced in these islands wound up on history's 'spike'. In February of this year, the *Tribune* looked destined for the same fate. Thirty years of journalistic excellence would gather dust in the National Library. The public would soon forget the *Trib*'s strident, honest voice.

In March, I floated the idea for this book with Y Books. How about a compilation of best bits from Nóirín Hegarty's tenure as editor? The timeframe would be 2005 to 2011, six of the most eventful years in recent history. We would ask the writers to choose four of their favourite articles. 'I'll whittle them down into a book,' I said. It sounded so straightforward at the time.

Soon my desktop was groaning under the weight of several hundred thousand words. Having such a wealth of top-quality material made the read-through one of the most enjoyable tasks imaginable. Having finite space made the editing process one of the most painful. Inclusion was eventually based on striking the right balance between human interest, analysis and humour. The positioning of columns and bylines doesn't denote any pre-eminence. This book is intended to be dipped into, not read from cover to cover.

These are the pieces the journalists most want you to read, and as a result *The Trib* is a kind of emotional bookmark – something that will prompt you to say: 'Oh, I'd forgotten about that,' and remind you of a moment or a buried feeling. Hopefully, it will engross you enough to make you miss your bus stop.

The Trib is dedicated to the only person who matters in the production of a newspaper: you, the reader, without whom we wouldn't exist. Or get paid. We hope you enjoy reading it as much as we enjoyed writing it.

David Kenny
June 2011

CONTENTS

Nóirín Hegarty

Foreword

It started with a phone call. Michael Roche's name flashed on the screen of my mobile. It was just after 8 p.m. on St Stephen's Day 2004.

'You know I've always valued you highly,' he began. It was news to me. Michael and I had enjoyed an adversarial professional relationship. His role as managing editor of Independent Newspapers was to limit expenditure, mine as deputy editor of the *Evening Herald* was to secure as much of the budget as I could.

'I'm going into the *Sunday Tribune* as managing director. I want you to be my editor.' I wasn't surprised. I was utterly stunned. 'You've hidden your admiration well,' I remember answering. The call ended with an instruction to keep our conversation top secret. We would meet in the coming days to thrash out the details.

My husband Frank came into the kitchen. I was still staring at the mobile phone in my hand. 'I'm going to be an editor,' I told him. He knew how badly I wanted this chance and how much it meant to me.

I had experience of many editorial environments, good and bad, and I knew that I wanted to do things differently. Just over a month later, in my maiden speech to the *Sunday Tribune* journalists I told them so. I wanted to preside over a meritocracy. I wanted to build a creative environment where entrepreneurial journalism was critical. They would work with me, not for me, and we would create a quality newspaper together.

Most of them just looked at me dumbfounded. I thought that everybody understood how detrimental tyrannies are to good journalism, but I forgot that most people at the *Sunday Tribune* had no such experience and didn't know what I was talking about. They were much more concerned that this unknown woman from the 'tabloid' *Evening Herald* would barrel in and wreck the newspaper they loved.

The early weeks in any new job are daunting. I was lucky. From day one I had a quiet, reliable, and wise counsel on my side in the shape of *Tribune* 'lifer', deputy editor Diarmuid Doyle. For the next six years he never wavered in his loyalty and support, and without it I would have been much the poorer.

The newspaper set up was schizophrenic. We had too many feature writers in specialist areas and too few news hounds. I had not one, but two previous editors looking over my shoulder – one at the far end of the newsroom who had just vacated my new office but remained working at the newspaper, and the other employed as a columnist.

Change had to be radical but could not cause consternation. Professional systems had to be put in place. We had to break stories, build credibility, and get some attention. The way the newspaper had been doing things wasn't working, so we had to do things differently. Some big names had to go and some new names had to come in.

Budgets were always tight and on many occasions huge sacrifices had to be made in order to attract fresh talent and ability. I saw it as a marriage between the high-quality writers traditionally associated with the *Tribune* and the new era. The only objective was excellence.

There were losses along the way – good people I had to make redundant for cost reasons. It was difficult, heartbreaking at times, but I had to concentrate on building a future for the people in jobs rather than focusing on the ones who had to lose out.

In spite of the limited resources, imagination was in ready supply, and when the economic picture darkened we became more and more inventive.

Everybody remembers the big stories the *Sunday Tribune* broke – John O'Donoghue, George Gibney, the Real IRA, Sean Quinn – and for those we have received much recognition. They are the easy ones. The real slog is in producing a relevant, exciting newspaper week after week no matter what. That achievement is credited to a top-class team of department heads. Deputy editor PJ Cunningham, who joined us that first year, greatly enhanced the newspaper and my term as editor with his strategic approach to management, sport and the newspaper business in general.

My best achievement was to assemble a team that far outshone my ability and made my job easy. Mick McCaffrey in News, Fionnuala McCarthy in Features, Maureen Gillespie in Photographic, Olivia Doyle in Arts, Neil Callanan in Business, Helen Rogers in News Analysis and chief sub editor Ger Siggins ran top-class departments and inspired all they worked with.

We made mistakes along the way, but we never wavered in our quest to become the best we could be. And in the pages that follow you will read the work of journalists who achieved that week after week.

Some good people left for new pastures – Stephen Collins, Kevin Rafter, Justine McCarthy, Emmet Oliver, Paul Howard to name just a few. I never liked to see them go, but I understood why they did, especially as our financial problems mounted.

When the end came it was via another phone call on the morning of 1 February 2011. I was in bed recovering from a chest infection when Michael Roche's name flashed on my screen. We had shared good and bad times in the intervening six years, but this time I had an ominous premonition.

'The day has come.' It was all he needed to say. I understood immediately. There was no reason for the *Sunday Tribune* to close now rather than at any other time in the previous twenty years of non profit. Michael and financial controller Fiona Falvey had managed our affairs better than anybody else could have, but there was no surviving Ireland's economic collapse.

As bad as it was facing into an announcement by the newly appointed receiver, Jim Luby, that we were in serious trouble, it was even worse twenty-four hours later when he told us that prohibitive libel insurance meant that we wouldn't be publishing again.

For the first week there was hope we would find a buyer. But as the days passed, reality dawned and then settled like a dark cloud. For the wind-down period journalists, advertising and circulation staff shared tribulations. Redundancy has no hierarchy and by 1 March we were all out of a job.

The greatest testament to the talent of the *Sunday Tribune* team across all sections is that they are continuing to find work – some achievement in the current climate.

The six years I was in charge as editor were the best of my professional life. We built a credible, vibrant newspaper through entrepreneurial journalism, a commitment to quality and drive. And we did it despite everything.

My thanks for conceiving and compiling this eclectic mixture of the best of the *Sunday Tribune* go to columnist and former associate editor, David Kenny.

And I will never forget the team who made it all work: PJ Cunningham, Diarmuid Doyle, Fionnuala McCarthy, Neil Callanan, Claire O'Mahony, Eamon Quinn, Ian Guider, Jon Ihle, Olivia Doyle, Ciaran Carty, Una Mullally, Martin Brennan, Suzanne Breen, Helen Rogers, Dave Kenny, Mark Condren, Joe Coyle, Paul Lynch, Gavin Corbett, Neil Dunphy, Ger Siggins, Mick McCaffrey, Maureen Gillespie, John Downes, Ken Foxe, Jennifer Bray, Ali Bracken, Mick Clifford, Shane Coleman, Conor McMorrow, Martin Frawley, Valerie Shanley, Mark Hilliard, Katy McGuinness, Ciara Elliot, Malachy Clerkin, Deirdre Sheeran, John Foley, Ewan McKenna, Miguel Delaney, Enda McEvoy, Liam Hayes, Neil Francis, Kieran Shannon, Ciaran Cronin, Eoghan Morrissey, Patrick Freyne, Eithne Tynan, Tom Dunne, Colm O'Grady, Celine Moran, Lisa Reilly, Lisa McGowan, Shana Wilkie, Nicola Cooke, Donna Ahern, Claire Dunne, Shane McDonnell, Ken Sweeney, Roisin Carabine, June Edwards, Julie Lordan, Ros Dee, Rita Byrne, Bea McMunn, Anne Marie Hourihane, Derek McKenna and Brian Hopkins. Niamh Roth, Ray O'Connor, Jim Clancy, Fiona Falvey and Michael Roche.

It was a hell of an adventure.

Nóirín Hegarty

June 2011

NEWS ANALYSIS

Diarmuid Doyle

Bertie is out of public sight but it's never been more important to keep an eye on him ...

9 January 2011

Brian Cowen was far more generous than he needed to be. Bertie Ahern, he said in a long statement of tribute to his predecessor, was the consummate politician of his generation, 'a person of rare ability and extraordinary talent'. Speaking after Ahern had announced he would not be running in the next election, Cowen waxed eloquent about the former taoiseach's 'immense work ethic' and superb negotiating skills. 'His fellow countrymen and women will always hold him in high esteem,' he concluded.

Ahern, of course, is currently one of our most toxic assets, so Cowen's willingness to speak of him in such glowing terms was politically risky and uncommonly decent. The past few weeks have been marked by increasingly routine and bland statements from the Taoiseach paying tribute to the latest rats to desert his sinking ship, and he would have got away with something similar on Ahern's retirement. Instead he opted for glowing tribute.

Three days later, as we all know now, he got his reward when Ahern, in his role as highly-paid media whore, went on the attack in the *News of The World*. Cowen was presented as a man of many mistakes, somebody whose main fault was that he didn't do it Bertie's way. From the chief political culprit for the economic downturn, it was farcically deluded and very nasty, although a timely reminder of the bile and bitterness which lies beneath that old Bertie bonhomie.

Timely, because Ahern cannot yet be consigned to history. In fact, now that he will be out of public sight, it has never been more important to keep an eye on him. He remains a menace and a threat to Ireland's prosperity through his significant, but little commented on, position as chairman of the International Forestry Fund.

So far, only the *Sunday Tribune* among the country's newspapers has paid close attention to Ahern's role in this private company. Independent TD Maureen O'Sullivan has asked a Dáil question, and Sinn Féin's Martin Ferris has thrown a few shapes about the former taoiseach's latest gig. But, as with John O'Donoghue's expenses a few years ago, it is taking the political classes a while to wake up to this issue.

Although the International Forestry Fund sounds like a vaguely cuddly group, which loves trees the way some of us love kittens, it is in fact a very profit-conscious joint venture between two private asset management companies, Helvetia Wealth and IFS Asset Managers Limited. It makes its money by acquiring existing forests on behalf of investors. As it says on its website, Helvetia has 1.1 billion Swiss Francs (€867 million) in assets 'following a number of very successful acquisitions in the UK, Germany and Ireland'. IFS currently manages in excess of €100 million of forestry assets on behalf of 18,000 private and corporate clients in this country.

In Ireland, most of our trees and forests belong to the state agency Coillte, which owns more than one million acres of land – about 7 per cent of Irish land cover. In July last year, Colm McCarthy issued his 'An Bord Snip Nua' report in which he suggested, among other ideas, that the government look at flogging Coillte as part of a mass sell-off of state assets.

This obviously piqued the interest of the cash-rich International Forestry Fund and five months later it announced that Bertie Ahern had been appointed as its chairman. 'Mr Ahern implemented bold economic initiatives that included corporate tax incentives and education reform', the Fund said at the time. 'His efforts laid out a welcome mat for international corporations, making Ireland an attractive location for foreign companies'.

Indeed. Seven months after that, in July 2010, McCarthy was given a new job – to look in more depth at the idea of selling off the state assets he had mentioned in his 2009 report. One of the companies specifically targeted was Coillte.

By now, the International Forestry Fund, with Bertie Ahern firmly ensconced at the top, was salivating at the prospect of getting its hands on Coillte and the 7 per cent of Ireland that comes with it. 'We would certainly have an interest in that regard,' Paul Brosnan, the Fund's director, told this newspaper last year. 'We have always had an interest in Coillte. It certainly would not be beyond the bounds of possibility that we would acquire it.'

Of the very many questions that arise from all of this, here are just some: why on earth would we sell 7 per cent of Irish land to private investors? Why is a former taoiseach heading up a company registered in the Virgin Islands that wants to profit from more than one million acres of the country he used to run? How much is he getting for whatever advice or help he will be giving to help secure this grand sell-off? Does the Green Party have anything to say? Will Bertie Ahern make a statement on the issue?

Many of these questions would be irrelevant if Ahern was to resign from the International Forestry Fund, or if the Fund was to confirm that it had no interest whatsoever in Coillte, now, or in the future. Such outcomes seem unlikely, however. The former taoiseach and the company he chairs are apparently both driven by an insatiable greed for money. They are perfect bedfellows.

✦ ✦ ✦

Had Fanning and Kenny been in charge of RTÉ for the week, we might have got some sense of proportion on Gerry Ryan's death

9 May 2010

What will we do when Gay Byrne dies? That day is still many years away, hopefully, but when Gaybo's time comes, how will Ireland mourn the death and celebrate the life of its greatest broadcaster? Now that the Princess Diana treatment – two books of condolences, a plethora of tribute shows, public tears and a live funeral attended by the President – have been given to a popular but much less historically important broadcaster, how do we pay appropriate tribute to the one person in RTÉ's history who might actually deserve such trappings?

To come at the question another way: had Gay Byrne died

suddenly at age fifty-three in 1987, at the height of his brilliant career, would his death have been greeted with the same hysteria that has marked the past week? There would have been shock, obviously, and tributes. But would the wall that separates private grief from public interest have collapsed as spectacularly as it did over the last ten days? Live funerals have traditionally been awarded to presidents and popes, as acknowledgement of their singular role in the histories of their nations. If they are to be handed out purely on the basis of celebrity, or the shock of premature death, or because the deceased worked in the national broadcaster and knew some people, it demeans the honour and renders it meaningless.

The decision to broadcast Ryan's funeral mass live on national radio reflects huge changes in Irish life over the last two decades. Celebrity and achievement are now regarded as sides of the same coin. There is no hierarchy of success. Everybody in the world of celebrity is treated the same way, which is to say nobody is regarded as being better or worse, or as having done a better or worse job, than anybody else. The result, which we've seen since Gerry Ryan's death, is that it becomes impossible for people to judge what is an appropriate tribute when somebody passes on. Hence the unbridled, over-the-top nature of the last week.

The media, naturally, has had a key role in creating the hype and hysteria. Ryan's death received more coverage in some tabloids on the day after his death then the September 11 attacks on the US did on 12 September 2001. The madness continued for more than a week. Even when there was nothing left to say, the media found a thousand different ways to say it. Dave Fanning, clearly devastated by the death of a close friend, seemed taken aback by the hysteria of the media coverage. 'Let's be honest about this,' he said during the week, 'Gerry could be a bollocks too. No question about that. He was self-centred in many ways.'

It was a rare moment of balance in the ongoing deification of Gerry Ryan, from one of the few RTÉ people to behave as though Ryan's death was not about them, but about his wife, children, partner and siblings. Pat Kenny was another. His tribute to Ryan on *The Late Late Show*, in which he described the deceased as one of RTÉ's holy trinity, along with Gay Byrne and Terry Wogan, was as kind and decent as it was wide of the mark. (Byrne definitely, Wogan possibly, Kenny himself maybe, but Gerry Ryan?) Had Fanning and Kenny been in charge of RTÉ for the week, we might have got some sense of proportion on Ryan's death. Instead, all was out-of-control hysteria, which actually did Ryan a huge disservice by completely overplaying his role in broadcasting history.

It wasn't just the media that was to blame, of course. One characteristic of modern living, which some Irish people share with the citizens of the UK and the US, is a heightened sense of entitlement in which every event is judged on the basis of how it affects the individual. When somebody well-known dies, therefore, Johnny or Julie see the tragedy primarily as something which affects them, though they may never have met the deceased. Grieving becomes a competitive sport: 'He was my radio husband'; 'I feel like I've lost a friend'. The demand to participate in something that has nothing to do with you, to be publicly validated by your display of grief, is overwhelming.

This democratisation of grief isn't a good thing. The funerals of public figures have generally been a reliable guide to the achievements of the deceased, and to the relative contributions they made to the places and communities in which they lived. The media-driven hysteria over Ryan's death and the frankly stupid coverage of his funeral in papers like the *Irish Daily Mail* and the *Star* makes it more difficult to proportionately and fittingly celebrate achievement in the future. The ante has been upped. And not in a good way.

✦ ✦ ✦

The journey of the public service employee from unambitious workhorse to shopaholic destroyer of an entire economy has been a sight to behold

29 November 2009

As RTÉ viewers and readers of Irish newspapers will know by now, public sector workers are the most evil, self-centred, lazy, opportunistic, stupid, dishonest and vile group of individuals Ireland has ever known. Their thievery knows no bounds and goes back generations. DNA tests on a nurse from Enfield recently discovered she is a direct descendant of a family of cruel kitten killers from the 1890s. Investigations into the background of a teacher in Kilkenny revealed that wealthy ancestors on his mother's side used to stand outside the homes of starving people during the Famine, munching potato salad sandwiches and feeding the leftovers to the local bird population. What else would he do with that kind of history but look for a job in the public service?

But of all the insults perpetrated by public sector workers over the years, perhaps the worst was their mass Christmas shopping outing to Newry last Tuesday. Luckily, the media was around to uncover the crime. The day of action, RTÉ confidently reported at lunchtime on Tuesday, had led to an influx of public sector workers who had abandoned their picket lines in search of cheap whiskey (they didn't quite put it like that, but it was clear what they were getting at). It was an arresting image, no doubt, and one backed up by no evidence whatsoever. I tuned into the *Six One News* later in the day to see if they were able to put any more meat on their story. Sadly, they were not, although that didn't stop them pushing an angle that was too attractive to abandon.

Three witnesses to the madness were interviewed. An Englishman who didn't work in the public sector thought the busier-than-usual shopping day might have had something to do with the work stoppage, although he didn't seem sure. A shopper from Dublin who didn't work in the public sector thought a fellow over there might be in the public sector, although there was no interview with the fellow over there to confirm that suspicion. An elderly woman who didn't work in the public sector was sure she was surrounded by public sector workers, their horns and pointy tails having completely given the game away.

RTÉ at least acknowledged that many of the people who arrived in Newry on Tuesday might have been the parents of children who had the day off (which, of course, was always the most likely explanation for the long queue of southern-registered cars meandering towards the town). Nevertheless the impression created and amplified in the following day's newspapers, was that thousands of strikers had used their day off – taken ostensibly on a point of principle – as an excuse to boost the economy of a foreign nation. The unstated analysis: what would you expect from the people who ruined the country?

The journey of the public service employee from unambitious, unimaginative workhorse to shopaholic destroyer of an entire economy has been a sight to behold. During the boom years, nobody worth their salt would be caught dead working in the public service. Our thrusting, creative, adaptable workforce demanded the freedom and excitement offered by the private sector to express themselves (whatever that means), win attention, secure promotion and earn lots of money. By contrast, the public sector was looked on as a kind of fusty fallback position for Denis and Denise Dullknickers, where they could toil away unrecognised by anybody. Judged by the rules and morality of the Celtic Badger, these people were unambitious, and therefore slightly weird, losers.

Now that the boom is over – wrecked mainly, let us not forget, by the private sector – the public service has been reimagined as the modern equivalent of Nero's Rome. Denis and Denise have been tried and found guilty of excesses likely to lead to a visit by the International Monetary Fund. A country's future depends on them being chastised for reckless behaviour they were never aware of.

To those people in the private sector who insist on the demonisation of public service workers, I would quote the great Roy Keane: 'Get over it!' If the public sector was the fantastic land of opportunity you say it is now, you could have joined at any point in your working past. But you made a choice to go the private route, as I did, and as did many of my colleagues who now so boldly lead the charge against the public service. Try as I might, I can't think of a single reason why public sector workers should be held responsible for that choice.

✦   ✦   ✦

TERRY PRONE

Wham, bam, thank you Obama

Optimism wins votes — now the opposition must peddle a vision of somewhere over the Rainbow.

24 December 2006

We constantly hear about political parties, including those on the opposition benches, paying for American pollsters and campaign experts to cross the Atlantic at high prices to tell them how to win the next general election.

We've heard rather less about something of much more immediate relevance to the upcoming general election: the Obama Factor.

The Obama Factor is what's fascinating American political observers at the moment. Illinois Democratic Senator Barack Obama, one handsome lump of African-American charm, is attracting bigger crowds, airtime, column inches and campaign money than any other potential presidential candidate. And he hasn't even declared yet.

It's happening for a number of reasons. He's young, good-looking and carries none of the baggage acquired by more experienced Democrats, who have to explain away problems like voting for the war in Iraq. He's clever and charismatic and possessed of a self-deprecating wit. He's black without any of the threatening rage issues that have crippled the hopes of men like Jesse Jackson.

But the biggest thing he has going for him is his ability to offer American voters something different, something hopeful. He doesn't keep dissecting failed Republican promises, showcasing Republican hate figures and reminding the voters of their responsibility for the creation of a now despised administration.

He may have peaked too soon. He may soon be exposed as all vision, no specifics. But — right now — he has cottoned on to a fundamental principle of election-winning: people vote for candidates who make the voter feel better about the voter.

Floating voters are always in the self-esteem business. They want to believe that they're risktaking idealists. That they can't be bought. That they care about more than back-pocket money and security. That their vote speaks to their faith in a better future and to their rejection of a squalid present.

It's that last consideration that, over the past couple of years, has hobbled the opposition in this country. They've been enthusiastically barking up the wrong tree, convinced that if they prove to the voter that Fianna Fáil is essentially and irrevocably corrupt and that the PDs are heartless fascists, all will be well. They've missed the positive future tense part of the equation.

They haven't been helped by Taoiseach's Questions. The format of this Dáil procedure requires them to put questions to the Taoiseach. Surrounded as the three opposition leaders are by advisers pushing the flawed notion of 'strong opposition', this has meant that, week in, week out, the three of them get delivered into the nation's sitting rooms, courtesy of TV soundbites, as boring, negative, eternally complaining whingers.

Inevitable? Not at all. Political leadership isn't just about inventing policies and keeping the troops motivated.It's about finding new ways to use – nay, re-invent – old procedures. During the Christmas break, the opposition party leaders would be well advised to figure out how to use the most frequently televised Dáil procedure in a way that doesn't continue to do them damage. It's a weekly opportunity to put the Obama Factor in play, and they'd better get the hang of it, smartish.

The Obama Factor is quintessentially future tense. It assumes people prefer the wide blue yonder of tomorrow to the recycled sock-smell of yesterday. Simple? Obvious? Not to the powers-that-be in some of the opposition parties, one of which, this week, as the rest of us were scissoring ribbons into curly fronds and trying to conceal parcels with giveaway shapes, was demanding time for a Dáil debate on the Moriarty Report Vol I. This is a bit like putting down a motion demanding the right to serve semolina pudding on Christmas Day: why the hell would you want to?

The answer depends on which bit of the non-tree you're barking up. If you're barking up the Duty of the Opposition bit, you believe a report so significant should not be allowed to pass without your TDs hammering home the implications. If you're barking up the Culture of Crookedness bit, you want yet another chance to point out to the plain people of Ireland that 'Haughey didn't do this all on his own, you know'.

Never mind that the people of Ireland, or at least those represented in opinion polls, are bored rigid by that stuff. Not to mention those for whom the events recorded by the Moriarty Report are distant history, belonging to the bad old days before Ryanair, cappuccinos in cardboard beakers and pre-Christmas shopping in American outlet malls.

The old management adage applies. If you keep doing what you've always done, you'll keep getting what you've always got. And, for Labour, Fine Gael and the Greens, that ain't enough.

If they keep doing what they've always done in the past year, they'll keep getting – post-election – what they've always got. Seats on the opposition benches.

✦ ✦ ✦

Mr Haughey, you'll do whatever you decide. I'm just telling you what you should do

20 January 2008

'Mister Haughey's on the phone, looking for Tom,' my assistant told me. 'But Tom's not here. Will you talk to him?'

My heart did a bungee jump. Forget that cliché about hearts going into boots. Mine visited my extremities, then bounced back and hit my larynx. Not that Haughey was ever unpleasant to any of us. It was just that if he was ringing at 10 a.m., and looking for Tom Savage, then he had a problem unlikely to be solvable by me.

I figured the problem had to do with the Progressive Democrats. The new party was only a few weeks old at that point. But for a tiny newborn, it was creating one hell of a stir – mainly by inspired timing. A high-profile defection from a major political party would occupy the national attention for one week. Then there would be a lull, during which that party would convince itself that the departure wasn't a loss but a gain. At the same time, media and public would wonder if that was the end of it.

It never was. Just as the national pulse returned to normal, a press conference or photocall or mass meeting would be announced, and a high profiler from another big party would join the PDs. Even if you had no interest in politics, you were reached by the dramatic tension. If you had an interest in politics, you got sucked into the latest conspiracy theory. Charlie McCreevy or Seamus Brennan were definitely going to be the next movers from Fianna Fáil, you were told.

When McCreevy and Brennan's posteriors stayed glued to FF seats, the explanation was that their tenure was temporary and that they'd be departing in a matter of weeks. Theories abounded, and the PDs did what Mary Harney later defined as their great strength: in media terms, they punched way above their weight.

It figured, therefore, that Haughey's problem related to this ongoing scenario. It did. In a tense growl, he told me that Bobby Molloy would be walking from Fianna Fáil within hours, his defection neatly timed to ensure that Charlie Haughey would be doorstepped at the entrance to (if I remember rightly) the Burlington Hotel by a phalanx of journalists wanting to get his reaction to the latest runner from the ranks.

Haughey had wanted Tom Savage's advice on whether he should simply walk past the media or say something to them, and if he was going to say something, what he should say.

'What's your own instinct?' I asked.

The question was asked, partly because only a half-witted consultant leaps into the breach, offering advice that's going to run counter to what the individual wants to do, before they've found out what exactly it is the individual wants to do. It was also playing for time. I hadn't been paying that much attention to the progress of the PDs.

Obviously reading from some notes, he monotoned his way through a litany of the proud history and present-day vibrancy of the Fianna Fáil party. (Whenever FF talk vibrancy, it's a dead giveaway.

They're goosed and know it. Whenever Fine Gael talk about the need for a national debate, it's a version of the same thing. They want two other people to argue with each other and come to the FG point of view.) 'No,' I said, suddenly certain. 'No, you won't say that.'

'I must send a strong message to the grassroots,' he responded.

'Frig the grassroots,' I said. 'The grassroots you always have with you. It's the waverers you have to reach today, and you're not going to reach them by making those kind of predictable threatened noises.'

With the infinite patience he could muster under pressure, he asked me what precisely I was recommending.

'No speech,' I said. 'No statement. You're going to arrive at the Burlo in high good humour. You're not going to rush past them. You're going to get out of the car as if it was a surprise birthday party. You're going to pick off individual journalists you know in the crowd and tease them unmercifully, by name. You're going to make the whole lot of them laugh and while they're laughing, you're going to wave and disappear into the hotel.'

'I would never do that.'

'Mr Haughey, you'll do whatever you decide. I'm just telling you what you should do.'

The conversation ended with a growl and a banged-down phone. A few hours later, my assistant slid an evening paper in front of me.

Big picture of the man, surrounded by microphone-holding journalists, with the caption 'An ebullient Charlie Haughey outside the Burlington Hotel earlier today'. The impact of Molloy's move could never be glossed over, but Haughey had at least stiffened his own party by appearing to be unbothered by this, the latest episode in a brilliantly planned wave.

Now, the process is happening in reverse.

The latest negative is the letter from one of the four founders of the PDs, Paul Mackay, urging members of the party to tell HQ that they had to get out of government in order to revive their fortunes. Mackay will have infuriated a good portion of the PDs and interested another portion of them. It doesn't matter. He's not only barking up the wrong tree, he's barking up the wrong shrub.

The PDs were a necessary, indeed vital catalyst in Irish politics. Mary Harney gave us smog-free cities, the party deregulated some

areas in serious need of deregulation, and tax was reformed. A lot
done.

The reality behind the electoral meltdown and the rumours that
one of their two TDs is now negotiating with Fianna Fáil with a view
to conversion, is that Fianna Fáil subsumes small parties and gains a
new sense of direction in the process.

Or put it another way: the PDs may no longer be necessary,
because Fianna Fáil has learned how to be them.

✦   ✦   ✦

David Kenny

Sometimes the growing pains never go away

16 May 2010

A story in the news last week reminded me of an old friend. Before I get to that story, I'd like to tell you about him. Forgive me for being nostalgic, the pay-off is important. Brian and I were thirteen the first time we met. I wasn't impressed. He looked a bit of a shaper as he marched around the schoolyard, clicking the studded heels of his George Webbs, with his hands in the pockets of an oversized Eskimo anorak.

We fought – I can't remember why. It was one of those 'hold-me-back' affairs, with a flurry of missed groin-kicks and the loser ending up in a headlock. Brian, as it turned out, was no hard-man: he was rubbish at fighting. It was something we had in common.

The scrap was a sort of pathetic, pubescent, bonding ritual. We became best friends, constantly messing about to disguise our terror at being weedy First Years, surrounded by giant, moody Older Lads. We slagged everything off – as all insecure thirteen-year-olds do to deflect attention from themselves. Clothes, hairstyles, even bikes were fair game.

Brian had a twenty-gear Asahi racer, while I had a crock of crap masquerading as a Chopper. He never let me forget it was crap – especially as it didn't have a crossbar.

'It's a girl's bike.'

'It's not. It's just ... streamlined. It's a streamlined Chopper.'

'But it folds in half.'

'It's a Chopper.'

'It's a girl's bike and you're a girl.'

The bike was eventually 'stolen'.

Our afternoons were spent listening to records or cycling around 'scoping out the talent'. At night we'd slip through back gardens, avoiding fathers filling coal scuttles, to steal apples that we never ate. We whispered instructions to each other on a shared set of walkie-talkies. Their range was about twenty feet. There was no need for them: we could have spoken normally and still have heard each other.

Brian and I learned how to smoke together. We could only afford cheap tipped cigars. They were disgusting and tasted like burning doc leaves (I once smoked a doc leaf). I accidentally stubbed one out on my arm while swinging from a tree, making monkey noises to annoy the lawn bowlers at Moran Park. The scar lasted for a year. I told my mother that it was a result of two wasps stinging me on the same spot, one after the other. She didn't buy it.

Brian and I rode around Dún Laoghaire with our cigars clamped between our teeth, thinking we looked like Clint Eastwood. We didn't see ourselves as two short-arses playing at being adults from the safety of childhood.

We went to our first disco together, herky-jerk dancing like mad to Bad Manners to impress the girls. The more we ran on the spot, the more they liked it – so local stud, Macker, told us. What he didn't tell us was that he had spread the word among the girls that we were 'special needs boys' from a care home.

'We're 'in' there,' I said, as one waved sympathetically at us. We ran faster on the spot to impress her even more.

Brian went on my first date with me. Not as my date, obviously – he came along to act as witness in the event that I 'scored'. When you're fourteen, 'scoring' is everything.

He cycled behind me to the venue, Sandycove train station.

'What's that smell?' he shouted at the back of my head. 'It's like oil and cat piss.'

'Don't know what you're talking about,' I cycled faster, knowing full-well what the smell was. It was the contents of a bottle of my dad's Eclipsol hair tonic. We skidded into the lane overlooking the tracks.

'What's up with your hair?' Brian was examining my forehead. A mixture of sweat and hair restorer was trickling down my nose.

'I haven't washed it for a week,' I said, 'and I used Ted's hair stuff. It helps to keep the bounce down.' Bouncy hair was for girls. My mother always said my freshly-washed hair reminded her of her own.

'You've got my hair.'

'No I don't.'

'Yes you do.' My father ran the palm of his hand over his bald head. 'Don't worry, you'll be like me some day. Then you won't have to worry about having bouncy hair and looking like ... Barry Manilow.' Bullseye.

Brian leaned his bike against the wall. 'Go on, then.' I could hear him chuckling as I nervously approached my 'girlfriend'.

'What's that smell?' asked one of her friends. 'It's like pee.'

'Why's your hair greased up like that? Are you trying to look like Elvis?' I had hoped I looked like Elvis.

'Did Elvis ever work as a toilet cleaner in a Pet Shop?'

'Or an old folk's home?' Brian fell over his bike laughing.

I didn't score. The love affair ended soon afterwards.

The day Brian moved down the country was the bleakest of my young life. I couldn't tell him I was going to miss him. You didn't say that to your mates. We played 'Baggy Trousers' on my Lloytron tape recorder over and over again as he unsuccessfully attempted to blow up his tree house with bangers. 'I'm not leaving it for the next family,' he said, despite my protests. Looking back, he was scorching the earth of his childhood.

Before he left, he handed me his half of our walkie-talkie set. I traded it for some now-forgotten item. I couldn't share it with anyone else.

Years passed and we lost touch. We picked up our friendship again when he eventually moved back. Then we both got night jobs and lost touch again. We orbited the same crowds, but never seemed to meet up.

In November 1992, Brian walked into his local and settled a few small debts. He was in good form. He was twenty-five. Later that night, Brian turned the exhaust pipe in on his car. He killed himself. No one had seen it coming.

I try not to think of his final moments. How alone he must have felt. How his family felt when they heard the news. How whoever found him felt. How I felt.

The fourteen-year-old who shared my growing pains was gone.

The reason why is not important now. I have other questions. What would his children have been like? Would he have enjoyed my wedding? Would we still be friends, tilting at the bar in Finnegan's?

Brian – that's not his real name – came back to me last Wednesday when I read that the Marks & Spencer model Noémie Lenoir had tried to kill herself. I was surprised at how hard that story struck me. Lenoir is young and beautiful: people like her don't kill themselves. People like Brian don't kill themselves.

Newspapers generally don't carry suicide stories because of the 'Werther effect', where reporting might encourage copycats. Sadly, Lenoir's attempt will have sown the seed in some minds.

The suicide rate here has risen by 35 per cent since last year (CSO) as more people succumb to depression. Two years before Brian's death, I suffered a prolonged period of desperate sadness. I was luckier than him: I learned from it. I think of what I could have said to him had I known what he was going through. I could have told him we all crash emotionally, but it's possible to walk away from the wreckage. I would have told him that he didn't really want to leave, he just wanted the pain to stop. I would have told him that the darkness passes.

I would have told him that he will always be my friend.

I would have told him that he was never really alone.

✦ ✦ ✦

'Manity' and the day I dyed for Ireland

23 January 2010

'Tell them what an idiot you are.' That was the curt instruction from the woman who edits this column. No political rants this week. Just explain to those who don't already know it that I'm an idiot. Here goes:

Men are idiots. Fact. Scientists proved this last week when they discovered that Man 'Flu actually exists. We exaggerate the symptoms of the common cold to idiotic proportions. We think we're the stronger sex, but we're not. We're also idiots who can't accept that ageing is inevitable. The Harley Medical Group has reported a 17 per cent rise in calls from men seeking Botox treatment since Louis Walsh admitted getting work done. Presumably hair weave enquiries also rose after Gordon Ramsay had his hairline restored. Men are idiots. Vain idiots.

The worst thing a man can do, next to wearing a wig or getting Botox, is to dye his hair. He is a preening knob if he does. He's cheating. Besides, grey is manly, grey is wise. Grey is the colour of silverback gorillas.

Grey is also bloody boring. I've an admission to make: I'm a preening knob. I dyed my hair last weekend. No, please don't turn the page; let me explain.

I've been letting my grey hair grow for the past year. I love taunting my baldy mates by draping it over their shiny heads. Over the past few months, however, it's been turning a horrible shade of green. This is something the Baldies love reminding me about. ('Look, it's the Not-So-Incredible Hulk!')

Sick of hearing me moan about it, my sister bought me a bottle of Super Silver Sensations. She promised it would sort the greenness out. I lathered half the bottle in, ignoring the instructions to rinse after five minutes. 'I'll give it forty,' I thought. To get it REALLY silvery. An hour later, my hair was purple. Silver Sensations turns out to be blue-rinse shampoo. My head looked like Barney The Dinosaur's crotch.

'No, you don't look like Barney,' my wife reassured me. 'You look like old Mrs Slocum. You idiot.'

Shortly afterwards, someone told me ketchup can rectify yellowness. It took fifteen minutes to apply because, being a man, I had to mess around, teasing my hair into various shapes. I let it dry into a two-horned, devil 'do'. Idiot.

The whang was appalling but I soon forgot about my saucy bonce as I caught up on household chores. Two hours later I went into the study to play with the cat. She shied away from me. 'That's odd,' I thought, reaching out to pet her. She licked my face and hissed again. I looked up to see the postman staring in the window. I waved. He slowly backed out the gate.

My ketchup 'horns' were melting down the side of my face. It looked like I was engaging in some perverted Satanic ritual with the cat. 'Come back, I can explain,' I called, which only made him run away faster.

Ketchup doesn't work, by the way. It turns your hair ginger. My pub-mates started calling me 'Rusty'. So I bought some Grecian 2000, but that turned my pillow brown, which was hard to explain to our disgusted (former) cleaning lady.

I bought a bottle of Just for Men hair dye, but I couldn't use it. I'm not that vain. I threw it in the bin. It came out again last Saturday in advance of an appearance on RTÉ's *Daily Show*. 'Don't put that in your hair. You'll make a mess of it,' my wife warned, forgetting that men are idiots. We'll always press the button marked 'Do Not Press This Button'. We'll always stick a knife in the toaster when it's plugged in.

I emptied the bottle onto my head. 'Two minutes is all it takes!' the label said. I left it in for ten.

My wife says the screams were up to *The Exorcist* level. My hair was black with red roots. I was a cross between Elvis and Bono. 'It's all YOUR fault,' I shrieked, as she locked herself in the bedroom with the cat.

I lathered Fairy liquid into it. I steeped it in lemon juice. It turned grapefruit pink. I shrieked some more.

It took my wife's hairdresser, Matt Malone, two days to rectify things. It still looks dyed though and I'm paranoid about it. The worst thing is when you catch someone staring at it and quickly looking away.

There's a lesson in this for all you fellow idiots who may be thinking of dyeing: don't do it. I really miss my grey hair.

The last straw came when I went for my first post-dye pint. A wag shouted: 'You can't come in here – it's Just For Men.'

I'm staying in until I go grey again. If anybody asks my wife where I am she's instructed to say I'm at home, under the weather.

Knowing me, they'll probably think it's Man 'Flu.

✦ ✦ ✦

Was it for all this the men of 1916 fought and died?

28 March 2010

My great-grandfather delivered Pearse's farewell letter to his mother. As the fires crackled around the GPO, the rebel leader wrote: 'Whatever happens to us, the name of Dublin will be splendid in history for ever. Willie and I hope you are not fretting for us ...' He sealed the envelope and great-granddad kept it safe. By the time he delivered it, Pearse was dead.

History sees Pearse's sacrifice in terms of bloodshed. My great-granddad, Matthew Walker, saw it in the face of a mother who had lost two sons.

You won't have heard of Matthew. He was one of those remarkable figures who prefer to work behind history's stage. You may remember from school that Parnell had lime thrown at his eyes during a rally. Matthew was the friend who shielded his face with his hat. Anonymous, forgotten.

On Easter Monday 1916, Matthew – who was sixty-nine – walked eight miles from Glasthule to the GPO. He was dressed in full Edwardian fig of topcoat and top hat. He also had corns on his feet, but his generation 'didn't grumble'. He was determined to play his part.

As he entered Sackville Street, Matthew would have seen the first casualties – two dead horses belonging to the lancers. He would have felt the giddiness of the slum bystanders waiting to see blood.

He would also have seen a tricolour flying over the GPO.

For Matthew – IRB man and publisher – Easter Monday was the culmination of his life's work. He was given the task of printing Pearse's *Irish War News*, as bullets ricocheted around the city. Each night, he bravely walked home through the cordons.

His Abbey actress daughters, Maire and Gypsy, were 'out' in 1916 too. Gypsy, my grandmother, lost her pacifist lover to a looter's bullet. A priest refused to marry the couple on his deathbed.

Despite the pain, their generation valued sacrifice. Their selflessness seems very remote as you survey today's Ireland.

Last week, the tricolour Matthew may have seen over the GPO failed to sell at auction. It had been valued at $500,000. I wonder how he would have felt about this. After the week we've just had with Brian Cowen's reshuffle and more turmoil with the banks, I wonder what he would make of the Republic he risked his life for.

If he was publishing a newspaper today, Matthew's editorial would probably compare our Taoiseach's power-at-all-costs philosophy to Pearse's. It would condemn the cynicism of hoarding power at the expense of the democracy people died for.

Coming from an age when people risked their lives for principles, what would he think of Beverley Flynn? Unprincipled Bev's belief that democracy should serve her was in evidence again last week. She said she deserved a place in cabinet. She would 'flower'. She couldn't understand why the media picked on her. Drop around Bev, I'll tell you why.

What would he make of the people who keep electing her? Or Michael Lowry for that matter? Or Mary Hanafin, who along with seven other deputies still refuses to give up her teacher's pension? Or smug Mary Harney, with no party behind her?

Let's be fair to politicians, though. They're not the only self-servers living in this great Republic.

Matthew would have led his newspaper with the Civil, Public and Services Union's go-slow and how they are denying people their passports. He would have been livid. A passport isn't a bargaining chip. It's proof of the citizenship fought for by people like him and Countess Markievicz.

Not that we care about the Countess any more. She would appear on Matthew's 'page 3' (with her clothes on). He would report that she isn't included in an MRBI poll of the greatest Irish people of all time. Neither is President McAleese. Louis Walsh is, though. What does that say about us?

Matthew would look at what the vacuous Tiger generation allowed happen to Tara and run a story warning about the same happening to under-threat Newgrange. How many would read it?

He would look at Seanie Fitz and wonder why we allowed a new landlord class of bankers and developers to be created.

He would look at the whole, sorry mess our Republic is in and scratch his head.

Over the next week, you'll hear a lot of misty-eyed manure about reclaiming the spirit of 1916. The Republicanism that Matthew and others strove for wasn't notional. It was based on the solid principle that your neighbour has a right to expect your help – as you do from him.

The current mess is being made worse by a general unwillingness to take some responsibility. We know who the chief culprits were, but we all bought into the Tiger crap to some extent.

If unity helped achieve our freedom, then it can help us maintain it. The refusal by some to take a hit is not acceptable. The new civil war of public sector against private has to end. We need to start behaving like a republic or stop calling ourselves one.

I wonder what Matthew would have said about that GPO flag being valued at $500,000. A copy of his *Irish War News* fetched €26,000 in 2007.

I'm sure he would look at that tricolour and see more than money. He would know its true value. He would know whether it was worth fighting for or not.

He would know whether we were worth fighting for. I hope we were.

✦   ✦   ✦

Michael Clifford

In FF, all has changed and nothing has changed

31 October 2010

There was a moment of déjà vu on the *Nine O'Clock News* last Monday evening. The cabinet was meeting in Farmleigh House to devise a budgetary plan. As the ministers were chauffeured in the gates, it brought to mind another gathering earlier this year.

Last February, the Irish bishops met in Rome to discuss with the Pope the problem of child abuse. There was something surreal, bordering on the ridiculous, about the pictures that were relayed from the Vatican.

The bishops, some of them togged out in cassocks, lined up to kiss the ring of Pope Benedict, resplendent in his white robes. From there, they retreated into conclave to discuss the damage wreaked by clerical sex abuse, and how best to address the issue into the future. The notion that these elderly men, their moral authority shot, could have anything to do with the protection of children in this day and age was absurd.

Yet once upon a time, their writ ran right across society. Power was wielded to great effect and had been abused with devastating consequences. Now they no longer matter. Even those who retain their faith and maintain connection through clerics on the ground, pay scant regard to the musings of an out-of-touch élite, clinging to an out-of-date notion of power.

So it goes with the current government or, principally, the Fianna Fáil element of it. Once, they considered themselves capable of walking on water. They had parented the imposter, which was then known as the Celtic Tiger. Regularly, media from other countries requested an audience in search of the secret of their success. How had they done it? Were they really men and women, or actually giants?

They lapped it up, buying into their own hype. Naturally, their remuneration, the mark of their greatness, had to be raised to levels commensurate with their amazing ability. Weren't they entitled to it?

The disconnect from the citizenry, which they forged through the bubble economy, should have become apparent to them three years ago. In September 2007, a government-appointed quango ruled that the Taoiseach should be paid another €38,000 on top of his then salary of €272,000, to make him the best paid leader in the developed world. Despite the gathering storm, Bertie Ahern saw the hike as his due for the great job he was still doing.

The optics were all wrong. People were already being thrust onto the dole. Ahern was accused of being out of touch. Let's give him the benefit of the doubt and suggest he was already ensconced in the bubble of delusion where he has since made his home.

That, however, is no excuse for the rest of them. The optics on Monday spoke volumes. As the country teeters on the brink of insolvency, highly experienced politicians saw nothing wrong in arriving in a cavalcade of state cars at Farmleigh, symbol of the old ascendancy, en route to determine the fate of the great unwashed. A couple of them stopped to toss out a few soundbites to the peasant media, before proceeding inside to determine who must suffer, whose lives are to be thrust into turmoil, and who gets off lightest. Are they really that out of touch, or is it that they are beyond caring?

Like the Church hierarchy, they remain in office, but no longer command any real power. That has been ceded to the German moneylenders.

Like the Church, Fianna Fáil has forfeited its moral authority. A party long possessed of a populist touch abused power to such a shocking extent that it mortgaged the State's future for electoral success.

The ranks of the faithful have also been greatly depleted. Last week's opinion poll puts Fianna Fáil at 18 per cent, the lowest point it has plumbed since de Valera's party was a pup.

The founder would not recognise what they have done to his

self-styled national movement. Dev saw austerity as an example he, as leader, could give to the citizens, conveying that he was their elected servant. He knew better than to get notions above his station in a country struggling to maintain economic independence.

Somewhere along the line, his austerity by example was replaced with a sense of entitlement. Charlie Haughey had his personal delusions of grandeur. The other right Charlie – McCreevy – raised the sense of entitlement onto a higher plane. Salaries, the Mercs, the perks, the pension set-up, all were bumped up to what might be expected in an oil-rich kingdom, divided between rulers and serfs. And now the sense of entitlement is so ingrained that it has blinded them to the most basic political instinct.

Neither is the disconnect confined to the Dáil. Fianna Fáil leader in the Seanad, Donie Cassidy, last week opined that senators were struggling to live on the €65,000 they are paid for a part-time gig. He apologised when the peasants reacted in kind, but his mindset was exposed.

It would be reassuring to conclude that the disconnect, the sense of entitlement, is confined solely to Fianna Fáil. But a suspicion arises that senior figures in the main opposition parties are just waiting in the wings to take their turn with the Mercs and perks. They may not suffer the same disconnect, but there is precious little to suggest they are equipped with what is required at a time of national peril.

Where are the signs of leadership on the most basic level? For example, what senior opposition figure has the guts to say something like, 'No member of the next executive should be paid more than €100,000 at this time of great upheaval'? Who is willing to declare that public office now more than ever must be about what can be put in, rather than what can be extracted as a sense of entitlement?

The old order is rapidly changing. Fianna Fáil and the Catholic Church, as we knew them both, are bound for the knacker's yard. The worrying thing is nothing has yet been found to replace them. Give us a shout if you hear anything.

✦ ✦ ✦

It's not going to be pretty, but in the coming years we're going to find out a lot about ourselves and our capacity for tolerance when the chips are down

22 February 2009

The flyer came through the door a couple of weeks ago. 'Are you looking for someone to paint your house? You have found the right people! We are a team of Professional Polish Workers who can cheaply and solidly paint.' It went on: 'We also provide high quality tiling services.'

The phrase 'Professional Polish Workers' was highlighted in bold typeface. There are two reasons why tradespeople would highlight their Polish nationality. In the first instance, over the last five years, Polish tradespeople have gained an excellent reputation in the workplace. They are not afraid of work and the combination of enthusiasm and skills generally provide a very satisfactory service. Like generations of Irish exiles before them, they use the hunger of the immigrant to push themselves on.

There is nothing unique about Poles. Immigrants from other eastern European states within the EU are similarly commended, but Poles are identified by sheer force of numbers. The other reason is cost. Through the bubble years, when the home-improvement market went through the roof, workers from the new EU states provided their trades at very competitive prices.

Work was plentiful. Many Irish tradespeople sniffed a market in which they could charge exorbitantly, and did so. Canny immigrants realised they could do the job profitably at lesser prices and exploited the fertile territory abandoned by the native boys. Everybody got a slice of the action.

Not any more. The work has dried up. Prices have come down, and everybody is flailing around in the same shrinking pool. In such an environment, tensions are going to rise and the grind of history has taught us that these tensions will inevitably be wrapped up in race. All the indications are that large numbers who came here when work was plentiful are now staying on. As of last December, 44,600 of those signing on were immigrants, representing about one-fifth of the total unemployed. A report in the *Irish Times* last Monday from a Polish church in Dublin confirmed that many have decided to stay on and see out the bad times.

Immigration is a highly mobile business these days with cheap air travel, but at the moment there is nowhere else to go. In any event, many who came here liked what they saw and have decided to nest. For parents of young children, or those at the foothills of family life, moving abroad again to the next job has added complications.

Handling this new reality is going to be no easy task. If our friends the Polish painters hoover up scarce work on the basis of cheaper pricing, their unemployed Irish counterparts will locate a vent in which to pour frustrations. The plight of PAYE workers is another concern. Through the boom years, employers sang loudly about the benefits immigrants were bringing to the country, principally cheap labour. There were cases of gross exploitation, ranging from mushroom pickers to construction workers. Now the market has turned and the employers hold all the aces. Inevitably, some will see the current economic distress as an opportunity. If the few jobs on offer end up being filled by immigrants, suspicions about pay levels and conditions will immediately arise. This sort of thing has already become a feature of the recession in the UK. Italian and Portugese unskilled workers have been imported to construct a power station in Lindsey Oil Refinery in Lincolnshire, prompting a series of wildcat strikes. The GMB trade union in the UK is claiming that two energy plants and an oil refinery are refusing to employ British workers.

Scarcity of resources is another area that will provide a flashpoint of tension. Currently there is talk of cuts to social welfare payments. If such a horrendous vista comes to pass, those at the receiving end will look around for somebody to blame.

It would be nice to believe that dear old Ireland will be able to keep tensions under wraps. However, if recent events have shown anything, it is that history keeps coming back to haunt just when you thought it had been dispatched once and for all. Leadership and tolerance are going to be at a premium to deal with what is coming down the line. Employers' groups and trade unions need to provide direction and vision. Both have been to the fore in usurping the job of governing through the partnership process, but this is an issue in which they could make a real contribution to society.

Leadership in the political sphere will also be vital, but don't hold your breath. With Fianna Fáil plunging in the polls, expect some of the more nervous nellies to exploit rather than attempt to defuse racial tensions. Noel O'Flynn has already been fast out of the blocks, publishing parliamentary questions he set down on permits for foreign workers. He's letting the frustrated element in his constituency know where he stands on the matter of Johnny Foreigner.

Some on the wilder shores of Fine Gael have a habit of drawing a few kicks at Travellers, and these politicians also can be expected to make hay on the back of racial vulnerabilities.

It's not going to be pretty, but in the coming years we're going to find out a lot about ourselves, and our capacity for tolerance when the chips are down.

✦ ✦ ✦

Once again, agencies of the State appear to have been more concerned with protecting themselves rather than the citizen

3 May 2009

THEY came for Michael Feichin Hannon early in the morning. He was awoken and told he was being taken away for questioning in relation to an alleged sexual assault of a ten-year-old.

What followed was a nightmare for a man who was just twenty-two years of age in 1997, when the matter arose. He was convicted of sexual assault two years later. Fortunately, his sentence was suspended for four years. He moved away from the area, in an attempt to come out from under the dark cloud that envelopes anybody convicted of sexual assault of a minor. In the ignorant discourse that often surrounds sexual offences, he could have been classified as a paedophile.

Last week, he received a certificate of miscarriage of justice following the retraction of the allegation by the girl, who is now a young woman.

A great wrong was perpetrated by the girl, Una Hardester, against Hannon, but he also suffered at the hands of the State. He had no complaint about how the case was investigated, prosecuted or tried. But his experience since the girl's retraction raises a recurring question about how the State conducts itself when innocent people have been wronged in one form or another.

Hardester made her retraction in a statement to a solicitor in November 2006. She had duped the gardaí, prosecutors and the jury at Galway Circuit Criminal Court into believing her story. (The trial largely hung on her word against Hannon's.)

Hannon only found out about the retraction by chance. His sister encountered Hardester at a petrol station in Galway. He contacted his solicitor, who got in touch with the local gardaí. They confirmed that Hardester had made a retraction.

The matter was straightforward. Hannon's solicitor should have been supplied with the statement, which would have allowed for an application to the Court of Criminal Appeal to quash the conviction.

The statement was not forthcoming from the gardaí. It was not forthcoming from the DPP, which had received a copy in November 2006. After numerous attempts, Hannon's solicitor, Michael Finucane, was finally furnished with the statement in March 2008. A letter from the DPP apologised for the delay, saying that the file had been mislaid.

The way was then opened up to have Hannon's name cleared in the Court of Criminal Appeal (CCA). Once the conviction was quashed, Hannon then applied for a certificate of miscarriage of justice. The certificate means that he is entitled to seek compensation from the State.

The DPP objected to the certificate being granted. The office's claim was on the grounds that the State or its agents had done no wrong in the case. The CCA rejected the arguments.

Judge Adrian Hardiman said that the issue was a narrow one – whether a man who was convicted and was now recognised as having been innocent all along was entitled to a certificate. He and his colleagues ruled that Hannon was entitled to it.

The delay in supplying Hannon with the document that would clear his name, and the objection to declaring the case a miscarriage of justice, show the State's agents in a harsh light.

A grave wrong had been perpetrated on a citizen. The State's function is to protect and serve the citizen. Yet there appears to have been a reluctance to acknowledge that something terrible had befallen an innocent man.

Once again, agencies of the State appear to have been more concerned with protecting themselves rather than the citizen, with serving the agency's interests, rather than those of the citizen.

So it was with Brigid McCole, the woman who was poisoned by blood supplied by the State, and fought all the way through the courts when she attempted to have the wrong righted. So it was with the McBreartys in Donegal, who had to fight the whole way to get the State to acknowledge how badly served, how badly protected they as citizens had been. So it goes in other cases, in health, in education, anywhere that the institution's function is questioned.

The culture of circling institutional wagons, rather than rushing to effect reparation is a damning indictment on a State that classifies itself as republican. Opposition politicians often point out these shortcomings. And then, when they join government, they quietly drop their objections. Somewhere along the line, the primacy of the citizen has been lost.

The other feature of the Hannon case is that it throws into sharp relief the might of the State in the criminal justice system. It is fashionable these days for comment on the system to focus on the rights of the accused versus the rights of the victim. This ignores the power of the State that is behind prosecutions, on the same side as the victim, although acting for all citizens.

In such a mismatch, safeguards, checks and balances are always going to be important. The fashionable view is that these safeguards weigh the system heavily in the defendant's favour, despite conviction rates of around 95 per cent. In Hannon's case, it appears there weren't enough safeguards to detect that something was amiss.

Then, when the wrongly convicted man and his accuser both moved to have the wrong righted, it was the State that foot-dragged and attempted to block the process of complete vindication.

The system needs tweaking to respond to the likes of organised crime in today's world. But caution must accompany every change. Nobody wants to be another Michael Feichin Hannon.

Una Mullally

Is this what we have regressed to now? An Ireland of magic tree stumps and of men patting the back of a sex criminal?

20 December 2009

When the London-based Irish comedian Dara Ó Briain appeared on *The Late Late Show* in November, he told an anecdote about his latest television series *Three Men in a Boat* that sees himself and two British comedians travel around Irish waterways. The other comedians, Gryff Rhys Jones and Rory McGrath, kept asking about the tree stump in Rathkeale in Limerick, which locals attested depicted an image of Mary. But Ó Briain played it down, mortified at the ridiculousness of it all, not wanting them to see that part of Ireland, the *Father Ted* Ireland, the Ireland from *The Field*, an Ireland full of ignorance and embarrassments.

After a decade of commentary on the Ireland we were living in, the 'real' Ireland was called for in moments of reflection, the 'old' Ireland, which apparently was something to be yearned for.

We got a glimpse of that 'real' and 'old' Ireland in a Tralee court-room last week when about fifty people shook the hand of convicted sex attacker Danny Foley as he awaited his sentencing. They queued in single file before the judge returned to the courtroom, squeezing his hand and embracing him, while his victim sat in the front row of the room accompanied only by gardaí, a rape counsellor and one friend.

'She cut quite a solitary figure,' a reporter for the *Irish Examiner* said. The incident is of course outrageous. What kind of person would sympathise with a sex attacker who, on CCTV evidence, carried a woman who was drunk behind a skip, forced her to the ground, pinned her down causing scrapes to her wrists and extensive bruising to her back, and pulled off her trousers? When gardaí spotted him crouching over her, he lied, saying he just found her there, semi-conscious. He referred to his victim as 'yer wan'.

On Newstalk's *Breakfast* programme on Thursday morning, Fr Sean Sheehy, a priest in Listowel – where the incident happened – who appeared in court as a character witness for the thirty-five-year-old bouncer Foley said: 'My Christian responsibility was to this person that I knew and to the person who is the object of, what I call, this extremely harsh sentence.' Sheehy didn't seem particularly concerned about his 'Christian responsibility' to a victim of sexual assault, but hey, she wasn't his buddy. Sheehy's shocking behaviour isn't that shocking in light of what we now know about Irish priests, but it does show their strange and disturbing attitude towards sex abuse isn't just confined to paedophilia.

Why dozens of men felt compelled to sympathise with Foley is a complex expression of many attitudes; attitudes to women, attitudes to sex, attitudes to community and solidarity. Perhaps they would have felt differently if Foley was in the dock for attacking their daughter, sister, mother, wife or girlfriend – or perhaps not. But it does show that many people refuse to accept that rapists are very often the supposedly nice upstanding and well-liked family men in our communities. It is rare that the face of sexual assault is an anonymous one in a dark alley; much more often, it's the Danny Foleys of this world – the blokes who go out on the lash in the hope of getting some young wan hammered enough to sleep with them. Sex attackers are our friends and our family members and our neighbours. The people of Listowel find that very hard to swallow.

And while Foley might be typical of sex attackers in Ireland, unfortunately, his victim is very much the exception as a sex-crime victim. She is the exception because she reported the attack. She is the exception because she went through with the legal process of bringing her attacker to court. She is the exception because after her case was brought to court, her attacker was convicted. And she is the exception because that conviction involved a jail sentence.

Despite facing total isolation from her community, she had the almighty bravery to follow through. In her victim-impact statement she said: 'I feel as if people are judging me the whole time. I've been asked by people I know if I am sorry for bringing Dan Foley to court. I am not sorry for it. All I did was tell the truth.'

It's commendable also that Judge Donagh McDonagh didn't listen to the 'character reference' from the priest about Foley's respect for women, but it's sad that he needs to be commended because his actions should be automatic.

Is this the Ireland that we want? Where a sexual-assault victim is judged by her community as though it was some delusional nation with an extreme vision of Sharia law? Is this what we have regressed to now? An Ireland of magic tree stumps, and eejits blinding themselves looking for a dancing sun in Knock, of people sympathising with paedophilic priests and colluding bishops, and of men patting the back of a sex criminal?

✦ ✦ ✦

Mown down by state and police, the students showed the rest of us what democracy is

7 November 2010

Just before 30,000 young people took to the streets in the largest student protest of their generation, my flatmate, also a student, hung a banner out the window. It read 'We Write The Future'. We all write the future, but none more so than a generation who have largely been ignored, disregarded and are now condemned either to unemployment or emigration. This is the moment we stopped confusing apathy with disaffection.

Last week began with a completely idiotic protest, an Éirígí councillor chucking paint on Mary Harney, which did nothing apart from provide a gift to sub-editors on the tabloids the next day. Éirígí was there again at the student protest, along with the Socialist Workers Party. They are to protests what liggers are to launch parties, turning up, constantly unwanted, hanging around, not getting the message that it's not their party. Both groups were instrumental in disrupting what was a peaceful protest. There is no doubt that those involved in causing aggravation at the tail end of the protest were completely wrong. But this protest took place in a context different from previous ones, a context of heightened emotions, anger, desperation, solidarity, determination.

Watching the TV footage, it was impossible to condone many of the gardaí's actions. They stood in rows, batons drawn, shields at the ready, as mounted gardaí assembled behind them. They bashed heads, bloodied noses. None of the protestors were armed or wearing protective clothing, yet even when they were sitting on the ground, the fully Robocopped gardaí saw fit to beat them with batons, knee them, and drag them across the ground by their hair. Eventually, by the time the protestors had reached Anglo Irish Bank on St Stephen's Green, gardaí on horses, again without warning, charged the crowd, who were simply making their way back to where they came from. They were backed up by charging gardaí on foot and armoured garda vans.

It was a totally disproportionate response, an ugly, unfair and unprofessional method of controlling a crowd that the gardaí should be truly ashamed of. These kids have been mown down by the State and when they try to make their voices heard what happens? They are mown down by the police. Eventually, two people were charged with minor offences. That means that only 0.0066 per cent of those involved in the protest were accused of breaking the law.

The issues behind the protest have been lost in the melee. This was about free education as a practical issue and also as an ideal. The lack of foresight in thinking that these problems will be solved by ramping up registration fees is astounding. There seems to be no interest in assessing the possibilities of means testing, a loans system or examining the corrupt grants system. Just whack up registration fees and hope people pay; act bluntly now, think vaguely later - the philosophy of our government.

People talk about students having a sense of entitlement. But the sense of entitlement to a job and a disposable income is slightly less intolerable than the sense of entitlement the real trouble makers on Kildare Street have. Students aren't a demographic that enamour themselves to the rest of the population. Their middle-class accents permeate vox pops on RTÉ radio, with 'likes' and 'bullshits', 'totallys' and 'whatevers' greeted with eyerolls by those who apparently know better. Their enthusiasm tends to be squashed by cynicism.

I had arguments with people last week online and offline about the value of protest. 'What's the point? Sure nothing is going to change,' some said. That attitude seems ridiculous to me. Isn't the reluctance to be involved in democracy – not expressing your opinions, lapsing on being a watchdog to this government – isn't it that lax attitude that made many of us (and not all, as we are told over and over again, but many) complicit in some of the economic terrors we are now facing? Plenty of people might slag off students for marching, but at least the students are doing something. What are you doing?

The failure of our democratic process to be fair and the failure of our politicians to communicate or listen has created a vacuum within which groups like Éirígí grow. Moderate voices need to be heard the loudest, and those are the voices of the students who didn't resort to scrappy behaviour. These are the people who will be shaping this country. Listen to them. We can't afford not to.

✦ ✦ ✦

If John Waters feels lost or disconnected from the new reality of Ireland, it's because this isn't his country anymore

12 September 2010

Last night I attended another emigration 'party' for two more friends of mine who are getting the hell out of Dodge and heading for the promised land of Sydney, where a sizeable number of this country's young people already reside. I've lost count of the number of farewells I've bid to friends and acquaintances this year, and indeed to my own brother who headed for Hong Kong. In almost all of these departures it seemed to me that those leaving this country were doing so in a fit of optimism, not desperation. But what for the poor eejits who stay?

John Waters grabbed a slice of youth culture pie last weekend when he hit the Electric Picnic festival. Writing in his column for the *Irish Times*, he despaired at the poor lost souls wandering around the site in Stradbally, Co Laois. 'The young Irish at Electric Picnic were in a place where they had been led to believe they might find what they were searching for, but they could not find it. And so they were guzzling soul-poison in the hope of locating it.'

Before you run to the nearest bar and shout for two pints of soul-poison and a packet of crisps, it's important to consider Waters' interpretation of young people, and indeed his own morbid summaries of what is essentially something called 'having a good time'. It's rather unfortunate that thousands of people attending a festival over the weekend had to suffer the projections of a man who sounds far more lost than any of them.

Waters' polemic seemed to stem from observations that because people younger than him were consuming alcohol and drugs in his midst, they were doing so because they had little else to consume in life. That's rubbish of course. Just because there isn't religion at a music bash (save for perhaps, the Dublin Gospel Choir on the main stage on Sunday morning) doesn't mean there's nothing to be enjoyed. Waters laments that those who were having fun at the festival, who were using a weekend in a field as an escape from the pessimism that hangs dense in the air, are somehow losing out on the greater meaning in this universe. As if a bunch of kids running from tent to tent to catch decent tunes and have a few beers in the process are some sort of empty vessels starved of meaning in life.

Personally, I'd rather be a godless hedonist than a god-riddled ascetic. There is generally lots of meaning at festivals: the music itself, dancing, random encounters, meeting up with old friends, sharing a laugh, letting one's hair down. Perhaps Waters would have been more suited keening outside the inflatable church at the other end of the festival and scorning those comely maidens who chose to dance past his confusing mental crossroads of muddled pious philosophising.

The commentariat make a living out of cannibalising youth culture and its trimmings and then complain that they are suffering from indigestion. Generation after generation give out about a spiritual deficit in those younger than them. But perhaps this is the first Irish generation who have purposely opted out of tormenting themselves by searching for some unattainable greater meaning and who have chosen instead just to live.

Religion and spirituality are crutches which many younger people have dispensed with in order to stand on their own two feet. The Archdiocese of Dublin used to deal with a few defections from the Catholic Church a year. Now there are so many, the Church has to come up with inventive administrative ways to make it seem as though it is stemming the tide.

As for spirituality, what of it? There is not much evidence of spirituality in the generation that makes up the establishment of this country. A generation of dishonest bankers, greedy developers and corrupt politicians. A generation that completely overstretched themselves, who spent recklessly, who applauded consumerism, who told their kids to take out giant mortgages and to study commerce, who bought second properties and pretended to be landlords, and who elected a series of inept governments.

This younger generation, who according to Waters are in the midst of a spiritual famine, are also attempting to forge a creative boom out of nothingness, and to reinvent community out of disaffection. Those in their teens, twenties and early thirties are bearing the brunt of this economic crisis through a combination of zero employment, emigration and negative equity, yet they are simultaneously the most active in attempting to restructure a country into one whose sole goal isn't profit-making.

Thousands have left. Those who stay should be allowed to have a good time without being told that their lives are empty. If John Waters feels lost or disconnected from this new reality, then it's because this isn't his country anymore. That Ireland is dead and gone. Thank God, or whoever.

✦   ✦   ✦

Shane Coleman

The opposition is skating on thin ice when it comes to the EU/IMF bailout. It needs to get real

5 December 2010

Now, more than ever, is a time for cool heads, but unfortunately there was precious little of that last week. The measured assessment of Ireland's situation by Ajai Chopra was a mini oasis of calm amidst the hysteria that dominated last week's debate.

The danger is that as the general election gets closer, the hysteria is going to get ratcheted up even further. We know Fine Gael and Labour are going to form the next government. But the divvy-up of cabinet seats has yet to be decided. And there are worrying signs both parties are looking to outdo each other in the anger stakes.

Describing Ireland as 'banjaxed' may make for good headlines, but it's hardly what the country needs to hear from the government-in-waiting. Nor does it help public confidence when both main opposition parties try to claim that the interest rate being charged to Ireland is higher than that paid by Greece when they know full well that three-year money as accessed by the Greeks is far cheaper than the longer term funding secured by Ireland.

Eamon Gilmore's angry insistence that he will not be bound by the terms of the agreement with the EU/IMF will certainly be a crowd-pleaser. But it is the most pointless piece of political posturing since Fianna Fáil's opposition to the Anglo-Irish Agreement in the mid-1980s. The government in which he will soon be Tánaiste will have to be bound by it.

In the current climate, there are obvious short-term political benefits to the opposition's approach. But Fine Gael and Labour are in serious danger of creating unrealistic expectations that they have no hope of satisfying when they come to power. The reality is that the deal reached with the EU/IMF was as good as could have been achieved. We were all out of options – the whole world knew it. The idea, which has been put forward in recent days, that we should have told the IMF and, more particularly, our European allies, to get stuffed is astonishingly naïve.

The European Central Bank has been propping up the Irish banks for some time now with emergency liquidity to the tune of tens of billions of euro. The merest hint from the ECB that Ireland's intransigence might cause this to change means our goose was cooked. So let's get real.

It is understandable that people wanted bondholders – particularly the €4 billion worth of unguaranteed senior debt holders in Anglo Irish – to share the pain. But once the ECB vetoed that move, for fear of contagion across the entire euro-region, that was a clear non-runner. But that hasn't stopped the calls for the government to revoke the full guarantee of the banking system, convert bondholders into equity holders and – even more dramatically – restructure the national debt and default.

Nobody can say for definite that matters won't reach a stage where Ireland – along with a number of other peripheral Euro countries – won't be forced to default. But to do so now unilaterally would be an extraordinary gamble with limitless potential downsides.

The highly respected *Financial Times* columnist Wolfgang Munchau made the sovereign default argument in an article in the *Irish Times* last week. But his forecast as to what would happen once we did that was less than reassuring. 'A default would cause havoc, no doubt, and would cut Ireland off from the capital markets for a while. But I would suspect that the shock would only be temporary,' he wrote.

That's great, so. Just as the real economy looks like it has finally stabilised – with exports and manufacturing increasing, unemployment edging down, the exchequer returns stabilised and even consumer confidence no longer dropping – we adopt a policy measure that will create 'havoc'. But don't worry, the suspicion is that being locked out of the capital markets will only be temporary. Munchau went on to argue that 'even Argentina was able to gain funding from investors a few years after its default'.

The reality is that Argentina defaulted in 2001 – setting the terms of its restructuring in 2005 – and nearly a decade on, the only international loan it has received is from Hugo Chavez's Venezuela at 11 per cent interest. It has relied largely on domestic savings to fund government spending, which is not an option in Ireland.

That hardly sounds like the model we want to follow. If you think the current credit crunch is bad, just imagine what it would be like if the Irish sovereign and our banks are shut out of international finance. Bank loan books would have to be reduced to the size of domestic deposits and that's making the very optimistic assumption that there would be no fleeing of depositors in the event of a default and a revoking of our bank guarantee.

In the piece, Munchau argued the government should assess its solvency on the basis of an estimate of nominal economic growth 'of no more than 1 per cent per year for the rest of the decade'.

If we do end up with nominal growth of just 1 per cent a year then we definitely will be screwed. But, given how the Irish economy's fate is so tied to global growth, presumably all the other peripheral Eurozone nations will be screwed too.

If we are to end up defaulting, surely it would be preferable to do so collectively with a number of our euro allies than for little Ireland to be the only guinea pig in what would be a hugely risky economic experiment where nobody has a clue what will happen apart from utter 'havoc' being created? For now at least, there is little choice but to go with the EU/IMF plan. If Patrick Honohan is right – and there are no more black holes in the banks – and if the economy can grow close to the rates set out in the plan, then our interest payments (which will account for between 25 and 28 per cent of total tax revenue) should be just about manageable.

Of course, they are two pretty big 'ifs' and it would be stupid to believe otherwise. But there is no potential solution to the current crisis – however alluring it might seem – that doesn't involve a whole raft of what ifs and maybes. We're long past the point of doing the right thing. It's now about taking the least wrong option.

✦ ✦ ✦

Tighter than a too-small bathing suit on a too-long ride home from the beach? Not this coming election!

2 January 2011

There's no question that the next general election will be seismic in terms of its impact on the political landscape. But for all that, there has never been an election where there has been so little doubt about the make-up of the next government.

Opinion polls only really began properly in the early 1980s, so before that point, predicting the outcome of an election was the political equivalent of pinning the tail on the donkey.

Even with access to polls, the outcome has generally remained in doubt up to polling day and often far beyond that, as various government formations were contemplated.

The three elections in eighteen months in 1981 and 1982 were very close affairs, although the November '82 campaign could be clearly seen to be slipping away from Fianna Fáil from the off. In 1987, it was felt that Fianna Fáil would win an overall majority, but that didn't happen. Ditto two years later when a totally unanticipated Fianna Fáil-PD coalition emerged. The 1992 election could have led to the formation of various governments (and ended up producing two different coalitions).

The 1997 contest was, to borrow a phrase from Dan Rather, tighter than a 'too-small bathing suit on a too-long ride home from the beach'. The Rainbow coalition should have won but didn't.

Fine Gael was obviously facing meltdown in the run-up to 2002, but there was doubt as to whether the next government would be a Fianna Fáil overall majority or a combination of Fianna Fáil with the PDs or the Labour Party (with most analysts plumping for the latter). Five years later most of the same analysts were predicting a Fine Gael-Labour-Green Rainbow.

But this time around is different. Unless something truly extraordinary happens between now and March (and even then it probably wouldn't matter), the next government will be made up of Fine Gael and Labour. The only questions are: how huge will their majority be? And what will the break-down of seats be between the two parties?

As of now, it looks as if they will have 100-plus seats between them and that Fine Gael will have at least a 60:40 advantage – although both these assumptions could change significantly in the course of a campaign.

But what won't change is the enormous prize on offer for the two parties. If they play their cards right, they have the potential to be in power for at least ten years (the best either has managed before is four and a half) and relegate Fianna Fáil forever from its status as the 'natural party of government'.

However, to do that they must avoid the mistakes of the past, most notably their disastrous coalition of the mid-1980s. For four interminable and depressing years, divisions between Fine Gael and Labour meant that tough decisions were shirked and the already awful public finances continued to decline.

Labour was the chief culprit that time around, refusing to countenance cuts in spending that were clearly unavoidable. But Fine Gael was not blameless either. A repeat performance a quarter of a century later simply cannot be countenanced, for their sake and for the country.

Ideally, the long and tortuous, on-off programme for government negotiations between the two parties post polling day would be truncated. Certainly, what we don't need right now is a programme for government long on aspirational and esoteric platitudes and short on the brutal economic realities.

Of course, political realities will dictate that we will have the charade of the programme for government negotiations. Fair enough. But after that, the new government needs to quickly show that it means business. It's about the economy, stupid, and it's pretty obvious what needs to be done and most of it is not pretty.

Right now there are large policy differences between the two would-be coalition partners, particularly on the speed in which the budget deficit needs to be addressed and the breakdown between tax increases and spending.

These differences definitely won't stop Fine Gael and Labour putting together a programme for government. But they do have the potential to lead to paralysis in government at a later date.

In that regard, the choice of finance minister is critical. He or she will have to be both politically skilful and tough – with the latter characteristic more important than the former.

In opposition you can wax lyrical about eliminating waste and taxing the rich. In government the reality is that spending is dominated by social welfare and public sector pay and the majority of tax revenue comes from the great mass of workers. Unfortunately, if you want to make savings, they're the areas you have to hit.

The common perception is that Labour will insist on the finance portfolio in the new coalition. But there is also a view within Labour that it should not do so because of what holding the job will entail. If that view prevails, then Michael Noonan will be the next finance minister and there is little doubt he understands what needs to be done.

Whether the same will hold true for the electorate and the government backbenchers is likely to prove much trickier. As US voters found after Barack Obama replaced George Bush, a new administration does not suddenly make everything alright. The ABFF (anybody but Fianna Fáil) sentiment that exists at the moment will help propel Fine Gael and Labour to power but it won't ensure their popularity for long when they have to make painful decisions.

And that could be difficult for government TDs to accept, particularly when up to half of them could be first-time deputies, unused to the rough and tumble of national politics. With such a large majority, the temptation for backbenchers to rebel against unpopular measures will be enormous.

It's difficult to know what, if anything, Fine Gael and Labour can do to head off such dissent. Ideally, it would seek to manage expectations between now and polling day as to what will be possible (or, more relevantly, impossible) when it comes to power.

With both parties striving for ascendency in the new government, that is probably wishful thinking. But that doesn't alter the reality for Enda Kenny and Eamon Gilmore that winning the election is going to be the easy bit. The big challenges will come after that.

✦   ✦   ✦

Sean Dublin Bay Loftus was a lesson for the hurlers on the ditch. He didn't moan or complain. He walked the walk instead of talking the talk

18 July 2010

Flying into our capital city over Howth and Bull Island, the natural beauty of Dublin Bay never ceases to amaze. In its own way, it's as spectacular as San Francisco Bay, yet nowhere near as lauded.

Part of the reason for that is we've never made the most of this extraordinary asset. Instead of having a beautiful harbour development, we have a huge area of brown-field development that is home to a major working port, an ESB power station and a sewage plant. In case that wasn't enough, there will soon be an incinerator there.

One of the biggest mistakes of the past forty years is that while Dublin expanded ever westwards, the opportunity to build a new city a mile or two from O'Connell Street was squandered.

If some government had had the vision and the cojones to shift Dublin Port twenty miles or so up the coast and redevelop the area with high density, urban living – serviced by high-speed rail links and restaurants and shops – the impact on the capital would have been amazing. Think Sydney Harbour or even a much bigger version of Dublin's stunning Grand Canal Quay.

To be fair, the much maligned PDs did trumpet the concept five years ago but nobody was listening. No surprise there as planning, urban or rural, has never been of huge importance in Ireland. Unless of course, it's about people demanding their right to build their 4,000 sq ft house wherever they want regardless of whether the land is suitable for a septic tank.

Corruption has played a large role in devaluing planning, but it goes much deeper than that. There are 440,000 septic tanks in Ireland compared to 100,000 in Scotland, which has a bigger population. That statistic speaks volumes about the respect we give to good planning here.

But amidst all the bad planning and chaotic decision making over the past fifty years, Sean Dublin Bay Loftus, who sadly passed away last weekend, stood like a beacon of light.

Loftus was an extraordinary man and an extraordinary politician for a number of reasons. He was Ireland's first environmentalist public representative. Without him, Dublin Bay – under-utilised as it is – would be far, far worse.

Loftus, who lectured in planning law, was one of the few politicians who understood town planning. He campaigned over many decades to protect the bay from the same kind of thinking that bulldozed Georgian Dublin.

At various stages, he fought plans for an oil refinery, a landfill to allow the expansion of the port and a motorway across Dublin Bay. All those crusades, mercifully, were successful and for that Loftus deserves much of the credit. He was a tireless campaigner and was light years ahead of his time in his use of PR. His decision to change his name by deed poll to incorporate the campaigns he was fighting was pure genius. When he finally won his Dáil seat in 1981 he was called Sean Alderman Dublin Bay Rockall Loftus.

His campaign literature with his face imposed on a bulldog always featured the tagline 'tenacity' and 'integrity'. Those two words summed him up. His integrity and sense of honour were beyond question – Loftus was a gentleman to his fingertips.

But it was his tenacity that will probably live longest in the memory. One of the things that is most annoying about the lazy dismissal of politicians that is so prevalent today, is that it ignores the sheer guts it takes to put yourself before the people and have them judge you. Sean Loftus did that on literally dozens of occasions in local, general and European elections.

He fought thirteen general elections, despite only being successful once. Undaunted, he kept campaigning, he kept fighting the good fight, he kept doing what he believed in. That tenacity deservedly got its reward when he served as Lord Mayor of Dublin from 1995 to 1996. No one has ever deserved the position more.

He continued his crusades well into his eighties. He regularly visited the offices of the *Sunday Tribune* to personally hand in press releases about his most recent campaign to stop the expansion of Dublin Port.

A few years back, I didn't hear from him for a long period before getting a letter from Sligo from him telling me he had taken ill there while on holidays. He told me that, as he was still recuperating, his wife had helped him write the letter. I didn't know anything about his family but I thought it was one of the most romantic things I had ever heard. I wasn't surprised to hear his family speak in such loving terms about him last week.

For the rest of us, Sean Dublin Bay Loftus was a lesson for the hurlers on the ditch who wring their hands and complain about politicians and a lack of leadership. He didn't moan or complain. He walked the walk instead of talking the talk.

In an era where volunteerism is constantly declining, his unstinting work on behalf of his community is a shining example of what one person can achieve and what is really important in life. It's customary when such an esteemed person dies to use the old saying, ní bhéidh a leithéid arís ann (there will never be his like again), ach tá súil agam go mbéidh, because, now more than ever, Ireland needs more men and women like Sean Dublin Bay Loftus.

Claire Byrne

Spot the difference: female models and model females

28 October 2007

Katie Price, also known as Jordan, is a woman who knows what she is doing. She uses her body and her fame to make money. Jordan is not an ambassador for charities, nor does she claim to represent a liberated feminist viewpoint or indeed recommend her lifestyle to anyone else. She just amasses huge amounts of cash by being a celebrity commodity.

The unfortunate side-effect of what Jordan does is that her persona is elevated to iconic status. The worst brand of celebrity magazine presents her and people like her as a representative of modern woman ... and the vulnerable, and perhaps the young, buy into it.

However, the wider British media do not present what Jordan is as an aspiration or ideal for all women.

She is broadly seen for what she is by most responsible publications and there is a distinct separation between someone who takes their clothes off for money and someone who should have social influence.

Here at home, we have a comparable example in model and celebrity Katy French, but the lines between model and moral authority have become dangerously blurred. Katy is everywhere, most product launches want her as their public face because her picture gets in the paper. She is in high demand as one of the most recognisable faces in Irish media.

That Katy French is sought-after as a model is no harm.

Good for her that she is busy ... take the work as it lands in your lap, Katy, and charge them top-dollar for the privilege.

More worrying is the recent development that has seen Katy's opinion held up almost as the voice of a generation. Her admission that abortion would be a better option than sacrificing her career for a baby and her vulgar honesty in relation to her sex life recently became frontpage, broadsheet news. The credibility this exposure gives to the musings of a model means Katy French now speaks for Irish women as a whole.

It is not necessarily what Katy says that is offensive, but that a responsible society gives her such a loud voice.

Katy French is a model who gets paid for posing in her underwear in the tabloids when the Dublin football team is playing in a big GAA match.

She should not be portrayed as a new feminist whose flagrant flaunting of her sexuality equals sexual maturity.

Most intelligent women are not, as she recently claimed, 'threatened by her sexuality' but instead cringe when her pronouncements are presented as being a bellwether indicator of what women think or want.

Even the most venerable in our society have fallen into the trap of using Katy as a role model. The aid organisation GOAL recently sent Katy French, the model, to Calcutta, where aid workers strive to alleviate poverty and rescue child prostitutes from the sex industry.

Do you really want to hear a model talking about her sex toys and sexual exploits one week and telling you about the plight of the Third World the next?

The use of Katy French by GOAL to garner some cheap publicity could be seen as compromising and it does devalue the real and valid work of the organisation. But perhaps modern society encourages such stunts because we want to hear how the trip affected the celebrity rather than the real issues behind the ongoing and dire poverty they experience.

Katy French is a free woman in a democratic country and her views are as valid as those of the next person. I'd imagine most of what she says is done with tongue firmly in cheek in order to elicit reaction. But if her crass pronouncements are read as an indicator of wider female opinion, it becomes damaging. Katy French is a female Irish model, not a model Irish female and should be treated by the media and others as such.

✦ ✦ ✦

Media outpouring of false friendship is an insult to Katy

9 December 2007

On Thursday night I sat looking at a newspaper photo of Katy French taken exactly a week earlier. That image was now tainted with another – that of her desperately sad death in a Co. Meath hospital surrounded by her family. This outspoken, but perhaps naïve, young woman whose antics had so irked me just weeks before was gone.

French's promotion by the media as a spokesperson for a generation prompted me to write in this paper about what she stood for. In a fairly hard-hitting piece, mostly directed at the organisations who exploited her for their own gain, I explained how I believed her deliberately provocative opinions were designed to buy her column inches and how the press fell for it every time. While I said I didn't object to her making a good living out of it, I objected to the media holding her up as representative of Irish women and giving her views such a loud voice.

Katy French's honesty led her to a place where the very organisations she used to get her on the front page of every tabloid newspaper here were starting to turn on her. Her birthday party, held just over a week ago, was mocked and described as being more akin to a meeting of the National Union of Journalists than a birthday celebration. The list of high-profile people who weren't there was published before the list of the attendees. It's fair to say she began to be ridiculed; her policy of giving herself completely to the media was beginning to backfire.

Until last week, media organisations continued to publish ever more daring photographs of Katy French and demanded ever more salacious soundbites. These were often accompanied by catty tales of gossip about her private life and her alleged cat-fights with her rivals.

Indeed, in the wake of the personal comments she made about

me in a Sunday newspaper, three tabloid journalists made contact asking for my response to the 'outrageous' and 'disgusting' attack.

For the record, I didn't regard the riposte as either outrageous or disgusting; it was amusing, and proved my substantive point. Since her death I have heard that she believed I wrote about her to garner publicity for myself. I wrote about her because I passionately believed young and vulnerable people were at risk of buying into the idea that it's okay to recklessly say and do what you like, regardless of the consequences, and expect to be feted as a result.

However, the news of her illness and subsequent death turned these journalistic foes into friends. The very journalists who took potshots at Ireland's only glamour model now told us they considered themselves amongst her closest friends.

In the sugar-coated tabloid world of celebrity reporting, friendship is a cheap commodity. Some of these new 'friends' explained that one of the main reasons they loved Katy French was because she made their jobs so easy.

We were told last week that most people on the Irish social scene are almost impossible to prise a story from. French provided a refreshing alternative to the gossip writers by giving them what they wanted. It was a mutually beneficial relationship and one which was abused on both sides. Now, however, we are expected to believe all of these people were genuine friends to the woman.

I don't doubt some of the people Katy French met through the media became close to her. Paul Martin, the *Irish Daily Mirror's* Showbiz editor, told the *Breakfast Show* on Newstalk on Friday that he and Katy concocted stories together, engineering photo shoots they knew would make the front page. They even went so far as to stage a reunion with her ex-fiancé.

One paper took the decision to publish comments from a website message board which were critical of Katy French. The comments were slated by the journalist who described the piece as 'disgusting'.

The decision to close down the thread was praised. This piece of journalism characterised the week's hypocrisy, coming from the same writers who laid in wait for Katy French to put her foot in her mouth. They who reserved column inches for the newspaper version of pointing and laughing at a personality they owned.

One can only but wonder if these people who claimed they knew Katy French really believed she would value their fairweather friendship?

The reaction of the red-top press to her tragic death has confirmed the stereotype. The only purpose Katy French served in most of their lives was to fill papers and make their jobs easier by being endlessly accessible. Professions of deep friendship and close bonds serve only to embarrass those who lay claim to them and insult the memory of Katy French. If French was even half as straight-up as she claimed to be, I am sure she would have appreciated honesty far more than faux friendship driven by guilt.

As it became apparent last week that she was not going to recover, a friend asked me if I felt guilty about what I had written about Katy French a number of weeks previously. My responsibility to honesty will not allow me to deny I found what French represented unsavoury and unpleasant.

I didn't know her personally and did not bear her any malice. Am I deeply shocked and saddened by her death? Absolutely, and I pray for her and those who genuinely loved her.

✦ ✦ ✦

Justine McCarthy

Cloyne abuse report: one hand washes the other

21 December 2008

I t is being said that Cloyne is another Ferns. It is not. It is worse. What has been going on in Cloyne for the last six months is the Catholic Church and the Irish State colluding at the uppermost levels to suppress the revelation that the diocese's elders were 'vulnerable to be seen as complicit' with predatory child abusers 'securing new victims'. By allowing priests accused of raping children to continue to wear their holy vestments and dog collars, Bishop John Magee and his now-sidelined enforcer, Monsignor Denis O'Callaghan, were giving an access-all-areas badge to criminals hunting for fresh young flesh, to paraphrase the excoriating report which the Church and the State nearly succeeded in burying.

When the game was finally up last Wednesday, thanks to local TD Sean Sherlock's persistence in the Dáil on behalf of victims, the Church and the State stuck with their fantasy tales, putting their own self-protection ahead of the protection of children and the appalling anguish of people whose complaints were never prosecuted by agents of the State or the Church. Bishop Magee, propagator of a faith that cherishes the 'little ones', and Barry Andrews, the minister who is supposed to look after the nation's children, could teach Pontius Pilate about washing one's hands of responsibility. Don't be fooled. The diocese of Cloyne did not publish Ian Elliott's report willingly. Nor was it Minister Andrews who ensured it was done. Our patrician State has done nothing but act hand-in-glove with a yet-again miscreant Church.

The report is out now, but the disinformation goes on. Minister Andrews, who gave his sole interview on the matter to RTÉ Radio's *Drivetime* on Wednesday, is still trotting out his ludicrous line about a separate HSE investigation. This phantom investigation had never been mentioned, either publicly or privately, in the last six months while this newspaper was repeatedly contacting Andrews' office to find out what had become of the Elliott report. The complainants in Cloyne had heard nothing about it and certainly had not been interviewed for it. Upon hearing about it for the first time on Wednesday, one complainant phoned Fr Bill Bermingham, O'Callaghan's replacement as Cloyne's chief child protector, to ask what he knew about it. The woman was told the diocese's knowledge of the supposed HSE inquiry amounted to a single phone call from a HSE official last Monday afternoon (15 December), enquiring how many Cloyne priests now stood accused of child abuse. Undeterred by the reality, Minister Andrews (who says he got the HSE report on 4 December), issued a statement to the media on Friday lauding the publication of Elliott's report and adding that he was still thinking about releasing his own beloved HSE report.

No doubt that one, unlike the Elliott report, will not expose the inauthenticity of the minister's original smokescreen about how his department never asked Elliott to do his damned investigation in the first place. Paragraph four of the Elliott report states unequivocably that the Department of Health and Children asked the chief executive of the Church's National Board for Safeguarding Children at a meeting on 15 February this year 'to investigate the circumstances outlined in the the complaint and to report back'.

On Friday night, the woman who had phoned Bermingham about the HSE report sighed exhaustedly on the phone and said to me: 'You know, this is a very sick country.'

At the same time that the nonsense was emanating from the children's ministry, Fr Bill Bermingham, a Youghal curate parachuted into the maelstrom last October as O'Callaghan's substitute – a direct consequence of the Elliott report, despite Bermingham's denials – was being equally disingenuous on national radio. In a pre-recorded interview (preventing any opportunity for debate), he stated that the diocese had decided to release the report on Friday because 'it's only in the last few days that questions have been asked about the report'. This is patent rubbish. Last July, this newspaper ran a page-one lead story about the suppression of the Elliot report, describing it as too hot to handle by either the Church or the State. The true reason why the report was finally published on Friday was because the bishop was made to understand that the demand for its publication was gaining momentum daily and the longer he prevaricated, the greater the damage to him and his Church. Why it was not published in the first place when it was completed last summer was because of 'legal concerns'. It was misleadingly hinted last week that these legal issues related to the danger of prejudicing any potential criminal trials arising from the allegations in Cloyne. This is another untruth and more crocodile tears for the victims. The 'legal concerns' preventing its publication until now was the threat that Bishop Magee and Monsignor O'Callaghan would pursue defamation proceedings; essentially suing their own institution (Elliott's office acts independently, but it was established by and is funded by the Catholic Church). How embarrassing would that have been for Ireland's cosy establishment?

The suppression of the report is now over. We are into stage two of institutional denial – the PR blizzard. Without any apparent concern for the emotional rollercoaster their actions were causing victims, Cloyne choreographed the release on Friday to ensure minimum damage for itself. While it was known in national Church circles on Friday morning that Cloyne was planning to release the report, a spokesman for the diocese was denying it to journalists. At that stage, they were going to release it exclusively to the *Irish Examiner*, the local newspaper where, perhaps, they hoped to get a kinder reception. (Unlikely, as the *Examiner* has recently been trenchant in its criticism of the diocese.) Next, we were told the diocese would post the report on its website at 4 p.m. Then it was 5 p.m. It came sometime after 5 p.m. by way of a press release, followed an hour later by a bland interview on RTÉ's *Six One News* with Bishop Magee. There was no press conference at which journalists who knew the details of the scandal and the cover-up could have asked pertinent questions.

Meanwhile, the facts are these. There is every chance that children, who could have been saved if Cloyne had acted correctly, have been added to the list of victims. A priest of the diocese who was abused as a child has left the priesthood. A woman who was abused by another priest and informed the bishop thirteen years ago is now dead.

While the diocese was immersed in its 'save-our-skin' exercise, another woman was routinely attending her counsellor on Friday morning to try to cope with the damage she is left to live with.

Yes, Cloyne is worse than Ferns because the minister and the bishop stopped the truth coming out. But it is also worse for this reason: Cloyne does not appear to have even heard of Ferns.

✦　✦　✦

Ferdia MacAnna

Nobody died, so the concert must have been a
success. But for a while in Punchestown last
weekend, it was touch and go

5 July 2009

You are standing with your twelve-year-old son in a field with 70,000 people. A small hyperactive fifty-three-year-old Australian with wild hair plays a storming twenty-minute guitar solo in teeming rain on a podium in the centre of the crowd while his bandmates stand on stage, dry as sticks. It is the climax of a wonderful concert by AC/DC.

You feel exhilarated, delighted to have had such a joyous communal experience and proud that your boy has had a good time, as has nearly everyone in the mixed, all-ages crowd – from teens to bikers to dads with their kids.

Afterwards, you trudge along heading towards the buses. The crowd from Slane had a terrible time getting home a couple of weeks back but the word is that all that has been sorted.

You take your place in the zig-zag queue like a good responsible heavy-rock citizen and wait your turn to board a bus home … and wait … and wait … and wait. In front of you, packed bus after packed bus leaves yet the queue doesn't move. Overhead comes the whirr of departing helicopters ferrying the artists and the privileged.

An hour and a half later, the queue hasn't budged. Few stewards in sight. No police. No announcements. No news about delays. No news about anything. People are fed up. The mood changes to anger.

Suddenly, the crowd at the far end breaks through the barriers and gallops for the buses. Now the crowd at the other end follows suit. You and your son, along with thousands of others, are cut off, trapped inside a series of steel barriers. The crowd surges forward

but there is nowhere to go. Where are the stewards? A group of
them stands huddled together in a far field, as though this mess is
now out of their hands.

Where are the police? Who's in charge here? Someone unhooks
a barrier and slips through. Others follow suit and now it's anarchy.
People skip the queues. Barriers are pushed over.

Thousands dash for the buses. Some shout abuse at the few stewards who are still around. You struggle to keep your feet. You worry
about your boy. Hold on tight. Keep your feet no matter what. Trip
and fall, and you will get trampled.

A lone cop tries to restore a barrier and he succeeds, but it's too
late. All discipline is gone as the crowds storm the buses. Rows and
arguments everywhere. Your son tells you that he is scared. You
don't blame him because you are scared too. You feel powerless in
the face of all this confusion, chaos and ill-feeling. You wonder how
it seems to him, to any kid. Panicked, angry adults everywhere. All
rules out the window. You see dads with little kids trying to find a
safe way through the mass of humanity. The organisation seems to
have completely fallen apart. It's a free-for-all.

Eventually, one of the bus stewards takes pity on you and flags
down a packed bus. Doors hish open and you pile on. A sign on the
wall notes that the bus holds ninety-one passengers. Here people
are squished two or three to a seat and sitting on the stairs or on the
floor. You don't care. Anything to get out of there. Your son makes
the trip home sitting on a luggage rack. You squat on the floor beside
a bunch of exhausted Germans.

You are lucky. The bus passes hordes of people desperately trying
to get home. How could things get so out of hand at such a joyous
occasion? Nobody died, so the concert must have been a success.

But for a while in the rain in Punchestown last weekend, it was
touch and go. All it needed was one person to start a panic. If people had tripped over a pushed-over barrier at the peak of the crowd
surge, they would have got trampled and crushed, perhaps killed.

Once when I was ten, my dad brought me to Dalymount to watch
Ireland play. Afterwards, we got trapped in front of a locked exit
gate. I remember elbows in my face, the smell of cigarettes and
beer, belt buckles scraping my hands. Each new push crushed the

breath out of me and took me further away from Dad's outstretched hand. I remember the awful feeling that my dad couldn't help me. It's a shocking thing for a child to realise that their parent is suddenly powerless.

Eventually, the gates opened and everything turned out okay, just like at Punchestown. But it doesn't take much to change a happy experience into a tragedy.

Festivals and open-air concerts are a big feature of the summertime. Oxegen is on next weekend and I hope that many thousands will have a wonderful time. I hope that there is no repeat of the chaos of Punchestown or Slane.

I love going to concerts with my kids. Usually we have a great time, despite the over-priced merchandising and the dire food.

However, after Punchestown I am going to give open-air gigs a miss. I don't trust them. I never again want to stand in a field and feel that I can't protect my kids. I don't ever want to feel like a ripped-off, tossed-away, worthless specimen of humanity just because someone somewhere took my money and then couldn't be bothered to organise the buses home.

✦ ✦ ✦

We took ourselves darned seriously. We spent as much time choosing stage names as we did rehearsing

3 January 2010

A week before Christmas I received a surprise email from the producers of *Killing Bono,* a new film based on Neil McCormick's memoir of life as Bono's best friend. I had visions of being offered a part in the film or being hired as a consultant. There is nothing like a brush with Hollywood to perk up a person's day.

Instead they just wanted permission to use an original 1978 poster of my band, Rocky de Valera and the Gravediggers, as background in some scenes set in Howth. Fame at last, if only as a fleeting image on the wall of someone else's film.

The poster shows six unkempt student types posing in the loo of the Belfield Bar in January 1978 – wannabes with a big new year's resolution to become the next Boomtown Rats. Though inspired by the energy and DIY attitude of the punks, most of us looked more like rejects from the film *Woodstock* than future new wave icons. Still, we took ourselves darned seriously. We spent as much time choosing stage names as we did rehearsing. I devoted inordinate energy to finding a suitable eye-patch for my image. Such attention to detail surely meant that our success was predestined. However, like most new year's resolutions, it failed. The line-up kept changing. By the end of 1980, all of the dreams had petered out and the band folded as though someone had put it in a drawer.

However, we had played a dozen gigs as headliners at Howth Community Centre, where Neil McCormick and his guitar-playing brother Ivan's band, Yeah Yeah, had often played support. The headlining gig was later taken over by U2 and we all know what happened to them.

Now Neil McCormick, ex-*Hot Press* hack and failed rock star, is destined to have his moment of fame on the big screen with a screenplay courtesy of Dick Clement and Ian La Frenais, who penned *The Commitments* and *Lovejoy* and who created *Porridge* and *The Likely Lads*. I remember Neil as an exuberant, speccy geek – he could have stepped out of the movie *Superbad* – and a chatterbox who seemed to be an expert on any subject under discussion. I had no idea that he was Bono's best mate. But then, once U2 had hit the big time, Dublin's pubs teemed with people who claimed to be Bono's pal.

McCormick, though, was the real deal and his memoir, *I Was Bono's Doppelganger* (retitled *Killing Bono* for the US market), is an honest, often painfully funny account of failing in the music business while enviously watching as his best friend's band becomes the biggest thing in rock.

I had mixed feelings when I read McCormick's book. I knew many of the people who were featured and I grudgingly related to the cartoonish but probably deadly accurate portrait of myself that appears fleetingly in a couple of chapters. Somehow it felt as though my teenage dreams of rock stardom had been hijacked. The book depicts a Howth that seemed about to become the epicentre of the rock universe. It was the world of my youth, and now Neil McCormick had made it accessible to everyone.

But I can't really complain. Howth has been on the silver screen before and I was partly responsible. *The Last of the High Kings*, based on my own coming-of-age novel and starring Gabriel Byrne, Jared Leto and Christina Ricci, was filmed in Howth in 1995. In a curious twist, Jared Leto has recently renounced Hollywood fame to become a rock star. He is now lead singer in his brother's band, 30 Seconds to Mars. Unlike other Hollywood rock wannabes such as Juliette Lewis and Keanu Reeves, Leto has made a decent fist of rock stardom and 30 Seconds are one of the hottest tickets on the planet. Just goes to show the power and allure of rock and roll.

It's perhaps fitting that McCormick's story is being filmed in January, a time when people make new year's resolutions and set out to change themselves for the better. Indeed, the new year seems to be the only time in the year when optimism becomes mandatory and people allow themselves 'what if' moments. What if I lost weight? What if I kept a tighter control of my money? What if I finally learned to play the guitar?

Except it's not really about losing weight or learning a musical instrument, is it? It's the one time in the year when we feel we can start anew, when we can reinvent ourselves, feel free to pursue a dream; when it's okay to think big.

But new year's resolutions, like rock dreams, rarely last. Statistics show that only around 40 per cent of people maintain their resolutions past January.

McCormick's story just goes to prove that you should never give up. Because even if the new film flops, McCormick is now a successful author as well as something of an official biographer to Bono and the lads. In a peculiar way, his rock dream has come true.

Each of the wannabe rockers from the 1978 poster turned away from music to carve out different careers for themselves. But I bet that, deep down, most of us would jump at the chance to become a rock star. However unrealistic they may seem, dreams give you something to aim for. And dreams can come true, but just not in the way you expect.

HELEN ROGERS

Expenses scandal discredits the entire Dáil

October 11, 2009

Ceann Comhairle John O'Donoghue leaves office on Tuesday, but he remains light years away from the transformed politician the electorate would like to see. He is not a man humbled by a moment of epiphany that allowed him to understand the ethical error of his ways. Far from it.

He is seething, resentful at having had to suffer the pain of public humiliation and, above all, angry that he was not allowed to have his say, to 'explain' just how he racked up a travel bill of over €100,000 in two years as Ceann Comhairle on top of his generous unvouched expenses, or just why, in this apolitical office, he needed to treble the size of his personal staff. (Never mind the fact this newspaper asked, asked and asked again for him to give his side of the story, only to meet with the worst sort of evasion, that of hiding behind the 'constitutional' bar on his making any sort of political statement. Mind you, he did send us a solicitor's letter claiming our coverage was 'inaccurate, misleading, exaggerated and disingenuous' and threatening to take further steps against us.)

Equally angry are, to their great discredit, his Fianna Fáil ministerial colleagues. To Willie O'Dea, Micheál Martin, Conor Lenihan and Brian Lenihan – to the Taoiseach – the Bull is a scapegoat, a lightning rod for anger, a fall guy for public fury that these days seems beyond persuasion by reasonable argument. He has been felled by grave-dancers who wouldn't wait for due process and whose only motive was to enhance their own standing in the eyes of a media-hyped public ravening for a scalp.

Of course, they are astute and pragmatic enough to realise the political momentum was against their former cabinet colleague and they knew O'Donoghue had to go. But why? Unfortunately for democracy in this country, they still don't get it.

Their gut instinct has been to deflect blame away from what is wrong with the way the Dáil is run and to try to discredit Eamon Gilmore for doing what the electorate and every scared FF back-bencher wanted: looking John O'Donoghue straight in the eye and telling him that his position was untenable and that he had to go.

The consequence has been a week of sour self-justification and bitterness between parties that disgusts the electorate as much as the lavish lifestyle enjoyed by O'Donoghue. The Ceann Comhairle was, as we all knew well, not alone in the level of indulgence he enjoyed. As we reveal today, the depressingly long line-up of cabinet colleagues for whom taxpayer-funded luxury was regarded as an enti-tlement is reinforcement of just how highly our ministers thought of themselves and how low their ethical standards had fallen. No wonder they felt uncomfortable about telling John O'Donoghue the jig was up.

But the inability of the Fianna Fáil leadership to look out, to lift its head above petty point-scoring and admit culpability, pledging a massive reform plan that will wipe out what have become known else-where in the public sector as 'legacy issues' adds to a destructive cyni-cism towards politics. And it comes at a time when we need hope in its ability to lift this country back to prosperity.

The truth about John O'Donoghue is simple. He was a greedy man who used the various high offices in which he was privileged to serve to finance a lifestyle for himself and his wife Kate Ann that he could never have afforded himself.

And the truth about the Dáil is simple. It too is a very greedy place.

The red-faced indignation of TDs and senators who insist they work hard for every cent they make and can verify the need for every cent of expenditure they stump up to selflessly serve their constitu-ents is genuinely felt. But it is a display of self-delusion by the body politic that is so deep-seated it is reaching the point of corruption.

We use that word carefully and advisedly. TDs have for the past dozen years enjoyed a regime of self-written rules and regulations which, in any other sphere, would be regarded as a blueprint for white-collar crime.

What workplace in what universe, for example, allows an employee to travel to work by train and then passes a law to make it perfectly legal to claim, tax free, for every mile never driven? What employee would be paid for phone calls never made? For mobile phones never bought? What employer would dream up accommodation allowances so generous it would be hard to find a hotel that charges enough to justify the payment?

The list goes on and on and the public is rightly angry about the level of unvouched expenses that have become a second salary to many – though not all – TDs and senators.

But, as much as the minister for finance tries to spin the truth by pretending he has been fighting a rearguard action to introduce expenses reform, it should be remembered that John O'Donoghue's political demise has not been caused by the unvouched allowances set by the Houses of the Oireachtas Commission.

It was his verifiable, vouched expenses that have got him into trouble because of their excess. Every flight taken, every suite luxuriated in, every meal digested, every drink savoured, every limousine he comfortably relaxed in was receipted, even down to the £1 donation to Unicef.

Today we publish the expenses of Mary Harney, Tom Parlon, Noel Dempsey, Bertie Ahern and even John Gormley, for God's sake. It makes for very uncomfortable reading. They have all, in some way, enjoyed a luxurious lifestyle at the taxpayer's expense – all of it signed off by the finance office of each minister's department and ultimately by the minister for finance.

John O'Donoghue is a fall guy all right, but only in the sense that so many of his colleagues, if they had an ounce of integrity, should resign along with him. As they brazen it out, they make him the lone scapegoat, not a public that wants root-and-branch transformation of the sleazy modus operandi of the Dáil.

The newly negotiated programme for government puts parliamentary reform at the top of the agenda. It is interesting that it proved one of the stickiest areas to negotiate. No doubt its terms will leave most TDs pale at the extent of the transformation proposed.

The fiasco of stonewalling the Freedom of Information Act at every turn must end. All expenses, whether they are vouched or unvouched, must be published regularly so taxpayers can see where their money is going and decide whether or not it is well spent. New regulations covering overly lavish accommodation, travel and dining arrangements must also be issued. And while there is an argument for some unvouched allowances, these should be kept to a minimum.

Nobody in this saga emerges with much glory. But it is to be hoped that, at last, a poisonous boil has been lanced.

It would have been better, however, if the lead could have been taken by the Taoiseach, who not once in this debacle has put it on record that the lessons have been learned and that our public representatives must clean up their own houses before asking everyone else to take a €4 billion hit for Team Ireland.

✦   ✦   ✦

Olivia Doyle

I felt no ill effects from the nurses' work-to-rule

8 April 2007

At about 11 p.m. last Sunday, a nurse bearing bad news entered the reception area of St James's A&E. To gauge when we might see a doctor, the thirty of us waiting should take our time of arrival and add at least ten hours.

The tourists who were accompanying their ill friend had already been waiting thirteen hours and the late-night casualties were getting rowdier, so we decided to cut our losses. As we left, the flushed nurse apologised to all present for 'this system' before comforting an elderly woman sitting in the chaotic environment. Nine hours to go before the work-to-rule by nurses would begin.

After a ring-around, my resourceful buddy drove me to Tallaght Hospital, hoping it might be less busy – and it was. By 1.30 a.m., I'd been through triage, had bloods taken and was on a trolley in a curtained cubicle on an IV drip. An ordinary sore throat had turned into a severe tonsillitis that had left me drooling, aching and unable to speak or swallow.

I've been in A&E units several times before, all but once, thank God, as a working journalist. Previously, I had seen a nurse not even flinch as she tended a stabbed teenager who drew his own blade out of his boot to 'show' her before spitting in her face. I had seen a nurse gently persuade a repeat attendee to acknowledge that she had not again 'walked into a door'. And I had seen nurses perform any number of clean-up jobs on drunks who thanked them with a stream of expletives and, once, an aggressive grope.

This time, I was the patient, and the nurses were as ever the ones making things bearable. One seemed to be with me for much of the ten hours I was on the trolley, her kindness as much of a balm as the drugs she was giving me.

And it was a nurse whose hand my fingernails were sunk into while a doctor stuck a very, very long needle down my throat to prod around.

By the time I was moved further in the A&E ward to a bed, the work-to-rule was well underway but I personally felt no ill effect from it.

What I did see was a nurse coax out of a badly-suffering patient that their pain was probably being exacerbated by their sudden withdrawal from an undisclosed alcohol dependency.

I saw a nurse embracing a young woman who was crying at the latest diagnosis a doctor had left her with. And I saw several visitors who seemed to interpret 'visiting hours' as the only period when you couldn't visit and 'two at a time' as the number of visitors who should stay outside, making it considerably harder for nurses to treat patients.

I was discharged last Wednesday and, on the way out, I saw about a dozen people on trolleys in the corridor and another two dozen waiting outside in 'chairs'. Any A&E I've ever experienced was invariably very busy and patients were invariably on trolleys, industrial action or not.

The Patient Focus Group has this past week reminded nurses that their main duty of care is to their patient rather than their union. I didn't meet any nurse who needed reminding of that fact. But I did meet the humane face of Ireland's ailing health service, doing on a routine basis for complete strangers the kind of messy, smelly, unpleasant tasks that most of us would have to steel ourselves to do for our loved ones.

✦　✦　✦

Kevin Rafter

Integrity and involvement, hand in hand

In matters of war and peace, refusing to sit on the fence
is not a denial of political impartiality.

27 July 2008

In November 1995, I travelled with Tommie Gorman from
Dublin to the Fanad peninsula in Co. Donegal. We were
attending the funeral of Neil T Blaney, the former Fianna Fáil
minister and longtime Republican independent politician.

I had written a short biography of Blaney a couple of years previously. But at the time, I was still learning my trade as a journalist in the RTÉ newsroom. Gorman had established a reputation
as a hardworking correspondent in the northwest region, and by
1995, he was RTÉ's Europe editor. Some years later, he would
swap Brussels for Belfast to become the national broadcaster's
Northern editor.

I was reminded of that day in November 1995 as I read Ed
Moloney's comments on speculation that Gorman played a role of
sorts in the Northern Ireland peace process. There has been persistent talk that Gorman facilitated contacts between the DUP and
Sinn Féin prior to the establishment of power-sharing at Stormont
in May 2007. Gorman has previously denied a role. But both Bertie
Ahern and Jonathan Powell, a long-time senior advisor to Tony Blair,
had referred to the involvement of the RTÉ journalist.

Moloney contends – if it is true – that Gorman crossed an ethical
line, and that the implications for Irish journalism are far-reaching.
I am not so sure.

There was a huge turnout on the bitter winter's day when Blaney
was laid to rest at the small graveyard at St Columba's Church. In

a graveside oration, another former Fianna Fáil minister, Kevin Boland, spoke of betrayal: 'Blaney is gone. There is no Nationalist, no Republican voice in the parliament of the twenty-six-county State. And there is no principle in it, either.' Given all that has happened in Northern Ireland over the past decade, Boland's words are from another world now.

Martin McGuinness was among the funeral congregation. The IRA ceasefire of August 1994 was in place, but the British had not responded with the same speed as their counterparts in Dublin. Demands for decommissioning and the attachment of the word 'permanent' to the ceasefire were, in peace-process language, creating an impasse to the invitation of Republicans to the talks table. Unknown to the wider world, there was a dynamic underway within the Republican movement, and one which played out so dramatically with the Canary Wharf bombing some months later in February 2006.

Gorman had a relationship with McGuinness. As I understand it, respect for Gorman had been formed some years previously when both men, for different reasons, were in attendance at a local court hearing. As cases waited to be heard, a traveller woman was before the court on some minor charge. She was a mother of several children and it wasn't her first appearance in court. 'Is there someone here to go bail for this woman?' the judge asked. There was silence in the body of the court. Then, rather than see the woman go to jail with the inevitable consequences for her young family, Gorman stood and said he would go bail.

After the Blaney funeral on the road to Derry, we stopped at a café. McGuinness and his driver had already ordered tea. I had not met McGuinness before. He eyed me warily. He was a man under pressure. 'What do you need?' Gorman asked. 'Talks, Tommie. We need talks,' McGuinness replied. And after a pause, he bluntly added: 'I could get a bullet in the head if this thing doesn't start delivering.'

McGuinness may have relayed the same information at meetings with Irish government politicians and officials. I don't know if Gorman passed on the conversation the next time he met a senior politician or minister. At that time, I wasn't in a position to have such access. But if I had met an Irish government figure involved in the peace process, would I have passed on my observations? Yes.

I have interviewed Ed Moloney on many occasions. He is a journalist whose work I respect greatly. I agree with his contention that journalists must not take part in politics nor do anything that raises questions about their professional integrity. I would not, however, be so confident as to state that these principles are widely applied. Conflicts of interest are not always declared. And it is regrettable that the purity which Moloney seeks does not universally prevail. The idea of a register of interests for media professionals is certainly worthy of consideration.

But a more pertinent matter concerns the belief that the non-intervention of journalists in political matters is an all-embracing principle. I do not accept that political purity is so easily applicable – or always justifiable – in an area of conflict-resolution.

Is it really unethical for a journalist to make his home and counsel available to rival parties in a political conflict so they can secretly meet to resolve their differences? I would say the answer is no. And it is certainly not unethical if the consequences of non-intervention are that the two sides fail to reach agreement and a return of conflict is a possible outcome.

I like Gorman. Like most television reporters, he demands attention and is driven by a desire to get his story on screen. But he is also motivated by tremendous compassion. And if he did play some small role in the latter stages of the peace process – describe it as being a player, if you like – then it was probably because moral responsibility overruled any ethical principle of the journalism profession.

✦   ✦   ✦

Liam Hayes

Me And The Big C

On 9 September GAA columnist Liam Hayes got a call that changed everything. Here, he writes about his diagnosis with cancer and his determination to overcome the biggest challenge of his life ...

17 October 2010

I sit into the large blue armchair, which is deep and comfortable, and a welcoming single piece of furniture. There are twelve such pieces in this large, well-lit spacious room. It is just after 2.30 p.m. I will be sitting down in this relaxing blue armchair for about four hours. It could indeed be very comfortable, because it can also offer me leg support if I wish to stretch out. I don't feel like stretching out. Sitting in my blue armchair, in fact, makes me feel quite like I am sitting in an advanced, quite luxurious electric chair or, more precisely, a chair which might accommodate the death of a very bad man by the quieter, slightly more humane, manner of lethal injection. Beside me, my wife is sitting on a tiny, wooden stool.

It is Monday 27 September, 2010.

To begin with, my over-riding thought, which charges an impulse to move and extract myself from this deep seat, is that they've got the wrong man, and more the wrong man rather than the condemned man necessarily. My long hours in this chair are not designed to kill me, I know that, even though I have also been informed that my time in this chair might transform me from a strong, fit, healthy, trim-enough forty-eight-year-old man into someone who is definitely going to look the worse for wear, and might also believe that he is actually quite seriously ill.

'It wasn't me!'

'I am not sick at all ... actually, I'm as strong as a feckin' horse. I could go for a two- or three-mile run and come back to you in fifteen or twenty minutes … believe me!'

That's what I feel like saying to those around me, those sitting in the other blue armchairs, and those walking around us, working smartly and brilliantly. My oncologist, I already trust with my life, literally, from my very first meeting. She is calm and certain, and embracing of myself and my wife in her words and her body language. All around her is efficiency and professionalism, and human kindness of an exceptionally high standard, except, of course, I feel unprepared and misplaced as a direct recipient of this attention.

'I'm a journalist.'

'A publisher … books, newspapers.'

'That's what I do.'

'I'm a former Gaelic footballer, that too.'

'Yes, used to play with Meath.'

'I'm a husband, a father.'

'I'm not a sick person at all … never have been!'

'I'm definitely not a patient.'

My right arm, however, is resting on a pillow, and some time ago my nurse had prepared the way, inserting a tube into a vein in the crook of my arm, from which extends a valve-like piece of plastic, taped firmly down on my skin. I'm all set, and awaiting the drugs which will be entering my body intravenously. In pouches and packets, they have just been prepared in a laboratory specially for me, and now they are on their way to the hospital. My name and date of birth is on each of those plastic packages.

'F**k it … you know what? Ladies and gentlemen – doctors and nurses – you've got the wrong f**king man here!'

Instead, I sit there, say nothing, and try to smile as often as possible. It's just before 6.30 p.m. when I finally lift myself out of my seat, and walk slowly into a toilet area, and stand, and pee.

And my pee is an interesting, alarming reddish colour, but I have been told some hours earlier that it will be so, and told not to be at all alarmed. The battle, like some battle from Tolkien's Middle Earth, as I like to imagine it, has commenced in my body, comprising evil little bastards of all sorts of shapes and sizes on one side, multiplying all the time most probably. And then there's my men, the good guys, hobbits and elves and cool, clean, square-jawed types played, of course, by Viggo Mortensen and other sword-wielding buddies of his.

One of the really important guys on my side of this battle (I think of him as Viggo himself) is a drug called rituximab, an extremely clever fella indeed, I am informed – a monoclonal antibody, who can recognise certain proteins that are found on the surface of some cancer cells, and once he sees them, he locks onto those cells, forever! My body's immune system then charges over the hill and gives the bad bastards a good kicking. Cancer cells don't like this. Sometimes, it happens that the cancer cells kill themselves before the rituximab and my immune system even get around to finishing the job.

The other lads on my side are cyclophosphamide, vincristine, doxorubicin, and a steroid called prednisolone. Quite an army, I feel, and, better still, they sound like they will not be taking any shit from anybody!

Eighteen days earlier, I was told that I had non-Hodgkin's lymphoma.

My wife was in Dublin city centre, doing some shopping. I was working at home. The previous Monday I had a needle biopsy taken from a lump, which had appeared from 'nowhere', and which felt as big and as hard as a golf ball, just below my left jaw. Anne was worried all week long and she wanted news of the result, but I wasn't at all perturbed, and had informed her and my doctors that the lump was the result of dehydration, which in turn was a direct result of my magnificent but failed attempt to beat the world record, during the months of July and August, for the consumption of fine Bordeaux wine.

For the previous three weeks, I had examined the lump every morning as I shaved, and because I had to look at it up close every morning I was, luckily, and thankfully, unable either to ignore it or presume that it might just piss off back to wherever it came from, voluntarily, and most generously.

On that Thursday morning, 9 September, I got a call.

As calls go, it was short, but sufficiently informative. Would I like to hear the results over the phone? Or would I like to come in and receive them face to face?

No good news was proffered.

Sitting down in front of my surgeon, who was not smiling, and who was not even thinking of chit-chatting on this occasion, trebly confirmed my certainty that I was indeed in big trouble of some description.

My surgeon was younger than me, and he didn't beat around the bush. He was direct, without too much emotion, but appeared genuinely sincere in the care and sympathy he voiced, after telling me I had 'B-cell, high grade, non-Hodgkin's lymphoma'. He made it abundantly clear in the information he provided me ('This will either kill you, or the chemo will kill it ... but this is not something you are going to have to live with.'), and also in the information he sought from me ('What age is your youngest child?') that I might be in very big trouble indeed.

He was excellent, I thought. Tough and excellent, and I felt then, and still feel now, that he was someone who was very good at his job of telling people that they might live or they might die.

The same man had sliced my neck open twice, under general anaesthetic, to examine my lymph gland, take away a piece of it, and finally extract it all. And, in my last conversation with him – which was about the results of a third biopsy which were better than expected – he did say to me, encouragingly, that my chances must now be as high as '85 or 90 per cent', which in all honesty, was not something I really wanted to hear or discuss for one minute.

What's a good percentage?

In my book, if you are in a life or death fight, as I now am, then even a 99 per cent chance of winning is not enough!

Driving home from hospital that afternoon, I asked Anne, what exactly did he mean by 85 or 90 per cent?

'85 or 90 per cent what?' I asked my wife. '85 or 90 per cent get better? The 10 or 15 per cent – what happens to them? They need stronger treatment? They what?'

Anne looked at me, dutifully, and lovingly.

'They die, darling,' she said, knowing that I was already aware of this, and needed to hear it, in order to be shushed.

In the last number of weeks, I have heard directly, and second- and third-hand, so many stories of people who have fought and won

the same fight I am now commencing. I know of several dozen people who are leading full, healthy lives. However, I also know people
who did not win this same fight, though my family and friends never
talk about them, it so happens.

Neither does anybody ever telephone me and tell me, 'I know
a man who had exactly what you have Liam ... and he died ...
unfortunately!'

Ten or fifteen people out of every 100 dying is not a percentage
that I like at all, thank you all the same.

If you put 100 people into a room, and announced that between
ten and fifteen of them are going to win the lottery in the next year
or two, of course they'd be delighted, thrilled by their chances of
winning. But, if you put 100 people into another room, and broke
the news that between ten and fifteen of them are going to lose their
jobs, and shortly after that lose their homes, they'd absolutely hate
it, and they'd all be pretty sure in their heads that they were bound
to be the unlucky ones to be rolled over and stood upon.

Between 10 per cent and 15 per cent can look very good, or it can
look very bad indeed.

I've never been in the running for 'Roman Catholic of the Month'.
I could explain why, but I'm not going to do so here and now. My
single greatest doubt about the Church into which I was born is
this: why, in the whole history of the Church, has a woman never
been asked to make a decision on anything, and why are women, still
today, never to be seen within 100 yards of the Pope?

I like women. I love them more than men. I trust them more, and
I personally know two women in particular, who are now in their
eighties, and who have given their whole lives to serving God, who
would do the job of Pope Benedict in the morning, do so brilliantly,
and in doing so make him look an awful, absurdly foolish old man.

All so quickly, I've just got Roman Catholics and people who do
not believe in any God at all 'praying' for me. Hundreds of the former, and a handful of the latter.

I know this, because my small, beautiful mother was heading off
to Lourdes with her beloved choir on the Meath Diocesan pilgrim-
age, when news of my big trouble first came through.

I am not a person who prays, and have not prayed for the last half of my life. But I do believe in good and evil. I also believe in the spirituality of our whole existence. Prayer, especially prayer by good people, I firmly believe has to be a good thing, and I am deeply, incredibly thankful for everyone who has thought of me, or better still fought for me, through prayer.

I am thankful, and I want it all.

I also believe, firmly, that prayer can help me. Maybe not save me in some wondrous way, but it can help me. My sister Carmel and my god-daughter Rebecca also prayed in Lourdes with my mother.

Rebecca is her mother's daughter. Life is straight lines for Rebecca and her mother, and you journey from A to B, and then from B to C, and you don't beat around the bush. Rebecca is ten years old.

As she waited to get into one of the brutally cold public baths, which they have in Lourdes for the pilgrims, and which scared her quite a bit, she very sensibly and earnestly, I'm informed, said to her mother, 'When I get into the water I'm not going to pray for a miracle for Uncle Liam ... I'm going to pray that he doesn't have too much pain, and that he then gets better!'

Sensible girl.

That sort of prayer might get a result.

I am not waiting to die, and I'm not even thinking of dying. But, I am waiting for some other things. I'm waiting, for instance, for my taste buds to temporarily retire from active duty. I was waiting, but I'm not waiting any longer, for my hair to fall out. On Tuesday morning last, I found enough evidence in my shower and bathroom sink to decide to spend that afternoon buying some headwear – two caps that I like to think of as more 'Guy Ritchie' than 'Jack Charlton'. On Thursday morning, I had my head shaved.

I'm not waiting for anything else. The different elements which make up my chemotherapy treatment, as I've happily stated earlier, don't take any shit from anybody or anything, and when I look down through the almost laughably outrageous list of possible side-effects it is clear that anything that moves, or beats, in my body is not entirely out of harm's way.

The strangest thing of all, however, and something I discovered within days of becoming one additional member of that massive tribe of people called 'the ill', is this: we have absolutely no other worries. Or very few all of a sudden.

Or no real worries at any rate, apart from the fact that we've all got cancer.

But that concern, amazingly, does not consume us or visibly present itself as some form of colossal fear on the faces of those who sit around me, as we wait for our 'bloods' or our 'chemo'. We don't complain about taxes or negative equity, or Seanie Fitz in sunny Spain, or Bertie in a dark cupboard. We don't even complain about waiting. I haven't heard one single person, over the last six weeks, not even once – honestly – mutter a single word of complaint. About ANYTHING.

And, believe me, we, 'the ill', do quite a lot of sitting and waiting!

In the early days, before I became a fully diagnosed member of this amazingly calm, civilised, happy-enough, hugely dignified group of people, I grumbled and put on a few 'why is it always me who has to wait' faces.

In hospitals in those early days, also, you'd never know who you'd meet or sit down beside, or worst of all, have just a drawn curtain away from you, in the bed next to you. One man my own age who entertained me in conversation in a pre-theatre waiting area in one hospital, each of us buck-naked underneath our hospital gowns, had a problem with the cartilage in his left knee.

One elderly woman, or at least she sounded lots and lots older than me, in another pre-theatre ward in another hospital, was being assured by her doctor that it would only take five or ten minutes to drain the fluid from her left ear, and she'd be hearing fine and tottering out the front door by lunchtime, God bless her. And good luck to her too, I say.

'The ill', of course, do not wish bad luck or harm to come to anybody else. We just don't need to be with 'the others' for long spells, or to be there for them if we can help it. That's not because we feel sorry for ourselves, because nobody appears to feel sorry for themselves when the tribe gathers. I certainly don't, which has also massively surprised me.

I feel good.

And, I feel, and this is going to appear completely weird, but it's the case: I feel lucky. The word 'weird' does not even do justice to that admission. I realise that! Am I slightly bonkers and definitely away with the fairies from time to time, due to the box full of medication I delve into, thanks to my wife's trusty Nurse Ratched-like reminding and disciplining, throughout my day? Perhaps I am, a little, but also I have never felt as clear-headed.

A lady I've met recently, who has survived her cancer, and who was unaware of me feeling 'lucky', shared with me her experience of feeling 'euphoric' in the time after her diagnosis. She explained that her life had been brought back to basics, and she could accept that she was now facing something huge, and vaguely unknown, and she felt euphoric about taking on that fight.

For me?

After forty-eight years of wondering, often enough to be honest, what this whole business of living is really about, I've now got some hope, faint though it may be still, that I might actually get to figure it out, or some of it at least.

And, yes, there is the strongest sense of being chosen, hand-picked even, for a right good fight.

✦　✦　✦

The weariness which has completely taken a grip on me is bone-deep

Life moves slowly when you're a member of the tribe they call 'the ill'. Senses are heightened; relief comes from unexpected places; the darkest thoughts jostle with a strange feeling of contentment.

19 December 2010

The batteries are gone. It's not that they are low, or that they are temporarily dead. THEY'RE GONE! As though somebody has unscrewed a large panel in my back and prised those two huge AA batteries out of their resting places, and taken them away somewhere. Today, I am as helpful and as mobile as a giant-sized Action Man doll that has had its batteries confiscated, without notice, without any discussion of any sort, by a godly, bossy ten-year-old. I have been like this for several days, it seems. Last Friday I took the last little heap of my twenty daily steroids, which bolster me, and which for the first five days of each twenty-one-day cycle of chemotherapy temporarily mask the fact that I have become something of a weakling, and on Saturday I felt okay. By Sunday afternoon, suddenly, totally unannounced, the batteries were gone. GONE, GONE!!!

This is my third cycle of chemo and the plan is that it will also be my last. I felt equally as low, and almost as entirely worthless as this, midway through my second cycle, but, definitely, when I was laid low and left mostly horizontal that particular week, the batteries in my back were still there. I knew they were still there, I could feel them. This is different. This time I feel vulnerable, completely at the mercy of somebody or something. I feel ... and this phrase is residing stubbornly in my head ... but ... I feel good for nothing. Whoever thought up that phrase? And why such complete dismissiveness?

I move around my home, which I am told I have not left for nine days, slowly and, usually, come eveningtime, with a blanket around my shoulders. I retire to my bed for one longish sleep every single day and also slip in two or three shortish naps on a chair. The tiredness and weariness, which has completely taken a grip on me, is bone-deep. I'm constantly tired and mildly nauseous, but I don't feel a physical sickness. Actually, I have no real physical complaints of any kind. Mentally, I'm alert and functioning alright ... I presume. But, right now, and these last few days, I know I am absolutely, entirely good for nothing. And not to be good for even one single thing is, right now, more alarming than frustrating, and offers me an insight that I would much prefer not to have of what a really serious illness must be like for some of those people I have been sharing large portions of my life with for these last few months. It is Tuesday 16 November, 2010.

I remained light and useless and completely good for nothing for about seven or eight days in total, which seemed an extremely long period of time, but now, on the first day of December, with the fluffiest, softest snow I have ever viewed or rolled in my hands covering everything in sight, my week without batteries seems, almost, incredibly, several months ago.

Life, and days, move slowly when you are a fully diagnosed member of the tribe called 'the ill', which is very good news indeed, is it not?

Who wants to have cancer, and have both hands on the clock on the wall engaged in some maddening and manic race? Days go slowly, I understand, because everything else has calmed and quietened down in the lives of 'the ill'. Our bodies move at a cautious pace. Our minds concentrate more, and our thoughts too. To have our daily existence dropping down from fourth gear (with the many ludicrous hours spent revving impatiently), to a comforting second gear, or even a completely self-indulgent and sleepy first gear, is exactly as it should be for every member of the tribe.

But, I need to put down on record something I have learned since first writing about my 'big trouble' (as I worded it) in this newspaper on 17 October last.

It is important.

It is this.

This tribe I talk about actually has two very different types of people. It has a dividing line down the middle of the camp. And wherever we camp, whether it is in the first of the tiny waiting areas of the oncology department in St James's Hospital (which, for the life of me, has me thinking that I am seated on one of the tiniest seats, in one of the tiniest departure lounges, in an airport hidden away in central Dublin), or in the slightly larger waiting area for chemotherapy treatment twenty yards further down the hallway, or in the treatment room itself (where we go from tight little blue plastic seats to our large, welcoming blue armchairs), there are always two very different types of people – 'the ill' and 'the very ill'.

I am in the former group. Fortunately. Thankfully. And those of us on that side of the dividing line in the tribe always need to remember to respect our situation and theirs, and always be aware that our understanding of illness, and of life, and definitely the ending of life, might be far less complete than those who have to count themselves amongst 'the very ill'.

Therefore, as someone with stage one of B cell, high grade, non-Hodgkin's lymphoma, I have to be careful about what I say and what I write. What do I know? However, I do know that when I spent my week without those two gigantic batteries packed into my back, I got to look down a road I had never even seen before then. I knew such a road existed, of course, but in November I actually got to look and walk down that road a few yards. That's all. Further down that road, closer to death, and touching upon the flick of a switch which comes with extinction, I can't imagine what it's like, and what people think about. I've heard people, who've been well down that road and who've come back up again, say that they have been in places, for periods of time, when they have not cared whether they lived or died. I can only imagine that that must be a place where feeling good for nothing is multiplied by a factor of ten, perhaps, or surely some far greater, even more unforgiving multiple.

Both 'the ill' and 'the very ill' wear the same clothes. And, upon first diagnosis, I had to make a quick change.

Turning up at the reception desks in hospitals – and I've been to a great number of desks in a large number of hospitals in the last three months (starting with the Hermitage Clinic where I first was told of the 'big trouble', and since then taking a long, slow tour of Mount Carmel, St James's, the Dublin Dental Hospital, and St Luke's) – in a sports jacket and shirt, finely creased slacks and business shoes is all fine and dandy for one day.

But day after day after day, two or three days per week?

Or, without fail, every single day of the working week until Christmas Eve, which is now my current treatment schedule (twenty minutes of radiotherapy, preceded by thirty or forty minutes reading Alan Sugar's large, brick-like autobiography *What You See Is What You Get*) in St Luke's?

All of us have to be relaxed, we've got to be in no hurry, and we've got to be seated as comfortably as we can possibly sit. The appropriate clothes are important.

Occasionally, I will still arrive at a reception desk and say 'My name is Liam Hayes, and I've got a meeting with ...' before correcting myself. There have been no business meetings for many months. There have been, in their place, dozens and dozens of appointments.

'I'm sorry. I mean I've got an appointment with ... My name is Liam Hayes,' and then I wait for my name to be located somewhere in the middle of a long list of people who have business in that same hospital at that same time.

Within one week of my diagnosis, my wife brought me for a speedy shopping trip. Jeans x 3, casual shirts x 6, pullovers x 3, comfortable shoes x 2. These are my cancer clothes. My wife will, of course, hate that phrase and tell me never to use it again when she reads this (same as, when she hears me tell people I'm thinking of keeping my head shaved when my treatment is over, she announces with sergeant-major like certainty that 'we will have no associations with cancer when this time passes') but the fact is that after fifteen years of mostly all work and very little play in my publishing career I had no clothing that could be considered suitable for a cancer patient.

A few weeks ago, when I appeared on *The Late Late Show*, having first questioned the show's production team if they honestly thought that talking about suicide and cancer back-to-back in one conversation with Ryan Tubridy would be an excellent recipe for good viewing figures, I made a big effort to get all dressed up – getting out an old business jacket, a good shirt, and finding a pair of slacks that didn't need much work done to them.

In make-up on the first floor, that Friday evening, I found myself in conversation with a fellow Meathman who very efficiently goes by the title of 'Hector'. We were sitting with our backs to one another, facing into mirrors, and getting along fine, but I definitely did think to myself that he might have bothered to put on a few clothes and not turn up in a pair of jeans and some old, worn tee-shirt.

Minutes later, my wife and I were chatting to Ryan himself, and he looked resplendent, if not absolute perfection, in the sharpest suit I have ever viewed that has not been positioned in a shop window. He's a nice man. And he was the perfect host in the green room – welcoming, and calming, and just exactly right in all the mannerisms that can oftentimes collide and cause disruption on formal occasions. He was actually the best-dressed man in the room, until Hector reappeared and dashed by in the direction of the bar in the newest, creamiest, shiniest three-piece suit I had ever seen.

Later, I stood behind the set, waiting to be introduced, waiting with the floor team, having some last-minute make-up administered, feeling like one of the best-dressed cancer patients in Ireland but also underdressed for the country's biggest TV show, thinking, 'Look down ... look down' when my name is announced and the band starts up and I have to negotiate all of those steps that every guest on *The Late Late Show* fears and targets with equal measure.

Life, officially, has been no fun since I was diagnosed on 9 September, 2010, which, if you like, has become my own personal 9/11, even though nobody has died. Yet. I'm not planning to die either.

For the first few hours, after diagnosis, I was convinced I was a goner. When I broke the news of my 'big trouble' to my wife and daughter, and my mother and sisters, I was fairly sure that I was marked down, by whomever marks down such things, to be done and dusted. Small things, during those first few days, struck me as forcibly as a medium-sized truck. As my youngest son, Stephen, came through the front door from school that first Friday afternoon, I felt immediately sad for myself, and for myself more than Stephen I have to admit, and firmly believed that such happy occasions as seeing his theatrical arrival home were already counting down.

My wife and daughter, supportively, like two happy tourist guides in the land of 'the ill' ask me, regularly, when am I next going to smile?

That always surprises me.

I think I am smiling most of the time. I'm actually quite happy and, definitely, not unhappy. And I'm happiest of all with a long glass filled with iced water. My favourite drink in the whole wide world is no longer the fine Bordeaux wine I had been lashing into during the months of July and August with the abandon of a mad, rosy-nosed Frenchman with his own private cellar beneath his kitchen floor.

Iced water, long glass after long glass of it in the eveningtime, is fulfilling and satisfying in a peculiarly nourishing way. And, I can genuinely catch more than a glimpse into the life of some poor wretch stranded on a desert island without any luxuries – and understand perfectly well how good, how breathtakingly cutting, a clean glass of water would be to such a man or woman on a hot, dry, desert island afternoon.

My senses are alive, and residing at a higher storey than I ever imagined existed. And not just my taste. My hearing has become intensely tuned to every slammed door in my home, every shout or scream, every X-Box game playing, every squeak from the television set. I have never lived a noisier life. And then there are my nostrils. These days I would fancy my chances in out-sniffing the most celebrated sniffer dog in Dublin airport. I smell everything. And everything smells stronger, and smells mostly repugnant, especially smells that are expensive to buy, like, for instance, big-brand perfume or some of the fancier liquid soaps in bathrooms. Within a few weeks of treatment, liquid soap had become my No. 1 enemy. It turns my stomach, doubles my nausea, and lingers on my fingers and the backs of my hands for hours and hours.

The disastrous state of this country's economy mostly uninterests me. I read only a little of the daily announcements telling me that Ireland is finished. I avoid all commentary on television and radio, and have done so since the earliest days of my diagnosis, and I understand fully why my dentist has the radio in his surgery tuned to a German station all through the day. But rather than switching to a foreign language for a reprieve from the life of this nation, I have actually switched the sound down on Ireland 2010 and have chosen to watch our politicians and bankers and businessmen moving around, and coming and going, like characters from a silent movie at the beginning of the last century.

In my old business life, I had bumped into almost all of these characters. I made presentations and discussed my business plans with almost all of them. With Sean FitzPatrick (and also David Drumm, whose Anglo Irish Bank business card I still have somewhere in my mini skyscraper of business cards, and which some day I might auction on eBay) and with Michael Fingleton and with Denis O'Brien. And, with my favourite rich man of them all, Dermot Desmond.

While Michael O'Leary still gets ten out of ten for returning my phone call one afternoon, and spending ten minutes informing me that he was not going to do business with me and was not going to give me any money, and then asking me what I could do for him that would not cost him a penny, Dermot Desmond got higher marks from me for his performance one afternoon when four of us rode the elevator to his boardroom in his offices in the IFSC, which were pristine, luxurious, and which had a library overhead and a telescope on a tripod, aimed at the southside of the city, on the balcony behind us.

When Dermot entered he sat at the top of the table. I don't remember him saying anything, but I do remember us starting to talk and, quickly, with more animation and passion than was probably necessary, racing through our presentation and our wonderful plans to make millions and millions of euros ... and stopping. Dermot didn't say anything. He sat there looking at us, ever so slightly interested, definitely bemused, but said nothing. And, so, we started again, the four of us, supporting one another, interrupting one another, filling any space that needed to be filled and – almost out of breath – stopping. And Dermot, still, didn't say anything. We needed to stop talking, but we couldn't. We needed to say goodbye to him, we needed to escape, but he was in no hurry to lift himself out of his chair. He eventually did stand, and invited us to leave, without having asked one single question in the forty-five minutes that had just passed.

Dermot Desmond, and O'Leary, together, with one or two others, might actually be capable of winning the confidence and the complete attention of a great many people living in this country, and also winning the support of whatever number of people out there are watching this country lose all confidence in itself. With Ireland nearly finished off, there's nothing to be lost from asking them to double-check whether the country really is at death's door or not.

The battle in my body, which previously I have likened to some battle in Tolkien's Middle Earth, has ceased. That's what I have been told. Last week, I was informed by my oncologist that the result of my latest Pet scan was negative, and that technically there were no more evil creatures hard at work in my neck, or hiding out somewhere else in my lymphatic system for that matter.

It was news I expected. I had always believed that I was doubly lucky – in having my cancer diagnosed early and in having my treatment commenced with such speed and professionalism. Add into that the prayers that people who pray have been offering up for me, and the surprising, humbling supply of good wishes and heartfelt support that has been directed my way by old-fashioned post, and also, hard and fast, by email.

I, purposely, have not replied to these people, or thanked any-one personally, believing that my chemotherapy and radiotherapy should be completed, and finished with, before being energetic with my thank yous.

I celebrated very briefly with a long glass of iced water the even-ing I was told this news. The celebrations will remain on ice. My daily radiotherapy treatment in St Luke's continues to Christmas Eve, and five days each week I am fitted with a plastic mask that fits over my head and neck, and which reminds me that, literally, helmets and shields should not be lowered just yet. I'm told I'm winning. I'm told there's a 10 per cent chance, only, of the cancer returning – once again, that same, sinister Mr 10 per cent.

There will be more tests in January. There will be three-monthly check-ups all through 2011. For the next five years, I am officially informed, we are not going to turn our backs on our opponent.

I only believed for a short period of time that I was going to die of cancer, and for the last couple of months I have been sure that I will not. I have always believed that, like my father, my heart will get me in the end. I will be better next year, and by the end of 2011 I am informed that, medically speaking, I will be healthy and energetic and no longer good for nothing. And then, potentially, it will be time to start worrying again about getting ill, and dying.

In the early days and weeks, after joining 'the ill', I accepted that this was how it was going to end. That may sound a bit dramatic, but when I sat on the side of the bed in my cubicle in the Hermitage Clinic, naked beneath a blue paper gown, and waited there, alone, for an hour or more, the one thought in my head (which, surpris-ingly, was not upsetting me as much as it should have been) was: 'This is how it is going to end.'

For a while, after being diagnosed with non-Hodgkin's lym-phoma, I didn't worry any more about getting ill. I stopped thinking about my heart, and my high cholesterol, and what might happen, when and how, without even a word of warning. For a little while, I was free of all my foolish worries.

I am tired and weary. The days are moving slowly. Christmas Eve appears to be many months away still. I am a free man, free of can-cer, but I have just popped three more anti-sickness pills, I have a blanket over my shoulders as I write, and the smells coming from downstairs in my home, where my wife has prepared a magnificent evening meal for us all, are intriguing and enticing, and at the same time mildly revolting. I only need to shave every three or fours days, and even then it takes three or four seconds rather than three or four minutes with an electric razor. I am bald. I am wearing my cancer clothes. I'm still, officially, a member of a quietly spoken, hugely dignified, calm and strangely contented tribe called 'the ill'.

I'm in no hurry to leave camp.

In its own good time.

✦ ✦ ✦

News Features

Michael Clifford

Chilled cat gets cream in court

It was more like a lesson in lingo for lawyers and judge alike,
but the bizarre case of the disappearing Prince ended
in settlement with one happy looking cat.

28 February 2010

There was no show from the little guy last week. For the second time, the artist once again known as Prince failed to turn up for an Irish audience. In 2008, a concert appearance he was due to give at Croke Park was cancelled at short notice. Last week, the fallout from that incident was played out in the High Court. The concert promoter, Denis Desmond's MCD, sued Prince for €1.7 million, but once again the little guy was nowhere to be seen.

All week in the Four Courts, we awaited his arrival. Perhaps he would amble in wearing a raspberry beret, the kind you find in a second hand store. But he didn't, and it was his loss, because he would have witnessed an interesting collision of cultures, between the music business, California-style, and the Irish legal system, as conducted in the historic setting of the Round Hall of the Four Courts.

At a time when the courts are filled with human misery and disappearing fortunes, a good old fashioned bunfight between multi-millionaires was just what the doctor ordered.

Desmond's outfit sued Prince for the lolly, but Prince claims the booking agent, Los Angeles-based WMEE, was not authorised to book the gig for him, so it was liable. As a result, WMEE was attached to proceedings, even though Desmond has no beef with the agency.

On Tuesday, Prince's lawyer told Judge Peter Kelly that the man himself wouldn't be making the trip. Neither would his right-hand woman, Ruth Arzate. Both had furnished witness statements, but that's a bit like lip synching on *Top Of The Pops* – it doesn't work in front of a live audience.

The lawyer Paul Sreenan told the judge about the no show.

'Well, what would Lady Bracknell say?' the judge replied. Nobody pointed out to the judge that the case was entering territory more familiar with Lady Gaga than Lady Bracknell and the bould Oscar.

The proposed gig saw the light of day in December 2007. Desmond contacted WMEE's Tony Goldring. Only the music business could produce a man by the name of Goldring. They checked it out with the little guy. A European tour was sketched. Offers came in for gigs at seven venues, including Croke Park, earmarked for 16 June. Prince was offered $3 million for the Dublin gig. In total, if he accepted the seven offers from across Europe, he was in line for $22 million for a week's work.

Of course, there were issues. The little guy isn't like you and me. He is an artist, subject to the whims of his muse and the moods of what was described in court as his 'gift'. Communication with Prince is through Ruth Arzate, who acts as an interpreter of his thoughts, as well as his interior decorator and personal assistant. Ruth is a busy woman.

'Ruth spent a lot of time interpreting Prince for us,' WMEE's Keith Sarkisian told the court on Wednesday. Sarkisian had flown in from LA. He is described as a 'responsible agent'. This really means he's the link man with the artist. But he was not allowed to go straight to Prince. He had to communicate via Ruth the interpreter.

Things got moving. In January, Ruth interpreted Prince and issued an email to Sarkisian, 'Dublin looks nice.' More emails followed and by late February the little guy confirmed he was ready to big it up in Croker.

WMEE got cracking. 'Are they cool?' Sarkisian wrote in one email, referring to another party involved in the promotion.

'What did you mean by, "Are they cool?"' lawyer Grainne Clohessy asked him.

'Are they good to go, up to date,' he replied.

'As opposed to are they trendy?' the lawyer inquired. Really, somebody needs to get down to the Four Courts and introduce these people to the Californian vernacular that has swept the rest of the world like a pandemic virus. Is we cool on that point?

Later, Sarkisian mentioned that he 'continued to reach out to them (concert buyers)'.

'What do you mean by 'reach out'?' the judge asked. Cue Diana Ross entering from the back of the courtroom, all big hair, trailing a sequinned dress and singing into a Big Mama microphone. 'Reach out and touch, somebody's hand, make this world a better place, if you can.'

Back on planet earth, the psyche of Prince was further dissected. Despite confirming for Dublin, he didn't confirm for any of the other European gigs. Everybody was trying to interpret what he wanted. In one email sent to Sarkisian, Prince was referred to as 'an incredible client'.

The judge wanted that characterisation interpreted.

'Is that that he was not to be believed or he was a good client?'

'Oh, it's that he was a very good client,' Sarkisian replied. 'He (the writer) was talking about his gift, as I understand it.'

On 12 March, Sarkisian was invited to Prince's house for dinner. 'Dinners with Prince are interesting, usually filled with lots of discussion about worldly issues,' he told the court.

'He was very frustrated with album sales. He was looking to do something to break into markets he hadn't been in in a long time.' Further correspondence through his interpreter Ruth elicited that the little guy didn't want any complimentary tickets given out for the Dublin gig. He wanted 'everybody to pay seriously'.

Through the evidence, a picture began to emerge of an ageing artist, well past the creative peak for contemporary performers, whose only solace was hoovering up large wads of cash, if only he could be bothered to get up off his rear end.

March turned into April. Desmond was putting Goldring under pressure for specifics from Prince. Once again, Sarkisian went to dine at the little guy's house. This time there were three others present, including Prince's female friend, who was some class of a singer herself. Sarkisian didn't want to discuss business in front of strangers, so the conversation presumably dwelt on worldly issues.

At one stage, Prince left the room. Soon after, his security man 'Raul' came in and told poor Keith that dinner was over and it was time to leave. Sarkisian was asked in the witness box why he didn't tell Prince to come back and eat his dinner.

'You can't tell Prince to come back to dinner, at least I can't.'

By June, everything was looking shaky. All eyes were on Prince's gaff, hoping for some smoke signals or the belt of a snare drum; any kind of interpretation at all that he might suggest he was willing to fulfil his commitment to gig in Dublin. Sarkisian and his boss Marc Geiger finally got an audience with him to explain that cancelling would be a serious problem. They outlined that Denis was over in Dublin getting his knickers in a twist.

'Tell the cat to chill, I'll figure it out,' Prince told them. The cat in question was smiling in the public gallery when that line was revealed. His €1.7 million in cream was looking more promising.

By Thursday afternoon, Judge Peter Kelly was clicking into the groove. At a break in Geiger's evidence, the judge remarked: 'There's no hurry, the rest of us are chilling.' Check out the dude who'd come a long way from Lady Bracknell.

Later, when reference was made once again to the function of Ruth the interpreter, the judge offered a description of Prince's assistant. 'His representative on earth, you might say,' Judge Kelly opined. Now we were sucking diesel.

On Friday morning, the case settled. By then, the lawyers were costing a king's ransom, even by Prince's extravagant standards. Judge Kelly asked the little guy's lawyer Sreenen whether he had confirmation of the settlement from his client.

'Does it mean the same in Princespeak as it does in English?' the judge asked.

Outside, Desmond expressed himself very pleased with the result.

'The cat is very chilled,' he said.

✦　✦　✦

The new courtroom dramedy from the makers of Airplane

Ryanair's Michael O'Leary met his match with Judge Peter Kelly in the High Court. There was always going to be one winner, and it wasn't the chief of spin.

28 March 2010

They got off to a bad start. Michael O'Leary bounded up into the witness box and took the Bible in his right hand. His left remained rooted in a pocket. 'Will you take your hand out of your pocket while the oath is being administered, please?' Judge Peter Kelly asked. O'Leary complied, but it was obvious from the off that these two boys would never be sharing a few pints together.

O'Leary was appearing in the High Court on Friday afternoon on foot of a request from the judge. On Wednesday, Kelly had been notified that an important letter sent by transport minister Noel Dempsey to O'Leary was not included in affidavits sworn by two solicitors on behalf of Ryanair. The airline, a frequent flyer to the courts, is involved in litigation over O'Leary's perennial bugbear – passenger charges at Dublin airport.

Judge Kelly felt he had been misled by the omission of the letter in question. He suggested that O'Leary hightail it down to the courts by 2 p.m. on Friday. Cometh the hour, there was the man, dolled up to the nines by his standards, in flannel trousers and smart jacket.

The attraction of a court appearance by O'Leary is obvious. When lawyers or a judge are performing their functions properly, facts are parsed and analysed in a cold, clinical manner in court. Spin is squeezed out. Spin is O'Leary's forte. He is by any standards a master communicator.

Just last month, he performed Herculean feats by spinning the construction of a Ryanair hangar in Scotland into a scenario whereby Mary Coughlan, Aer Lingus and the Dublin Airport Authority were ineptly allowing jobs to flee the country. Different class, as our footballing brethren might say.

Peter Kelly is no slouch at his own business. He presides over the Commercial Court. For the last eighteen months, he has been sifting through the embers of the Celtic bonfire. All manner of wide-boys, shysters, fools, not to mention lawyers and accountants displaying the ethics of vultures, have been parading through his court. Through his public comments and his work in general he has delivered a devastating critique of what transpired during the madness. He is a rare species at the current time, somebody who draws his authority from the performance of his duty rather than the status of the office he occupies.

O'Leary told the court he was there on foot of the court report in the *Irish Times* the previous day (Thursday). The judge's suggestion on Wednesday that he was misleading the court obviously didn't prompt any underling to contact him that evening. He just read about it in the papers.

'I'd like to add my own apology,' he said, referring to the words of sorrow expressed by the two solicitors who swore the offending affidavits.

'How is it that both of them were unaware of the letter?' the judge wanted to know.

'I did not give them the letter. They didn't check the file,' O'Leary said. He launched into one of his standard soliloquies about the crazy bureaucracy Ryanair has to endure from the assorted arms of the State. He said that if he had seen the affidavit he would have amended it in relation to a sentence which implied there had been no communication on the relevant matter with Dempsey, but he wouldn't have included the letter anyway because it wasn't relevant.

Four times the judge asked him whether he would have included the letter.

'Was I going to be told in affidavit form what the minister had decided?' Kelly asked, with growing exasperation. O'Leary's lawyer got up and tried to explain where his client was coming from.

'You're fencing with me now,' the judge said. 'He's the chief executive of Ryanair. He calls the shots.'

At one stage, the judge told O'Leary, 'You're contradicting yourself.'

'I'm not contradicting myself,' the spinmeister replied.

O'Leary and his company have form with the judiciary. In 2005, Judge Barry White threatened to jail the Ryanair chief if he didn't comply with a court order to reinstate a pilot to a roster. O'Leary drew back at the last moment.

In 2006 Judge Thomas Smyth said that for only the second time in his career, he felt compelled to rule that witnesses had given false evidence under oath, referring to two Ryanair executives.

Despite the rarity of the ruling, no charges of perjury were ever forthcoming from the DPP. Neither were the executives sanctioned by Ryanair. The ruling didn't affect the bottom line, and beyond that, who, as Mickser himself might put it, gives a fiddlers?

On Friday, the fireworks exploded when a lawyer for the Dublin Airport Authority produced a separate letter that O'Leary had written to Dempsey beseeching the minister to organise a review of the airport charges.

'Both Judge Kelly and the DAA lawyers were critical of your delay in appointing an appeals panel,' O'Leary wrote. Kelly hit the roof. He had made no criticism of Dempsey.

'You are representing to the minister something you say I said. Where did I say that?' he wanted to know. O'Leary made what the judge later referred to as a 'pathetic' attempt to justify the comment. By then, the spinmeister was transmogrifying into the squirmmeister.

O'Leary said the offending passage was a misquote.

'It is not a misquote, it is a lie,' the judge said.

The DAA lawyer Cian Ferriter produced a press release Ryanair had issued calling the minister 'dozy Dempsey' and 'doolittle Dempsey'. This was two days after Dempsey had written a letter to O'Leary undertaking to set up the review panel.

Ferriter put it to the witness. 'There is a pattern of mislead. You misled the court, the Commission for Aviation Regulation, the minister, the public and [Ryanair's] solicitors ... it shows a disregard for the truth.' O'Leary rejected the multiple misleadings.

Judge Kelly was more interested in how he had been misrepresented. O'Leary said he would apologise. 'It's not just enough that he apologises to the court,' the judge replied.

O'Leary's lawyer took the hint. 'Do you wish to apologise to the minister?'

'Yes I do.'

The judge was taking no chances. 'Hadn't he better write to the minister and tell him that I didn't criticise him ... I want to see the letter before it is sent.'

At the end of the proceedings, Judge Kelly told O'Leary he was lucky the matter wasn't being treated as contempt. He put back the substantive issue, allowing the DAA and others time to apply to strike out the action on the basis of Ryanair's conduct. He wants to see O'Leary's letter of apology to Dempsey by Tuesday.

Outside, Mickser was visibly shaken. He said he would write the letter of apology that evening. After a few questions, the reporters drifted off. 'Is that it?' he asked, looking like a man who badly needed a microphone to crank up his self-confidence and restart the spinning machine.

He will be back in court on Tuesday with his draft letter for Dempsey. It might be fitting if he turns up in short trousers and school tie and cap. And he would be well advised to have everything in order. Any excuses about the horse eating his homework won't wash with Peter Kelly.

Meanwhile, if you happen to see Noel Dempsey this weekend, he will most likely have a smile on his face as wide as the Shannon, a spring in his step befitting a mountain goat. The smart money says he will get the letter framed and hang it in a choice position in his loo.

✦ ✦ ✦

Livingstone case shows An Garda Síochána at its best ... and at its worst

In April 2008 James Livingstone settled a legal action against An Garda Síochána over the manner in which the force had dealt with him following the murder of his wife, Grace.

13 April 2008

The investigating gardaí knew who was responsible for the murder of Grace Livingstone. All they were missing was the evidence. Here is what happened, according to the deductions of the investigating gardaí.

Grace was murdered by her husband James on 7 December 1992. He arrived home from work to The Moorings, Malahide, at around 5.50 p.m., a few minutes after dropping off a colleague. He and his wife had a row, probably because she didn't have his dinner ready.

They went upstairs to their bedroom, where James kept a number of firearms. He bound her hands, feet and mouth with adhesive tape.

Then he shot her with a double-barrel shotgun.

He placed the weapon in bushes outside the house. He ran over to a neighbour's house, got no answer, went to another neighbour and ran back to his own house, whereupon he phoned the emergency services at 5.58 p.m. All of this occurred in the space of eight minutes, at the very most.

There was no sign of a break-in. Nobody heard the shot. Nobody among the procession who entered the bedroom in the following minutes ... the neighbour, gardaí, the ambulance crew ... detected the smell of cordite. Livingstone's clothes tested negative for gunshot residue.

There was circumstantial evidence pointing towards a young man acting suspiciously in the area around 4.30 p.m. that day, when Livingstone was at work in the city centre. Some neighbours heard a loud bang around the same time. But the gardaí didn't give that too much thought. They had their man.

The husband did it, whatever about his lack of opportunity, not to mention motive.

James Livingstone is, by his own account, a 'hard man with a fondness for guns'.

He had eight firearms on his property on the day in question. He was a long-time member of the FCA. He was employed in the special investigations unit of the Revenue Commissioners, a job that required a dogged and committed operator to do the State's work.

He is not a man given to public displays of emotion.

His personality did him no favours in the weeks after his wife's murder, but the gardaí are supposed to be concerned with evidence rather than impressions.

On the night of the killing he gave a statement in which he listed his guns. They were taken away. He admitted that he may not have a licence for some of them.

On 3 March 1993 he was arrested under the Offences Against The State Act, on suspicion of having an unlicensed firearm, which had been in possession of the gardaí since the previous December. The basis for the arrest allowed for his detention for up to forty-eight hours. He was kept in custody at Swords garda station for two days.

He claims he wasn't asked about the firearm during his detention, but repeatedly questioned about Grace's demise. He says he was shown photographs of her naked body during this period.

He was charged with possession of the unlicensed firearm. He pleaded guilty and was fined. A separate file on his wife's murder was sent to the garda commissioner, but not the DPP. Livingstone was never arrested in connection with his wife's death.

In August 1993 Deputy Commissioner Tom O'Reilly asked Detective Superintendent Tom Connolly to review the file. Connolly is an oldschool cop ... understated, dogged and with a career of unblemished investigation behind him. He was joined on the case by Detective Sergeant Tom O'Loughlin.

Soon after his appointment, Connolly met the leading officers on the case in Malahide.

'I was left in no doubt that Jim Livingstone was the culprit for this murder and they just didn't have sufficient evidence to charge him,' Connolly remembers.

He went in search of hard evidence. There was an issue over the time of death. A GP who attended at 6.35 p.m. on the day said the victim had been dead for two hours.

State Pathologist John Harbison was at the scene at 11.30 p.m. and he estimated the time to be around 6p.m.

A reconstruction of the shooting was set up in the Livingstones' bedroom. The shooter's garments tested positive for gunshot residue.

Another actor, who entered the room five minutes after the shot was fired, also tested positive.

The neighbour who attended on the day of the murder, and the two officers who were first on the scene, entered the bedroom fifteen and twenty minutes after the discharge. The neighbour detected the smell of cordite in the bedroom.

The two cops detected it on the landing outside before even entering the bedroom.

The result raised a vital question: How could Livingstone have shot his wife – as the initial investigators believed – and no cordite be detected within minutes of the incident?

The four neighbours who had heard a bang at 4.30 p.m. were also in situ that day.

High winds meant they didn't hear the shot during the reconstruction. A second reconstruction was set up on a day with similar weather conditions to 7 December 1992. Three of the neighbours heard it. The fourth was unavailable, but a garda taking her place also clearly heard the bang. The conclusion strengthened the proposition that Grace Livingstone might well have been shot at 4.30 p.m., while her husband was working in Dublin Castle, twelve miles away in the city.

Gardaí in the original investigation had put the bang down to work being carried out by cable TV installers who were in the neighbouring Seapark estate that day. The workmen also attended one house in The Moorings, but the cops hadn't even checked which house.

There was evidence that pointed to another suspect, an unidentified long-haired man. Four sixteen-year-old girls had seen this man in the estate around 4.30 p.m.

On the day in question, Philip McGibney was a landscape gardener working in the cul-de-sac where the Livingstones lived. He packed up around 4.30 p.m., got into his van, and turned the vehicle around outside the Livingstone home. As his van's lights shone onto the Livingstone's house, he noticed a young man with long hair straightening a plant inside the glass porch.

The investigating gardaí considered him a truthful witness, but were convinced he had mistaken the youth for middle-aged Grace Livingstone, who wore her hair in a bun. Connolly gives far more credence to the accuracy of McGibney's account.

There was a sighting of a long-haired man getting into a red car and taking off at speed nearby. There were also sightings on the far side of Malahide of a red car driving erratically later that afternoon.

Then there were the fingerprints on the adhesive tape with which Grace Livingstone was bound and gagged. One print on the tape was unidentified.

'The finger impression is, in my view, most likely to have been put on after the tape was unrolled,' Connolly reported.

Charity collectors who were going house to house on the day in question were quizzed. One, an Englishman, had previously been suspected of stealing from homes. The second investigation went to England to interview him, but it came to naught. His prints didn't match those on the adhesive tape.

Connolly's report concluded: 'It is my opinion, having carried out the review and further investigation, that the chances of Mr Livingstone having murdered his wife are very slim indeed. One other reason why I feel Mr Livingstone is very unlikely to have murdered his wife is the time available to him, to assault his wife, tie her up, shoot her, call to two neighbours' houses and return home to make a phone call (to the emergency services) at 5.58 p.m.'

Last Wednesday, Livingstone and his son Conor and daughter Tara settled their case for damages against the State, following a day of legal argument. Lawyers for the State read a statement saying Livingstone was entitled to the 'full and unreserved presumption of innocence'.

There is no case law in this area, and if the judge had ultimately ruled in Livingstone's favour, it would have had major repercussions for the manner in which gardaí can investigate crime. The *Sunday Tribune* understands that he didn't receive any compensation but was given a contribution to his legal costs.

The seventy-one-year-old retiree feels vindicated. How did he manage to carry on with a cloud over his life for fifteen years?

'Maybe I'm thicker than most,' he says. 'It wasn't easy, but I had great support from my family and from Grace's as well. And the FCA was like a second family to me.'

Livingstone believed for a long time that the murder was associated with his work, which included investigations of fuel smuggling in border areas. He now accepts, in light of Connolly's investigation, that this is unlikely. He has written an unpublished book on the affair, entitled *Lies, Leaks And Layabouts*.

Tom Connolly says he feels vindicated that his belief in Livingstone's innocence has been shown to be correct.

'He has been through an unimaginable ordeal. He should have been eliminated as a suspect after a day or two, but all the energy and focus of the investigation remained on him. His wife was brutally murdered and a large section of the community were given to understand, through rumour and innuendo, that he was the culprit. If the investigation had focused on the credible evidence, which became available early on, this crime could and should have been solved.'

The case illustrated the worst and the best of the force. It wasn't the first time that officers put the cart before the horse, identifying a suspect and looking for the evidence to back up their hunch. The review showed An Garda Síochána at its best, doggedly investigating a crime, and letting the evidence speak for itself.

The case of the murder of Grace Livingstone remains open.

✦ ✦ ✦

Time to choose between lies and coincidences. No matter the findings on Ahern's evidence, it is certain that something does not quite add up

22 June 2008

And so the journey into the heart of darkness ends. Last Tuesday saw what should be the final detailed examination of Bertie Ahern's finances. Praise the Lord for eventual, if not happy, endings. Last week, we visited the former Taoiseach's house in Beresford Avenue, in the heart of Drumcondra, from whence the greatest of them all was sprung, and where the seeds of his possible destruction were sown.

We won't bore you with the details this time around. Suffice to say, it's more tales of the unexpected, the bizarre, the quite unbelievable. If Ahern's renting of the house in 1995, and subsequent purchase two years later, is as he claims, then he hasn't offered a single plausible explanation as to why it appears as if his landlord- cum-friend, Michael Wall, acted as a front for him to buy the property in 1995.

In terms of themes, it was déjà vu. Big lumps of sterling cash, money moved around accounts, a change in plans to explain lodgements of sterling and a change of details from earlier explanations. Celia Larkin is again at the heart of his affairs. So is Wall, who, Ahern alleged on Tuesday, had a bit of an obsession with security.

On a previous occasion, Wall told the inquiry that he left a bag with stg£30,000 in a hotel wardrobe when he went off to Bertie's annual fundraising dinner in 1994. Maybe he wasn't on the ball that evening, as he was looking forward to the grub, which he was denied on that other fundraising occasion, the alleged whip-round in Manchester.

In its totality, Ahern's evidence over twelve days, allied to bank documents and the evidence of his assorted friends, paint a number of scenarios. Three are offered here, which, it is hoped, draw fair conclusions from what we have heard.

The first is the most benign. Ahern is largely telling the truth. His complicated finances can be put down to the fallout from his marital break-up. He has embellished or fudged the story here and there in an effort to retain some privacy about his personal affairs. Such a course would be in keeping with his conduct in public life, when, at times, most of us weren't sure what he was saying and whether he meant to say it.

His slowness to co-operate could be attributed to an abhorrence of having to deal with personal matters in a public forum. He wouldn't have been the first tribunal witness who tried to conceal stuff on the basis that it exposed him to attention in other forums, but which had nothing to do with the inquiry's terms of reference.

If the judges were to rule that his transgressions were of that order, he could expect sanction in the report, but nothing major. He would, to a greater extent, be back where he was in September 2006 when the story first broke. The fullness of his contribution to public life would negate in the public mind any perceived minor transgressions.

The second scenario, one which he rejects out of hand, is not benign but, perhaps his supporters would claim, isn't a hanging offence either. Let's say he had a hidden bank account or facility, during his marital break-up, most likely outside the State, possibly in Manchester.

He wouldn't be the first spouse in a break-up situation to hide money away. In some quarters, there would be tolerance for such a move. Into this facility he would have poured his savings between 1988 and 1993, which, according to his accountant, could have amounted to £80,000. The subsequent cash lodgements were merely the repatriating of the funds after his legal separation was finalised.

In such a scenario, there would be no question of him getting funds from any other source. Despite the dishonesty involved, it would have been entirely a personal matter that would not have impacted on his public duties.

The digouts and whip rounds would have actually happened, even if the shaky evidence suggests they did not. He wouldn't have any tax issues to worry about, as the money was taxed at source.

His main problem would be in failing to give a sworn inquiry a truthful account of his affairs. That is a serious criminal offence, albeit one that is difficult to prosecute. He could expect severe sanction in the report, but sections of the public – particularly in his own party – might be more forgiving. His reputation would be damaged, but he could call on the capital he has built up over his three decades in public life. The damage would be serious, but not fatal.

The only problem with the above scenario is the sums don't add up. It would require confirmation that his stories about relodgements, and the yarn about Wall plonking thirty grand sterling on his desk, were true. It would require a series of coincidences and changes of mind to be just that. And it would require that the biggest coincidence of all – one of his lodgements equating to $45,000 – to be nothing more than bad luck. It would require a very benign interpretation of the cumulative evidence. But it is possible, however unlikely.

The worst case scenario is also one that he rejects out of hand. He received large sums of money, much of it sterling, from sources unknown. The evidence about relodging large sums, which crops up again and again, is false. The coincidences don't add up. His slowness to co-operate was an effort at obstruction, a path well worn by previous witnesses.

This scenario would have involved a major conspiracy to obstruct the tribunal. The dig-outs and whip-rounds, as presented, were fantasy. He was, in fact, the beneficial owner of the house in Beresford from day one. He failed to pay tax on the income. And the Dobson interview, his testimony to the Irish people, was lies from start to finish.

The damage to his legacy would be severe. A constant refrain from Ahern's supporters has been that whatever money he got, he wasn't corrupt. This is a mere play on words, a belief that he didn't agree to do anything specific for money that was given to him. It implies that a minister for finance can compartmentalise in his mind personal payments when he is making decisions that could affect his benefactors. It is hogwash.

If the three judges were to find anything of the order of this scenario, Ahern would forever find his name corralled with those of Charlie Haughey and Ray Burke, his only saving grace being the absence of any visible extravagant lifestyle.

The three judges of the tribunal now labour under a heavy burden, even if they're well paid for it. Much of the rest of their report into planning corruption should be relatively straightforward. Minor reputations will be damaged and the culture of zoning for bribes put firmly on the record.

The report into Ahern is of a different magnitude. The three judges – Alan Mahon, Gerard Keys and Mary Faherty – were appointed by Ahern's government for the task at hand, largely because no sitting judge was willing to take it on.

The three are relatively young. While nobody doubts their integrity, it would be reasonable to assume they are ambitious. Mahon, for instance, lobbied unsuccessfully to be elevated from Circuit to High Court status last year. They hold in their hands the reputation of the most popular politician of the modern age, a well-liked former leader of the permanent party of government.

Stout hearts may well be required if their deliberations point towards negative or even devastating findings against Ahern. Either way, a thorough report is the least that can be expected in light of the financial cost and political fallout from the whole affair.

✦ ✦ ✦

The People vs Padraig Nally in name only

Overt appeals to the emotions from within and outside the court succeeded in turning the Mayo farmer from defendant to victim in a jury's eyes at his manslaughter trial.

17 December 2006

In the old courtrooms, in the round hall of the Four Courts, the accused sits on the end of a bench, removed from the general body of the court. The dock as a concept has long been abolished, but the accused in a criminal trial usually sits alone, opposite the jury.

Throughout the Padraig Nally manslaughter trial, his sister Maureen sat beside him. That was highly unusual. A tourist entering Court Three on a casual basis might conclude that the man and woman were both on trial for killing a burglar.

Early on in the trial, a number of Nally's supporters slipped onto the far end of the bench.

Judge Kevin O'Higgins requested that they vacate the seat. Visually, such a vista could be loaded. In the trial of The People vs Padraig Nally, it might be confusing as to where the people's allegiance lay.

During breaks in the proceedings, new friends and complete strangers approached Nally in the Round Hall to wish him well. Each day, when he and his supporters made the short trip across the Liffey to lunch, hands reached out to shake his. Since his release from prison in October, the reception for him in rural circles has been even more voracious. At times over the last few weeks, it appeared as if the system, and not Nally, was on trial.

He had the cut of a man who was enjoying the celebrity, whatever about its provenance. The farmer from a rural outpost in south Co. Mayo, who lived with his parents until their respective demise when he was in his fifties, was now the focus of affection and admiration from people who got to know him, literally, through the barrel of a shotgun.

The bereaved family of the man Nally killed on 14 October 2004 was nowhere to be seen at the trial. The only one of the late John Ward's eleven children to show up was Tom, who was with his father on the day he died. Tom Ward was brought to the court from his place of detention to give evidence against Nally.

The twenty-year-old traveller is serving an eleven-month sentence for theft offences. He told the court that his father's killing has driven him to attempt suicide on a number of occasions. Neither his plight, nor that of his family, has attracted much sympathy. In killing John Ward, as the traveller limped, possibly crawled away, Nally, in the eyes of many, became a victim. First of criminal travellers, then of the system.

THE EVIDENCE:

By October 2004 Padraig Nally was living in fear. 'The man was demented with fear,' his neighbour Michael Varley told the court. 'I cried last Sunday after my sister left,' Nally told the guards on the day of the killing. 'I said that there would be changes when you come back. I had a premonition.'

The rational basis for his fear is highly suspect. Nine months before the killing, in February 2004, a chainsaw was stolen. Drawers in the house were ransacked. Understandably, the sense of violation traumatised him.

Between that time and the killing, he wasn't raided. Now and then, strange cars came by, and he noted down the registration. Others in the rural community did likewise as a precaution.

Three weeks before the fateful day, two travellers in a car stopped and asked Nally directions to the nearby lake. He suspected, quite reasonably, that they were up to no good. But he wasn't raided.

The incidence of burglary in the area wasn't particularly high at a time when the overall incidence had fallen nationally since the 1990s. Nally's neighbour Varley, the father of three small children, told the court that he wasn't afraid. Yet Nally was 'demented'.

His primitive shotgun was held together with a bicycle tube. He moved it from his bedroom to a shed lest raiders would come in, overpower him and shoot him. The sixty-two-year-old farmer spent long hours at night in the shed with the gun, watching over his stead, waiting for them to come.

'About an hour I slept last night thinking it was going to happen,' he told guards after the shooting.

He lived alone through the week while his sister was away teaching in Ballina. He didn't have a telephone in the house. He never married. All he had was his farm, that which defined him, and plenty of time alone, long hours in which the imagination can draw a dark veil over all thoughts. There was no evidence in the trial that his sister or friends had any concern for the level of fear he expressed and whether or not it was rooted in reality.

And fear was what Nally said was the impetus for the killing of John Ward, as he limped, or crawled, down the road, fleeing for his life, after a failed attempt to rob the farmer.

Nally had feared attack, yet it was he who shot Ward on sight when he saw the traveller trying to gain entry to his house. Fear drove him to beat Ward with an ash plant, inflicting serious head wounds, to ensure that he himself wasn't killed. And when Ward limped or crawled away, fear that he might return drove Nally after him.

The farmer reloaded, and put another three cartridges in his pocket.

'It was done with a degree of coolness,' prosecuting counsel Paul O'Higgins told the court. 'He had taken three cartridges out with him. He was ready for action again.'

Ward was moving down the road when Nally came up behind him. He shot the traveller from a range of not more than five yards. The trajectory of the fatal shot was downwards, which suggests Ward was crouched, or maybe crawling. He may even have begged for his life.

'I said to myself he wasn't going again,' Nally told the cops afterwards. 'I've so long been raided, this was going to be the last time.' He was raided once, nine months before, but in his mind the raids may have multiplied and thus justified him in shooting dead a man who resembled the burglar that haunted his waking hours.

Nally didn't take the stand in his manslaughter trial, as was his right. In the original murder trial in Castlebar, he did give evidence.

Back then, he had much to gain by personally appealing to a jury. This time the jury members would have been aware of his plight unless they had just arrived from Mars. To give evidence might have been to expose himself to the harsh glare of cross examination, so he declined, as do most defendants in his position.

The respective summing up of the case by O'Higgins and defending counsel Brendan Grehan illustrated the crux of the issue. O'Higgins delved into the law and the facts. Grehan, for the most part, appealed to emotions. In the best traditions of advocacy, he made the most of what he had, telling the jury that 'trouble came looking for him [Nally]', and 'a greater contrast between two individuals you will not find than between Mr Nally and John Ward'. And in reference to the one burglary that did occur:

'When they stole his chainsaw, they stole his peace of mind.'

He also tapped into the debate being conducted beyond the confines of the court. 'Maybe the law has lagged behind community standards and maybe the impetus should be to change the law.'

Judge O'Higgins also made references to the debate. Charging the jury, he held up a copy of the recent Law Reform Commission document on defending the home. 'They're thinking about that,' he said, of the commission. 'And maybe they even are in Leinster House.' But, he told the jury, they were obliged to concentrate only on the facts of the case.

'The law in this country protects nice people and not so nice people,' Judge O'Higgins told the jury. 'A man with eighty previous convictions [as Ward had] is entitled to the same degree of protection as the Lord Mayor of Dublin.'

After nearly sixteen hours' deliberation, over three days, the jury decided that Nally had acted reasonably in following Ward out onto the road that day and shooting him dead.

The eight men and four women were charged to consider only the facts of the case, but it must have taken a huge effort to keep the world outside from seeping into the jury room.

When Nally was sentenced to six years for manslaughter after the first trial, all hell broke loose. A law that would send a man to jail for defending himself and his property was decried.

The facts were conveniently overlooked, as there was capital to be made on the killing, and the jailing of a man of impeccable character.

There had to be 'rebalancing of the law', a political term currently in vogue. Nobody said that Nally should have been protected by the law in his actions, but that subtext informed the debate. Some grubby politicians suggested that homeowners would now be in fear of defending themselves or their property in their home.

Then the Law Reform Commission produced the paper referred to by the judge. Cue more fire and brimstone, more waffle about 'rebalancing' and ludicrous suggestions that this was the homeowner fighting back.

The reality was that the Commission merely clarified what 'reasonable force' entailed. Legislation following on from the recommendations won't change the amount of force permissible, but will clarify it in respect of homeowners. It always has been legal to use a reasonable amount of force. (Ironically, if such clarity had been in the law at the time of the killing, Nally might have found it more difficult to defend his position in court.) Against this backdrop of heightened fear, the retrial was conducted. Then as the evidence closed, and deliberations began, another element of crime exploded. The recent gun murders sparked further debate. The court system was called into question once more. In the battle against crime, the system is being portrayed as protecting the criminal rather than society. That such an analysis is top-of-the-head stuff, purveyed by vested interests, is glossed over. The desired message is getting though.

And in the Nally trial, a large section of the public mind had the dead man cast as the criminal, the accused as victim. To some, convicting Nally would once more be playing into the hands of criminals. Against this backdrop, the jury raked over the killing of John Ward. Charged to consider only the facts, their long spell deliberating indicates they did that in some detail. Any suggestion that the world outside seeped into their collective sub-consciousness can only be speculation.

THE AFTERMATH:

Nally said afterwards that he was 'surprised' at the verdict. So were his supporters. So was almost anybody who sat through the trial. Now, he will return to his farm outside Cross in Co. Mayo and attempt to rebuild his life. Few would wish him ill luck. Prior to Ward's attempt to rob him, Nally led a blameless life.

Ward's widow Marie reacted to the verdict with dismay. Earlier this year she married a Ghanaian asylum seeker and now lives in Longford. The court heard that she intends to pursue a civil action against Nally.

She and the wider travelling community see the outcome in stark terms. For them, we may all be equal before the law, but some are more equal than others.

✦ ✦ ✦

Iceland melts down under unfriendly fire

Like the Celtic Tiger cubs, Icelanders lived on the economic never-never. Then their country became a byword for disaster, and the streets resounded not with building work, but protest.

15 February 2009

It's eight below zero and the racket is echoing across the low roofs of the old town in Reykjavik. There is the sound of a hooter, powered by a barrel of oxygen, the rhythmic beat of drums, the clang of aluminium and the sporadic popping of fireworks. Most of all though, there is the sound of saucepans being battered with all manner of implements. Welcome to the saucepan revolution, and don't forget your earplugs.

Last Tuesday morning, around fifty recruits were wringing the last out of the revolution. Positioned outside the Central Bank, they flailed away at making noise, stomping feet against the bitter cold, attempting to drive the governor of the bank from office by sheer force of cacophony.

Across the road, against the backdrop of sun and snow on the hills ringing the city's quay, four tower cranes are silent and redundant. They stand over a half-finished building that was to have been a retail paradise. Scaffolding testifies to the abrupt halt of work. The money just ran out.

Back on the streets, the saucepan revolution is on a roll. It acquired its name at its height last month when thousands raised a racket by making noise outside the parliament building, using whatever means possible, but principally banging saucepans.

Their efforts drove the prime minister from office and prompted the resignation of their financial services authority. Now, they have set their sights on the man many see as the architect of Iceland's descent into bankruptcy, David Oddsson. He is a former prime minister who implemented neo-liberal policies and then moved on to police the policies with the lightest of touches. It would be akin to having Bertie Ahern as the financial regulator during these turbulent times.

'This country was run for decades by a minority who have become very rich by fooling the majority,' says Horour Torfason, one of the main organisers of the protest. The people are claiming their country back, but the question hanging in the cold, clear air is whether or not it is too late.

The comparison between Ireland and Iceland is growing tiresome. British media types love to trot out the line that the only difference between the pair is one letter and six months. In November, the International Monetary Fund was called into Iceland. The Brits and our own harbingers of doom predict that we're next on the list. Last week, *The Economist* ran a piece on Ireland's woes headlined 'Reykjavik on Liffey'.

In all of this, Iceland has become a byword for disaster, a name that is not to be uttered in front of small children lest it brings on nightmares. Some of the fear is justified. In Stansted Airport near London, the money changers are refusing to buy or sell the Icelandic kroner.

'The currency is too volatile,' a stern money changer says, as if worried that the kroner and its people may soon disappear up the North Pole.

On paper, comparison s can be made between the lands of Ice and Ire. Iceland used to prosper on exports, principally fish. Around six years ago, the big banks were privatised and credit went through the roof. The whole country began to live on the never-never.

'The banks kicked up their heels like cows in spring and went on a lending spree,' economist Thorvaldur Gylfason explains. 'A few

years later the house came crashing down. This would have happened even without the credit crunch.'

Construction became an end in itself. Tower cranes darkened
the sky as estates and shopping malls began mushrooming around
Reykjavik's perimeter. House prices shot up and the traditional habit
of long-term renting was dismissed as foolishness.

This explosion in the illusion of wealth was even more pro-
nounced when placed in context. Reykjavik is about the size of Cork,
accommodating half the national population of 320,000. Iceland's
land mass is as big as England.

Polish migrants arrived to do the heavy lifting. Range Rovers
were all the rage and shopping was elevated to an art form. So far,
so similar.

Much of the lending was done in foreign currency, which was
fine and dandy because the Icelandic kroner was sitting pretty on
the back of all that prosperity. As a nation, Iceland had no problem
believing that it was invincible, an economic powerhouse punching
above its puny weight, just like the mythical Celtic Tiger further
south in the Atlantic.

In terms of scale, however, Iceland's turmoil is of a different
order. Danger lurked beneath the surface for a long time. Those at
the top of politics and finance were the best of buddies. In terms of
crony capitalism, these lads make Seanie Fitz and his homies look
like recruits for the Vienna Boys Choir. And crucially, the banksters
had little in the way of experience, having been only cast adrift in the
free market in 2002.

When the house did come crashing down, the reaction echoed
with that of Brian Cowen's administration.

'The government dragged its feet,' the economist Gylfason says.
'Gordon Brown told our prime minister of the danger as far back as
April last year. But they didn't act. They lost precious months and
this was a serious case of negligence.'

On 9 October last, the nation awoke from its slumber to hear that
the biggest bank, Landsbanki, had been nationalised. Two others
followed. The economy began to shudder. Interest rates shot up six
points to 18 per cent.

Now the Poles are going home, unemployment is creeping up

over 10 per cent, cranes no longer lurch and creak against the sky and the IMF has set up shop in town. The kroner is heading south, which in turn is hugely exacerbating the personal debt of the credit card and mortgage holders who took out loans in foreign curren-cies. One calculation has it that the party is going to cost every man, woman and child in the country around $25,000 a head.

Reykjavik is an unlikely spot for a popular revolution. Its narrow streets twist between three- and four-storey houses of clapboard and aluminium cladding, and quaint shops and pubs. In recent months, as the shoppers thinned out, the disaffected began making them-selves known.

Every Saturday since last October a prominent artist, Horour Torfason, protested outside the parliament building, a small two-storey stone affair which would sit comfortably into a basement cor-ner of Leinster House.

Torfason invited the public to have their say. 'I had a microphone and I asked people to express themselves,' he says. 'Unfortunately, we had all become part of the problem. We had been led to believe in this absurd way of living on credit and materialism.'

The crowd began building. By January, it was in its thousands and growing angrier by the day. Riot police were deployed for the first time since 1949, when there had been protests about the govern-ment's decision to join Nato.

Yet, for the greater part, there was little violence. The protes-tors took to wearing orange labels and armbands to emphasise their peaceful intent, and to echo the 'orange revolution' in the Ukraine a few years ago.

'We had four demands,' Torfason says. 'We wanted new elections, the government to step down, the financial services authority to go and the central bank directors to go.'

The government conceded elections first, now scheduled for May. Then on 26 January, the prime minister Geir Haarde resigned, followed soon after by the financial services authority.

A new government was formed the following day, a socialist/ Green alliance led by the world's first openly gay prime minister, Johanna Siguroardottir.

There was no shifting the top man in the central bank, David

Oddsson. For many, he epitomises the crony capitalism that has banjaxed the country. He instigated the bank-friendly policies while prime minister, privatised the institutions and then moved over to policing them.

Oddsson's refusal to yield led to the protest moving to the central bank last week. While he stewed inside, the saucepans and hooters and drums rented the freezing air without. Somewhere else in the nondescript building, the bogeymen – staff drafted in from the International Monetary Fund – were hard at work, trying to extract Iceland from the mire.

Relations between the protestors and the complement of cops rarely descended to the level of tense. Individuals on both sides are wearing balaclavas, not in an attempt at disguise, but to keep the freezing temperatures at bay. One of the female protestors has a wok dangling from her belt, like a carpenter's hammer, or a policeman's baton.

Jensson Johanson is carrying a placard depicting a man bent low by an invisible weight. He is fifty-six years of age, a school librarian by training. 'I was working for a state school and last December they let everybody go,' he says. 'The small man cannot bear all the weight of this problem. Too many people are losing jobs. Rent is going very high. We need to have change.'

He points to a young man hammering away at a drum kit nearby. 'My son, he is an electrical engineer. He lost his job last month. Educated people like him have no work now.'

The plight of the young is one which also resonates with this country's economic woes, both past the present. The prospect of immigration is one of the most worrying aspects of the crisis, according to the economist Thorvaldur Gylfason.

He is a professor at the University of Iceland, where, he points out, they have proportionately more staff with PhDs than anywhere else in Europe.

'We always had a tradition of people going abroad to get qualified and then returning here,' he says. 'Whether that can be sustained when we have unemployment in double digits – something we have little experience of in this country – is worrying.

'If people have to emigrate and don't return, there will be severe long-term implications for the country. The main challenge for the government is to inspire enough confidence to keep the young people loyal.'

Haukur Magnusson is one of the generation to which the economist refers. He is twenty-eight, and was present for most of the protests. 'We are the group who will be paying for all of this and nobody consulted us on how to run society. We weren't invited to the party and now we're being asked to pick up the tab,' he says. Magnusson, a journalist, is philosophical on where the future lies. He points to a recent story in a Norwegian newspaper that suggests Icelanders are the new Poles, on the move, looking for work.

'Unfortunately, there is some poetic justice in what has happened. Iceland had become a nation of nouveau riche fishermen with their cellphones, looking down on the Poles, who have a fine culture of their own.

'Now people are thinking what kind of society we really want to be rather than chasing after Range Rovers and flat-screen TVs.'

✦　✦　✦

DAVID KENNY

The West's afloat

Hugh O'Donnell lost his Co. Galway farmhouse in the floods of 2009. His wife Kathleen lost her photos of her mother. What was taken by the surging water went beyond bricks and mortar.

29 November 2009

The beige-brown fields of Beagh have stopped trying to absorb the blows of the past week. They flinch as your boot sinks into them. Invisible hands snatch at your ankles as if you are stepping in a wound. The sky seems to mock the land. The sun shining one minute, the rain pelting down the next.

'The muck will never come over the rim of your boot. Sure, it's solid underneath. Move slowly, that's the trick.' Hugh O'Donnell is surprisingly upbeat for a man whose farm is under water. The suspicion is that he might still be in denial about what has happened to him.

He leads us over slippery, green stone walls and ditches for half an hour, throwing stories of drunken bishops and legendary postmen over his shoulder.

After half an hour we are looking down at a scene that epitomises the suffering the West is enduring: the abandoned O'Donnell farm is Atlantis, with broken turf stacks for fallen columns. Water is up to the windows, a car is submerged beside the kitchen door, a kettle in the window hints that family life and all its treasures are trapped inside.

'It's gone down a few feet,' says Hugh. Moments later, he too is in the water, wading out to check on the house he was born in. He is deep in the freezing swirl. Up to his neck in it, as is his home town of Gort.

He's getting used to it, and so are his family. O'Donnell's eighty-seven-year-old mother Mary is currently recovering in a nursing home after being air-lifted from her flooded home by helicopter.

O'Donnell and four members of her family were winched 100 ft into the air as unprecedented water levels swamped their home. 'I'm feeling an awful lot better now, but I got an awful fright,' she told the *Sunday Tribune*. 'I went to bed and said my prayers. I said a rosary for my late husband. The next thing, Kathleen [Hugh's wife] came in at about 3 a.m. and said, "Nana, you have to get up. The house is full of water." It was a terrible shock to get. They tried to come in to the room, but it was too deep for the wheelchair. So I went out and up and into the helicopter. I had to lie down [in the stretcher] ... well, the pains in my arms ... The crew were very nice to me. They landed me on the hurling field and [local publican] Florry [McCarthy] and my son landed me here in the nursing home.'

When asked if she ever planned to ride in a helicopter again, Mary O'Donnell joked: 'I don't know if I'll live that long – but I certainly don't want to again.'

Hugh recalled the moment the helicopter arrived. 'The man in the helicopter was great. He sat down with my mother for a couple of minutes and relaxed her – told her everything that was going to happen. If she was living alone she was lost, there are no two ways about it.' O'Donnell, together with his two children Oisin and Suzanne and his wife Kathleen, were also rescued by the air crew.

Miles away, up in the town square, John Counihan looks down Crowe Street, where a river runs past his front door. 'We've pumped 120 million gallons of water in the last week. We're working around the clock.' For all its efforts, Gort is merely sticking its finger in the dam. Manhole covers have been lifted by the force of the water and lie on Crowe Street like huge pennies in a filthy brown fountain.

Counihan lives halfway down. The torrent swept past his front door and ruined everything in its path – except his house. 'We have a step,' his wife Mary explains, at the twenty-four-hour coffee station at her front door. She points across the street to the grey stain which is the high water mark of her neighbours' misery: the flood had reached up to their window sills.

A middle-aged man is wading disconsolately through the water.

'That's Brian Honan,' Mary says. 'He's lost his antique furniture shop and his house was flooded too.' Both are on either side of Crowe Street.

Honan's face is grey and drawn. 'I export antiques all over the world. Now I've lost 75 per cent of my stock.' Is he insured? He shakes his head. 'Sure what insurance would you get? You put in a claim ten or fifteen years ago and they won't cover you. I'm covered for the house, but not the shop.' His neighbour Michael Finn's shop is destroyed too. Debris is spread around the sodden floor.

For families like the Honans, the floods have been merciless, destroying livelihoods and cutting off the last line of retreat – the family home. Even when the waters recede, they retain a presence in the air, in the stench of dampness and raw sewage.

'It's very difficult for people, very stressful,' says Fr Tommy Marrinon. 'They don't know what's going to happen next.'

This fear is everywhere across the submerged West. The fear that the rain will strike again. The fear that this is permanent. That nature is reconquering the land of Cromwell's refugees.

'To hell or the rock-pools of Connacht.'

It starts to rain again and the drains throw up a fresh batch of sewage. Toilet paper is floating down Crowe Street. Along the pavements new cracks are showing.

New cracks are also showing in the walls of Ballinasloe. The River Suck is roaring through the chicane it has made between the public lavatories and the flooded, abandoned townhouses on their right.

Up on Main Street, Pierce Keller pulls back the plastic sheeting over the basement entrance to his family furniture business. The smell is eye-watering. 'It came all the way up here,' he says, pointing halfway up the walls. Files and carpets squelch underfoot. He walks past dozens of soiled couches, armchairs and beds. Outside the floor-length windows, the river still forces its way uphill.

The fifty-year-old business has lost 81 per cent of its stock. On top of that, Pierce's brother Bill says they lost €31,500 of purchased goods that were due to be delivered last Saturday, one of their biggest days of the year. The flood's timing couldn't have been worse.

Behind Kellers, Woodslip Quay is abandoned and still semi-submerged. Sacks of discarded food from nearby Costcutters are piled on a trolley. A Polish reg-plate car is up on blocks.

Pierce looks up at the spire of St Michael's Church, on the river-bank. 'The church didn't flood but the priest said Mass in the Church of Ireland chapel instead, just in case it did.'

Derrymullan, on the edge of town, wasn't as fortunate as St Michael's. The football pitch off Station Road is still a lake. The goals look like discarded fishing nets. The six-foot-high wall beside it was no protection for the residents of Ashfield Drive.

'Water came cascading over the wall into Daddy's garden,' Michelle Devlin says. It went over the shed, under the house and up through the floors. She is visiting her father, Eamonn, who has has moved back to the deserted district to protect his property from looters. 'They caught two of them the other day,' Michelle says with disgust.

'All the houses are destroyed along here. Four members of my family have been affected. The elderly people in the bungalows had to be evacuated at 2 a.m. last Thursday when it surged over from Deerpark.

'The woman down there was destroyed for the third time. She's lost everything. She had paid off her mortgage and had no cover. Another lady, who is separated with children, had her home and business hit. The townspeople have been great, helping her out.'

This sympathetic community spirit is evident all over the affected areas, with people frequently citing other stories that are worse than their own.

'It was more traumatic for the elderly and little children. A family near me with two small children had to be evacuated by boat. The five-year-old was so upset he didn't speak for three days.'

Her parents' house was insured. Inside, carpets are pulled back off warped floors and household items are propped up on blocks. A settee is perched on the kitchen table. 'We were lucky with Santa, though,' jokes Michelle. 'He was safe upstairs.'

In the front bedroom Michelle points to a new crack. 'It goes all the way through to the outside wall.' The story is repeated at the back of the house. Eamonn and Theresa Devlin stand beside a bed, among their rescued memories. Eamonn stares at the cracked wall.

'This has been our dream home for twenty-two years,' he says.

'Because of the floods, we may now have to knock it down.'

His words are echoed in Kathleen O'Donnell's as she pours tea for her husband Hugh, the underwater farmer from Beagh parish, Gort. There are cracks in their farmhouse too. It may have to be 'knocked'.

'It isn't easy, there are so many memories there,' she says. 'All our possessions are in the house.' Like photographs of deceased relatives.

She leans forward a little. Her confession is quietly devastating. 'I lie awake at night and wonder if I'll ever see a picture of my mother again.'

It starts to rain. The West's awash, again.

✦   ✦   ✦

Una Mullally

A farewell to McGahern, 'who loved life, but did not fear death'

2 April 2006

Hundreds of mourners filled St Patrick's Church in Aughawillan, Co. Leitrim yesterday for the funeral of John McGahern, who died on Thursday. The remote and beautiful setting was fitting for the burial of a man who found acclaim by describing the simplest elements of Irish life and its landscape.

McGahern died in the Mater Hospital in Dublin, and it was there that his journey back to Leitrim began early yesterday. Friends and family, amongst them the broadcaster Mike Murphy, Labour TD Joan Burton, actor Mick Lally and journalist Eddie Holt gathered in a small room in the basement of the private hospital.

With the red eyes of morning and mourning, anecdotes were thrown around like coins in a well of remembrance. The hearse was followed out of the underground car park by a black car with tinted windows. It carried McGahern's wife, Madeline Green, and the writer's siblings.

Beyond the N4 Motorway, the brown and beige fields of Leitrim, interrupted by gorse, pointed the way to where McGahern spent most of his life walking the countryside, taking pleasure in what it offered him.

In Roosky, the swept reeds alongside Kilglass Lough and the marshy fields preceded the winding road from Dromod to Mohill, where people gathered at the crossroads on Lower Main Street. By Early's and Carroll's Public House, a butcher in a striped red apron chatted to elderly men in caps. As the hearse passed by, they quietened. A book of condolence was set up outside Carroll's, the peace just briefly disturbed by an excitable dog jumping amongst waiting children.

Beyond Mohill, past lanes enclosed in tunnels of joining branches was Garvagh, where rain threatened and clouds rubbed the hilltops that looked down over the lake. In Fenagh, crowds lined the paths beside Quinn's pub, leaning against the moss-topped stone walls which led to Ballinamore, and then up and down hills to Aughawillan.

Most people parked at the national school, and walked down the lane to St Patrick's Church as dark clouds shifted over Garadice Lough. The old, white, pebble-dashed church was already full three-quarters of an hour before mass. As the minister for the arts, John O'Donoghue, signed the book of condolence, McGahern's admirers and friends from the arts community arrived.

They included Brian Friel, Seamus Heaney and Eugene McCabe. Hundreds of local people lined the walls of the church, eyeing the novelty of crowds of press photographers and TV cameramen.

A loudspeaker was set up outside the church, so the many who could not fit could hear the mass, which was said by McGahern's friend Fr Liam Kelly. Kelly, also a cousin of the author, said it was appropriate that the funeral took place in St Patrick's as it was here where McGahern first came to church as a child, where he learned to say mass and where he experienced 'his first brush with discipline' when he was denounced from the altar for rattling his beads too loudly during prayer.

Fr Kelly told those gathered that McGahern was very aware of his impending death, and spoke openly about his funeral plans in the weeks leading up to it. 'He wanted no fuss, no frills, just a simple mass'. And that is what he received. As the coffin was brought from the gates of the church through the crowd, no music played. No music played either when his sisters Rosaline, Margaret, Monica and Dympna brought up the gifts of the offertory, or at anytime during the service.

In a touching sermon, Fr Kelly praised McGahern's writing: 'His work, like all good art, is essentially spiritual.' He said McGahern tapped into 'the minutiae of life, the things that others see, yet never notice ... only a person with a great gift and deep spirituality could produce such fair and lyrical prose about ordinary days in ordinary places'.

Fr Kelly, originally from Leitrim but now based in Cavan, reminded mourners of the lane just outside the church door, quoting from McGahern's Memoir: 'I must have been extraordinarily happy walking that lane to school.'

Fr Kelly spoke about the last few weeks he had spent with McGahern, a man he counted as a dear friend for more than thirty years. 'He loved life, but did not fear death. He liked to quote Achilles: 'speak not soothingly to me of death'. He was never one to run away from the realities of life and death ... to him, one was as natural as the other. He was completely at peace in his last few days,' Kelly said, as a couple of drops of rain fell outside and then stopped. 'He never complained about dying. A great writer and a good man has died and we are all the poorer for it.'

As the coffin was carried just the few yards outside the church walls, the crowds gathered around the plot where McGahern was to be buried alongside his beloved mother. The grave was blessed. And heavy sleet fell as the dirt hit the coffin's wood to the sound of a rosary being said by those who loved him. As the crowd were invited by family to the Landmark Hotel (one of McGahern's last wishes), the priest repeated the writer's final reminder: that there was to be no sympathy offered.

✦ ✦ ✦

JUSTINE McCARTHY

They didn't rescue me

When Kelly Fitzgerald was dying from neglect, she asked her sister
Geraldine to tell their story. Most parents comfort a child after a
nightmare; the Fitzgeralds' parents were their nightmare.

3 June 2007

The last time Kelly spoke to Geraldine – maybe the last time
she spoke to anybody – she said she was going to die soon.
The children were sitting on the ground at the back of the
house in Carracastle. They looked like Dickensian urchins; Kelly
(15) and Geraldine (12), skeletal and shivering in their nighties
while the rest of the family wallowed in the ample glow indoors on a
winter's night in the West of Ireland.

'She was saying about death. She asked me to promise if anything
happened to her to tell what was going on,' Geraldine remembers,
dry-eyed. 'She was so calm about it.'

After that bleak conversation, Kelly stopped talking. 'One minute,
I noticed she had diahorrhea and she was sick. The next minute, she
was whacking her head off the wall. It was like she couldn't help it.
That's all she did, day after day after day. I can hear her head whacking against the wall. She was doing it and she was crying. One day,
my father caught her and said: "Right, if you want to whack your
head, I'll whack it for you."

'He brought her into the house and started whacking her head
against the wall. He was whacking her head inside. She was whacking it outside. She didn't shake, didn't scream, nothing. When I
looked in her eyes, it was blackness. It was like she was gone. Not
even blinking. Just dead. The next day, I went to school. I was very
upset. I told the social workers and they went to the house and asked

to see Kelly but my father said she was in bed sick. They left soon afterwards.

'My father rang Uncle Gary in England and he said to put Kelly on the first plane to London. The night before she went, my father brought her in to eat. She couldn't lift her arms or hold herself up. Tears were streaming down her face. Everybody else went with her to the airport the next day but I was sent to school.

'That's my last memory of Kelly. Looking into her eyes and seeing nothing. Nothing. I don't think I'll ever get over her dying. Every time I think about it, I feel the same pain I felt then. I have to deal with that and live with that for the rest of my life and nobody has any idea how that feels and nobody gives a shit.'

On the table, as she speaks, lies the only possession of Kelly's that Geraldine managed to salvage from her sister's life. It is a child's miniature diary with tiny blank pages and the title 'Zoe Zebra' printed on its little plastic cover. She keeps it on a green string in her handbag, always. The written entries are sparse. On the first page, Geraldine has recorded: 'Kelly RIP February 4, '93'. Page two reads: 'Better by far you should forget and smile, than you should remember and be sad.'

The only other entry is for 13 June next. It says: 'Kelly's thirtieth birthday today ... if she wasn't killed by our parents. I will always love you.'

The life and death of Kelly Fitzgerald was described in Dáil Éireann by the former Minister for Justice Maire Geoghegan-Quinn, as 'the most horrific abuse case in the history of the state'. Kelly died, aged fifteen, in a London hospital from blood poisoning, triggering an avalanche of recriminations, much of it aimed at the Irish welfare authorities who had been alerted by their English counterparts that she was officially registered as at 'high risk' by Lambeth Council before the family came to live in rural Co. Mayo in 1990. The first indication of her maltreatment had been recorded when she was four months old and admitted to a London hospital in a state of emaciation and dehydration. After Kelly died, her parents Des and Sue Fitzgerald pleaded guilty in Castlebar Circuit Court to a charge of wilful neglect and were sentenced to eighteen months' imprisonment.

Lambeth Council had warned that another child in the Fitzgerald family was also on the at-risk register. The official minutes of a case conference at St Thomas' Hospital in London in March 1990 described this second child as 'withdrawn, losing weight, marks noticed on her when doing PE, eating excessively, reluctant to go home from school at the end of the day, clingy, wants affection, pale, ghostlike eyes, sad and scared'. She was the Fitzgeralds' third-born child, Geraldine, three years younger than Kelly and already stealing sandwiches from her classmates' lunch boxes at Larkhall School at the age of nine. Preparatory notes for a Western Health Board case conference about Kelly and Geraldine on 5 February 1993, under the heading 'Suspected Neglect', noted that at school in Scoil Iosa, Carracastle, 'both had a frightened look about them'. In the welter of media coverage following Kelly's shocking death, Geraldine was obliquely mentioned in reports but never identified and then, wraith-like, she receded from the public's mind and ultimately vanished.

Fifteen years on, she is still underweight and riddled with bad health. Her lungs have collapsed twice and she has undergone surgery for a life-threatening condition classified as spontaneous pneumothorax. She has bad eyesight and suffers from asthma, migraines, irritable bowel syndrome and occasional kidney infections. She takes Valium and sees a psychologist every week. She believes her illnesses are associated with the trauma she has suffered throughout her life. She still bears scars on her back from the ritual beatings she says her father administered every day when she was aged ten, eleven and twelve.

Alienated from her parents, who remain in Carracastle, she lives in the West of Ireland with her husband Wade Thompson, a South African who has lived in Ireland for fourteen years and whom she married in September 2001. That was before she finally severed the communication cord with her parents. Initially, after their release from Mountjoy Prison she kept in touch, primarily to maintain contact with her siblings, including her baby sister who was born while Sue Fitzgerald was serving her jail sentence.

Geraldine invited her parents to her wedding reception in a hotel in Castlebar. Her father arrived late, dressed in mechanic's overalls, and told the bride: 'You look like shit.'

'She is intelligent, attractive, distrustful, dignified, angry and strong-willed. She has no qualifications to pursue a career, having dropped out of secondary school when she went into 'self-destruction mode' while in care. She receives €185-a-week disability allowance and Wade receives the same amount in job seeker's allowance. Community Welfare contributes €74.50 to the couple's €150 weekly rent. They have fallen behind in repayments to the credit union for the loan they got to buy a car so that Geraldine could keep her appointments with the psychologist every week. 'I've asked Community Welfare for money for clothing and food but, apart from once, they haven't given it to us. The rent allowance we get keeps going up and down. At one stage, we slept in the car for three nights. We'll soon be in serious debt.'

Her dearth of knowledge about officialdom's dealings with her own case and with Kelly's is deeply disturbing, despite amassing a file of official documentation under the Freedom of Information Act, largely emanating from the Western Health Board. To date, she has failed to acquire her medical records from either Castlebar Hospital or St Thomas' in London and only discovered eight weeks ago that a Western-Health-Board-commissioned report exists, entitled 'Kelly Fitzgerald: A Child Is Dead'. Last Tuesday, she learned for the first time that the London coroner had formally concluded that Kelly died 'from natural causes'. It is as if Geraldine Fitzgerald has lived in a twilight zone all her life.

'I've got dreams. I've got ambitions,' she says, 'but my life hasn't changed. I'm doing this [interview] in the hope that my life can change. I'm twenty-seven years old and I feel my life is over, not beginning. I'm so sick and tired of it. I think I deserve something and I think she [Kelly] deserves something. I've fought so hard to be here all these years and what have I achieved?

'I am literally tired from the amount of times over the years that I've appealed to people to help me. I explain to them who I am and what I'm going through and it still doesn't make a difference. The way I see life: you get born, you get f**ked, and then you die.'

'She believes the reason she was singled out for what she describes as torture by her parents, from the age of five, was because she used to play with Kelly. 'My father told us not to talk to Kelly, to pretend she didn't exist, because she'd been bold. Me and Kelly were separated from the others [there were three other siblings at that time]. We weren't allowed talk to them or play with them. We didn't get the treats they got.'

At first, when they moved to Carracastle from London, Kelly stayed behind, residing with her grandparents and thriving for the time being. In Mayo, Geraldine was isolated. At night she was put outside the back door in her nightdress to sleep on the step with the dogs, until the dogs grew raucous with the cold and were brought inside. After her parents were informed that Geraldine had been breaking into neighbours' houses in the middle of the night, wrapped in a blanket, to steal bread, they put her to sleep in the bathroom with the door locked from the outside.

'Most of the time, I wasn't allowed into the house,' she recalls. 'While the rest of them would be having breakfast, I would be cleaning out the cowshed, restacking the turf and clearing up after the dogs. I had to walk the dogs every morning in my nightie – wind, rain or snow. I was never given anything extra to wear, except if somebody came to the house. I had to pick up the dog poop with my bare hands. If I missed any, my mother would take off her shoe and hit me on the head with it and then I'd have to clean and dry the shoes of the person who had stepped in it.

When the chores were done, my father would make me do press-ups and run around the house.

'He used to stamp on my bare feet and hit me if the others fell over or hurt themselves. Sometimes, to make him stop hitting me, she (her mother) would slap me to make me cry.

'I never sat with the family for a meal. When they were eating, I was left outside. The only time I would be with them at mealtime would be when my father would tell me to stay and watch them eat. He'd offer me something on a plate but, when I went to take it, he would either put it down for the dogs or else throw it on the floor and tell me to eat it off the floor. Sometimes he made porridge and put a whole bag of salt in it or gave me dog-food and held my nose and forced me to eat it.' A teacher in Scoil Iosa, noticing that Geraldine was coming to school with no lunch, apportioned some of her brother's lunchbox to the girl but Sue Fitzgerald went to the school and instructed the teacher to stop.

'My mother and father brought me to the bathroom every day and told me to take off all my clothes and he would beat me with his belt. The more I cried, the more he beat me. These beatings happened every day for three years.'

(In a Health Board document outlining beatings suffered by Kelly at the hands of her father, it is repeatedly noted as 'worrying' that Des Fitzgerald admitted he was sexually aroused during these beatings.)

'He hit me with a black pipe he used to have for the cows,' Geraldine continues. 'He said he hated me and I was a bitch. He said it was in the Bible that a father could take the rod to his child and that I made him do it. I was always warned by my parents to keep my socks up at school to hide the marks on my legs. Sometimes, after beating me, he'd fill the bath with water and put me into it and hold my head down under the water.

'On the school bus one day, I was crying and a girl in my class asked me what was wrong. I said I was afraid to go home but my parents found out and my father beat me with his belt.

'When the child psychologist used to call to the school, my father coached me in what to say to her. Sometimes, when I couldn't walk, I was kept home from school. I tried telling the neighbour, Mrs Duffy – she's dead now – and my parents beat me again.

'My brother, Rory (seven years younger than Geraldine), used to ask my mother for biscuits and he would bring them out to me but I was frightened for him. I used to be nice like that to Kelly and I got beaten for it and I couldn't let that happen to him. I told him not to play with me or talk to me.'

After a fortnight away from the family, Kelly returned to live with them in Mayo for five months, until she was put on a plane at Knock Airport in a wheelchair and sent back to England.

'The social workers came to the house one day after that and we were all told to take ourselves off while they talked to my parents,' Geraldine recalls. 'My parents were really strange that day.

'They were really nice, and that wasn't good. I got to sleep in a bed and have food. In the middle of the night, the phone rang. My mother answered it and she started crying and I knew. I could feel it in the air. I asked my mother: 'What's wrong with you?' She just said: 'Kelly's dead.' The following day, we were taken into care.

'We were brought to the hospital in Castlebar. We were all in the same ward. We wanted to torment the doctors. One of us would put two others on a trolley and go wild, crashing into doors.

'It was the first time I felt like a child, happy. The social workers said we would be going into care and I said I'd rather go home and be beaten because that was what I knew. It didn't feel right at first, not being beaten. They said there was something wrong with me to feel like that.

'I went to a family in Tubbercurry with my younger brother, Rory. I had clothes and I had food and I had hugs whenever I wanted them. I had friends. I got my ears pierced. But the social workers said I should be upset because my sister had died. Everybody kept talking about Kelly and everybody was feeling sorry for my parents.

'When I tried to talk about me, they [her parents] said I was an attention seeker, that I was trying to take the attention away from Kelly. Nobody gave a continental about me. I started taking overdoses. I took a lot of them. If they had listened to me, I wouldn't have done that.' She has not harmed herself since meeting her husband, Wade.

Geraldine and Rory were split up and sent to different families and, in her words, she 'went out of control'. She started smoking and drinking, self-harming and missing school. For most of the following six years, she stayed from Monday to Friday at St Anne's, a residential centre in Galway for children with psychological, behavioural and emotional problems. Her weekends were spent at another children's centre, Aiglish House, in Castlebar.

'In 1996 I tried to make a complaint [to bring charges against her parents for the abuse],' she says. 'I was in fear of my family but they were allowed have contact with me and I ran away from Aiglish.' A Health Board note of this time records that it was 'no surprise' that she withdrew her complaint, following contacts with members of her family. Surprising too that, as the garda investigation of her parents was underway, Geraldine and her siblings returned to the family home for three days that Christmas.

'We went to visit them once a month in Mountjoy. The social workers hired a mini-van and we would go up to Dublin and go back to Mayo in one day. My parents would say hello to everyone – 'How's it going? How's school?' – but they wouldn't want to know anything about me. While they were talking in one corner, I'd be sitting in another corner.

'An extra visit was arranged because it was my birthday. They were getting a cake and soft drinks and presents. I approached my mother for a hug and she said: "Oh, I saw you the other day."'

The agenda for a social workers' meeting about Geraldine, dated 3 March 1997, four years after Kelly's death, records: 'Geraldine continues to be abused by her parents. While we have been able to protect Geraldine from the physical abuse that she experienced at home, we have been unable to protect her from the power and domination of her parents, particularly her father.' The Health Board files attest to 'the visible, ongoing rejection' of Geraldine by her parents on access visits.

'They didn't rescue me,' she insists. 'It was only when Kelly died that I was taken out of there. Even when I was in care, nothing was done without the consent of my parents. When the social workers wanted me to go to court to give evidence about what was done to Kelly, my father refused to give his permission.

'Even if it kills me, I am going to have my say now. The reason I didn't do it before was I thought I was to blame. People say that if you have been abused, you become an abuser yourself. I want people to know I'm not like that. I'm embarrassed; I'm ashamed of my life. People will say, "Why is she doing this to her parents?" But the only thing I can think of is a voice saying:

"Please, Daddy, don't hurt me."'

✦   ✦   ✦

'My dream was to swim. He ruined my life'

In 2007 the *Tribune* tracked alleged child rapist George Gibney to Orange County, Florida. Here, one of his alleged victim talks about how he ruined her life.

18 March 2007

After the detectives came to break the news, she walked to a field in the grounds of a religious order's house and hung herself from a tree with her scarf. Inside, she felt dead already.

For years, the prospect of seeing the man who raped her being convicted by a court of the land and sent to jail had kept her engaged in living. The gardaí were optimistic.

Three other girls had sworn statements that he had sexually abused them too. These crimes were much more recent than the seven alleged rapes he had got away with in 1994 when the Supreme Court had ruled that they were so old he could not adequately defend himself against the charges. This second case file was watertight. The gardaí had worked assiduously, ever since she first went to them in 1997. They were talking about having him extradited from the US. Her counselling sessions were concentrated on getting her psychologically prepared for the ordeal of being cross-examined.

At first, after the guards sat with heavy surrender in her living room and told her that the state had decided not to apply for George Gibney's extradition, all she felt was relief. She would not have to go to court after all. Would not have to see his face ever again. Would not have to recount to an audience of strangers the intense details of that day he raped her in a hotel room in Florida when she was just seventeen.

It was a priest who cut her down from the tree two years ago. Her parents got the call from a hospital emergency room. They were sorrowfully practised in the drill.

The hospital calls had become part of their lives. Often she would get up and leave the house in the middle of the night and wander aimlessly abroad. Sometimes she was admitted to A&E bleeding copiously after cutting her body indiscriminately with a knife or blades. Other times it would be an overdose of pills.

She had never tried to hang herself before, though.

It was the anger, she explains in a leaden voice. The raging anger that boiled inside her once the initial relief receded and which she could not express. She was left to drift like flotsam after a catastrophe in the sea. She who was once a future Olympic swimmer. The girl who cut through the water so fast that bystanders on the bank turned to one another and asked what was her name. A name to watch out for in the future, they would nod. That name lost to her now as she reluctantly chooses anonymity for a veil of armour. As if to compensate, she only ever alludes to George Gibney by his surname.

'I think he saw a vulnerability in me,' she agrees.

Her destiny was decided when she was five, after her mother was taken to Peamount Hospital with TB and remained there for six months. While her father would visit his wife at the hospital, the child would be sent to the house three doors down, where other little girls about her own age were minded by their live-in grandfather.

'If you tell anybody, your mother will die and it'll be all your fault,' the grandfather threatened her after the first time he sexually abused her, aged five-and-a-half.

The abuse was a regular occurrence, becoming increasingly severe and rough. Once, when she was seven, she came home with scrapes and bruises and had to make excuses to her parents. When she was nine, her parents, worried about her psychological withdrawal, brought her to Temple Street Children's Hospital. It was supposed that her symptoms were a natural response to her mother's prolonged absence from home.

Her parents hired a private tutor to come to the house because she had fallen behind academically in school. All the while, the abuse continued, not stopping until she was eleven, when the other family moved away from the locality.

When a swimming pool opened in her neighbourhood and she went there for the first time, she discovered a means of escape. 'It felt like I was flying,' she remembers. 'Like I'd been freed. I put everything into it. I really focused. It happened so quickly. One year, I wasn't able to swim. Within a year, I was breaking Irish records. People were wondering who I was.'

One day, a swimming coach phoned her parents after seeing her swim and told them she had the potential to be a great champion. Trojans Swimming Club in Blackrock was recommended, the citation eulogising its founder, George Gibney, the Irish Amateur Swimming Association's national coach when she joined in 1990 and Olympic coach to the Irish team in Seoul two years earlier. In 1990, most of the club's most accomplished swimmers left Trojans, their puzzling departure barely whispered in swimming circles. (It has since emerged that, in 1990, a male swimmer informed a senior swimming official that George Gibney had raped him when he was eleven.) Even though the pool was eighteen miles from their home, she and her father rose from bed at four o'clock every morning to be at the pool by 5.15 a.m., as stipulated. While her father slept outside in the car, she was swimming her heart out inside.

'I was so driven. All I wanted to do was to go to the Olympics at any cost. That was my dream.'

Gibney showered her with attention. Promised her he would make her a star. Gave her swimming togs and tracksuits and hats and goggles. Hugged her every time she swam well. That year, at the national championships, she streaked home first in the 50 m freestyle, the 100 m freestyle, the 100 m breaststroke and the 100 m butterfly. She was sixteen years old, perfectly poised to be selected for the next Olympic games in Barcelona in 1992.

Then the sun went in. She was competing in Holland with the club. After one of the swim meets, she returned to her hotel room to dress for a disco that was part of the swimmers' itinerary. 'Gibney came to the room and started saying how bad I was and that I was never going to go anywhere. Suddenly, he jumped on me. He pushed me down on the bed and then left the room. After that he completely ignored me for a couple of weeks. I was wondering what did I do wrong. Back home, at training, he'd act as if I wasn't there. I felt all this guilt. I was swimming my hardest, training extra hard to get his attention.'

In 1991 Trojans organised a training camp in Tampa, Florida, to prepare for the National Championships in Belfast, where swimmers would be selected for the Olympics. The swimmers were assigned to host families, returning for a daily siesta to their houses after morning training and before the afternoon session. One day, her host family was away and she remained at the poolside with another girl after everyone dispersed.

'Gibney appeared out of nowhere and said, "Come on, we'll go for breakfast." The three of us went for breakfast. Then he drove us to a hotel that I didn't know. He brought me to a room and said, "You, get in there," and he went off with the other girl. I don't know where he brought her.

'He comes back and starts ranting and raving that I was so bad at swimming and how disappointed in me he was. I was sitting on a double bed. He jumped on me and raped me, there on the bed. He said if I told anybody, he would sue my family and nobody would believe me because he was George Gibney and he would bankrupt my family. Then he left.

'When he was gone, I just sat on the floor in the room. I couldn't leave because I didn't know where I was. He came back about three hours later with his wife and loads of kids and said: "Come on you, we're going swimming now."

'People saw me crying but nobody came near me. None of the swimming managers who were there approached me. My host family asked me what was wrong and I said I was homesick. I rang home and I told my mother that Gibney locked me in a room but I didn't tell her he raped me.'

At the National Championships in Belfast that year, her legs shook so much standing on the starting block that she could not swim.

'Even then, I kept crying all the time. I couldn't stop.'

Finally, in 1994, her trauma reached crisis point. She feigned an injury to get out of swimming in a competition and was referred to a doctor appointed by the Olympic Council of Ireland. The dam burst. She told the doctor about the prolonged abuse by the grandfather when she was a child and about being raped by Gibney.

She made a statement to gardaí about the first series of abuse. Two other females came forward and alleged that they had also been abused by the man. He fought the prosecution through the courts, seeking a judicial review but finally pleaded guilty in 1999. He was sentenced to five years' jail on conviction of seven charges of child sexual abuse of the three girls. The man is dead now. She heard he died in prison of natural causes. In passing sentence, the judge remarked that it was probably no coincidence that one of the girls was later abused by her swimming coach.

'I felt I got a bit of justice,' she says. 'It wasn't my imagination. It wasn't me going mad. It wasn't all in my head.'

That experience encouraged her to make a statement against Gibney. He had eluded seven rape charges on the technicality that they were too old to defend. Yet, most of the Gibney charges pertained to the same years (or post-dated them) as the charges against the convicted grandfather.

The explanation she was given for the DPP's decision not to seek Gibney's extradition on foot of the second investigation was that he was entitled to insist on having each of the four complainants' cases tried separately. Again, this had not arisen in the case of the grandfather or in the vast majority of sexual-abuse prosecutions.

'The guards were absolutely brilliant. They couldn't have done enough,' she says.

She is pursuing a civil action for damages against the Irish Amateur Swimming Association, the Olympic Council of Ireland and George Gibney. (This journalist has seen the legal statement of claim lodged in court, despite a denial by Swim Ireland that any such legal action exists.) Meanwhile, she is left to cope with the devastation. She takes six pills for her mental well-being every night, attends a psychiatrist every week and a cognitive counsellor twice a week. She does not socialise and has never had a proper romantic relationship. She has suffered from anorexia, dropping to under five-and-a-half stone at one stage though she stands 5ft 10" tall, and has had surgery for the scars left by her self-mutilation.

She is too embarrassed by the cut marks on her skin (the most recent episode was last November) to ever swim again.

'I'm sorry to say this,' says her mother, sitting beside her on the couch, holding her hand and looking searchingly into her daughter's empty eyes, 'but, sometimes, she's like the living dead.'

✦ ✦ ✦

Valerie Shanley

Profile: Adele King (Twink)

They're behind you! The banks are behind you!
Will there be a fairytale resolution to the latest unfortunate
twist in the Panto Queen's life?

21 February 2010

As the number of house repossessions rises, there are the ordinary folk out there finding some reassurance that the rich and famous are not immune from losing their homes either. Idrone House, a 300-year-old Georgian mansion in Knocklyon, South Dublin, fell under the public spotlight last week due to proceedings issued by Bank of Scotland (Ireland). The owner is the actor, comedian, veteran pantomime star, and recently turned 'sugarcrafter', Adele King.

It's not the first time Twink, as King is better known, has faced a repossession order. Back in 1993, she nearly lost her former home in Rathfarnham due to what she claimed were debts accrued from her dealings with jailed solicitor Elio Malocco. In 2006, the fifty-eight-year-old and her former husband David Agnew (forty-eight) had to pay a joint court judgement for €19,000 after being sued by a firm of builders for unpaid debts. One of the alterations to Idrone House in recent years is the creation of what King has described as her 'sugarcraft loft for big little girls'. The room was originally her ex-husband's office, and is now a confection in pink in every sense. This is where she now crafts her 'edible art'. But she long ago gave up trying to ice over the cracks in her marriage.

King's personal as well as professional life have been played out on the public stage practically since she became a 'Gaiety Kiddie' at the age of five. But expletive-laden lines delivered to Agnew's answering machine after their twenty-one-year marriage broke down in 2004 have typecast her in a new role – that of wronged, and very fearsome, wife – ever since.

The tirade allegedly resulted from the failure of Mr Twink, or, as she dubbed him in that infamous message, the 'fat, bald, middle-aged dickhead', to attend the birthday party of their eldest daughter Chloe (20). The message spread like wildfire via email, and went around the world and back again as a YouTube hit.

Undoubtedly she is what might politely be called 'high octane'. Someone who has met her professionally over the years describes King as 'draining. That said, I really like her. She's our Cher, the kind of star you rarely see in this country. Once you can get beyond the fact that she always seems to be 'on', she's a very bright, well-read, informed and talented woman.'

She looks after herself, too. And you won't find her eating any of that cake she ices – she hates the stuff. Sweets, likewise. One gym member recalls seeing the formidable panto queen in action.

'She really doesn't do things by halves and would go at the gym equipment like a woman possessed. Definitely not the sort of person you want to have a row with.'

In interviews, she invariably comes across as a resolute self-promoter. Who doesn't know that Twink wanted to be a doctor, can write and direct panto, do serious acting (*The Vagina Monologues*, *Menopause the Musical*), impersonates everyone she refers to, and ices cakes like a sculptor? Then there's the collecting passion, from dolls' houses to dogs. Among her many adored 'mutts' is one 'Bertie Ahern' who she found abandoned and tied to a lamppost under an election poster.

Shouldn't the star herself be deserving of some public sympathy just now?

'I don't think we like people who are that 'full on' in this country,' says a former showbusiness colleague. 'And some people will secretly be pleased she's having financial problems. She doesn't deserve that.'

The woman herself doesn't harbour delusions about the fickleness of public affection. 'I know people think that I'm brash, arrogant, full of meself,' she has said. 'But that's only one side of things, and most entertainers are terrible cowards underneath it all, terribly shy, insecure people.'

She views motherhood as her most important role; she frequently refers in interviews to daughters Chloe and Naomi (15). Her relationship with her eldest, a successful singer in her own right, is like that of 'an auld married couple'. King has said they were both very protective of the younger girl when news broke of Agnew's relationship with clarinetist Ruth Hickey (32), and the impending arrival of their child. Naomi was 'very crushed, terribly hurt, particularly by the news of the new arrival. And they both felt he did not understand that he wasn't just cheating on me, he was cheating on them.'

But she recently revealed that on the day their divorce was finalised, both she and Agnew exchanged sympathetic looks. 'We both started crying, and he wrote me a lovely card.'

Now her formidable focus is not only on writing her autobiography to raise funds, but building on that sugar-crafting business. Recent commissions included christening cakes for Gay Byrne's grandchild, Harry, and Lucy Kennedy's baby son, Jack. But the bank is closing in, assessing those debts on Idrone House, formerly valued at €2 million. And that's an awful lot of sugar.

✦ ✦ ✦

Profile: Simon Cowell

This Briton's got talent ... for making a £100 million fortune.

24 October 2010

Supposedly the richest man in television, Simon Cowell is the Brit who's got talent for raking it in. Worth £100 million (€113.7 million) at the last count, he's arguably also the reason why a nation too broke to head to the pub instead tunes in every weekend for the diversion of seeing this latter-day Svengali of pop make another hapless wannabee redundant.

Having just turned a well-preserved fifty-one, displaying an impressive chest rug curling over one of his trademark V-necks, and with a smile more menacing than genial, Cowell pretty much sums up the current popular music industry in one neatly-coiffed package.

The object of *The X Factor* 'is not to be mean to the losers, but to find a winner' he has claimed, but Cowell is smart enough never to underestimate the public's taste for that thinly-disguised meanness. Unlike excitable Louis, tearful Cheryl, or Dannii Minogue, he's the judge all the contestants dread.

After all, he has his bad-boy image to maintain. When invited onto BBC Radio 4's *Desert Island Discs* four years ago, he said, if stranded, his one luxury would be a mirror 'because I'd miss me'. Former girlfriend Jackie St Clair likely wished him marooned indefinitely when he presented her with a life-sized oil portrait of himself for her fiftieth birthday last year.

As an extremely eligible bachelor, he's also known a string of ex's. His engagement to St Clair's replacement, Afghan make-up artist Mezhghan Hussainy, has reportedly just broken up, while his longest relationship – six years with Terri Seymour, the US *Extra Extra* presenter who became Cowell's ex-ex in 2008 – ended after she finally admitted defeat in breaking his resolve never to marry or have kids. She was given $5 million cash and another $4.6 million to buy a Beverly Hills home.

Inevitably, there has been speculation about Cowell's sexual orientation, and that he might be gay or bisexual. He has refused to refute such rumours, sensibly telling one British newspaper that denial 'would imply that it's some sort of evil' and given that there are 'plenty of gay people working in television, so if I was, it wouldn't be a problem saying I was'.

Cowell is no working-class hero, despite having left school at sixteen. He attended public school, and his parents weren't short of a few bob. But they insisted he use his pocket money for ice lollies when they went on luxury holidays, and instilled in the boy the need to make his own lolly as an adult. He's made no secret of that devotion to money – 'as much as I can get my hands on'. He famously told *Rolling Stone* magazine he regretted not being around in the 1960s to sign The Beatles – not for Lennon and McCartney's timeless music, but for the timeless royalties.

Another of his crimes against humanity was Robson and Jerome's cover version of *Unchained Melody*, which blocked *Common People* by Pulp from the number one slot in 1995.

Still, as the nation huddles around their tellies from now until the austerity Christmas ahead, it's unsentimental Simon who will go on, like a murdered ballad on an endless loop, bringing a glow to the nation's cheeks each weekend.

✦ ✦ ✦

Profile: Jeremy Clarkson

Clarkson's way with words has once again put him and the BBC in hot water.

9 November 2008

When the opening bars of The Allman Brothers' 1973 hit 'Jessica' strike, it's the signature tune for viewers to either crank up the volume, or change channels at turbo speed. *Top Gear* is one of the BBC's most enduringly popular series, with motoring presenters James May, Richard Hammond and Jeremy Clarkson a winning team. Of the three, it's self-confessed petrolhead Clarkson who provokes mirth and moral indignation in equal measure.

For some inveterate telly addicts, his all-round 'ordinary bloke' persona bears an uncanny resemblance to spoof TV presenter Alan Partridge. The Lexus-driving, failed chat show host Partridge is the comic creation of comedian Steve Coogan. On a guest appearance on *Top Gear*, Coogan declared his indebtedness to Clarkson as part inspiration for caricature, cringe-inducing *I'm Alan Partridge* sketches, such as the programme idea for *Crash! Bang! Wallop!* – a show about car crashes – or when Partridge quotes from the pages of *Top Gear* magazine to rubbish the make of car belonging to his wife's lover.

When motormouth Clarkson performs such stunts as testing the crumple potential of a pick-up truck by slamming it into an ancient horse chestnut, torching a detested caravan, or describing the Ferrari 355 as being like 'a quail's egg dipped in celery salt and served in Julia Robert's belly button', it's easy to see why *The Daily Mirror* dubbed him 'the dazzling hero of political incorrectness' in 2000.

The 'dazzling' bit turned out to be somewhat prescient, funnily enough, for Piers Morgan. The former *Mirror* editor was doused with a glass of water during an argument with Clarkson on a flight; then, at the British Press Awards, Morgan was sworn at and punched in the face by an enraged Clarkson, who claimed his privacy had been invaded. None of which seemed to do the presenter's testosterone-fuelled image any harm. Even in the Channel 4 viewers' poll listing the *100 Worst Britons We Love to Hate*, Clarkson was placed a reasonably respectable sixty-sixth.

To lighten the techno jargon of his supercharged pronouncements on all things motoring, Clarkson, on occasion, drives a metaphorical truck over the sensibilities of quite a sizeable group of innocent bystanders, which include women, the gay community, environmentalists, and Korean car manufacturers.

And, in eerie coincidence with Partridge's turn as Radio Norwich presenter, a 'We Hate Jeremy Clarkson' club was set up by residents of Norfolk after he said people living in the 'flat and featureless' area were backward and would point and exclaim, 'Hey, look, it's a car!' whenever he drove past. Hyundai complained to the BBC about his comments at the Birmingham Motor Show after he said one of their designers had most likely 'eaten a spaniel for lunch'. He agreed with an audience member that a car could be 'a bit gay', or as he put it, a bit 'ginger beer'. 'Eco-mentalists' as he calls them, are just a bunch of 'old trade-unionists and CND lesbians'.

His concern about the tough lot of lorry drivers on last week's *Top Gear* has added more fuel to the general debate about editorial standards at the BBC. 'Change gear, change gear, change gear, check mirror, murder a prostitute, change gear, murder. That's a lot of effort in a day,' exclaimed Clarkson in one scene. There is no doubt that Clarkson delights in winding people up, particularly what he calls 'lefties', 'Guardianistas', and 'those of a sandal persuasion'.

So is he just having a laugh? Is he wittily exposing extremes of political correctness? Or is Clarkson a prime example of the arrogant pub bore, an ethnocentric chauvinist embodying the worst aspects of a certain English stereotype, a man accused by more than just Korean car-company executives as being 'bigoted and racist'?

Clarkson attended Repton, one of Britain's elite public schools. His working-class parents – teacher mother and travelling salesman father – are said to have paid for the fees through the success of their soft toys' business. Eventually expelled for 'making a nuisance of himself', the teenage Clarkson nonetheless fitted the profile as he played the role of a public schoolboy in a radio adaptation of the Jennings novels.

His career in journalism revved off on a local paper in his native Yorkshire. Writing has continued to be a major source of income, with a stint on *The Sun*, and a regular column in *The Sunday Times* to this day. But his passion for motoring, combined with a way with words and childlike enthusiasm, made him a natural as presenter of *Top Gear*.

Last week saw two forced resignations and a suspension at the BBC over the offence caused during a prank call [Jonathan Ross and Russell Brand's offensive phone call to Andrew 'Manuel' Sachs]. Clarkson is now part of the general debate about editorial standards with regard to maverick presenters, free speech and comedy's right to breach boundaries. The corporation has responded to the latest criticism by asserting that most *Top Gear* viewers know exactly what to expect from Clarkson and that he was 'comically exaggerating and making ridiculous an unfair urban myth about lorry drivers'.

So that's sorted, then, for anyone troubled over suitable targets for humorous focus at the Beeb: respected seventy-eight-year-old actor = offensive; murdered prostitutes = fair comment. In the past, Clarkson has dismissed as nonsense any perceived influence on what he says: 'I enjoy this back and forth, it makes the world go round. But it is just opinion.'

At this stage, the forty-eight-year-old anti-eco, pro-hunting, Countryside-Alliance-supporting Clarkson is unlikely to undergo a socially liberal conversion anytime soon. Especially, as he so unreservedly exclaims: 'God, I love being middle-class!' An incurable road hog too, he won't even accept the need for something as innocuous as a bus lane: 'Why do poor people have to get to places quicker than me?'

Crash! Bang! Wallop! it is then ... on bags or tee-shirts, owning property abroad, or going on spending sprees in New York. And that identity is priceless.

✦   ✦   ✦

Ken Sweeney

Profile: George Lee

Merry Lee on high. It's all gone horribly right for George, the man 'who told us so'.

6 July 2008

Last week, the BBC's former economics editor, Evan Davis, claimed that UK journalists could have done more to warn the public about the credit crunch that triggered Britain's current housing price crash and general financial turmoil.

'I do ask whether we did our best to warn people of impending problems during the upswing of the [economic] cycle,' Davis said at a radio festival in Glasgow.

Such a question could never apply to RTÉ's George Lee, the station's economics editor, who has been predicting an economic Armageddon twice nightly on the TV news for as long as anyone can remember. Often accused of turning glum into a fine art, his nearest TV equivalent is *Dad's Army's* Private Frazer who was always howling 'We're doomed, I tell you. Doomed,' at Captain Mainwaring in the BBC comedy.

His pessimism did not go unnoticed. 'George Lee could tell you that you'd just scooped the Lotto jackpot and still leave you wondering how you were going to pay your mortgage,' one commentator wrote at the height of the boom. 'Why can't he enjoy the good times like everybody else?' His tendency to see clouds where others see silver linings has brought him to the attention of political satirists as well. Today FM's *Gift Grub* and 2FM's *Nob Nation* have both milked great humour from Lee's instinctive glumness.

But it seems Lee was right all along. Educated at Coláiste Eanna in Dublin, he graduated from UCD before getting a scholarship to study for an MSc at the London School of Economics. He then joined the Central Bank, from which he moved to the ESB as a treasury economist. While there he started writing an economics column for the fledgling *Sunday Business Post*. Bitten by the bug, he jumped when offered a chance to join the newspaper full time, even though it meant taking a 40 per cent pay cut. He is the first to concede the transition was difficult. 'I can put my hand on my heart and say that the communications learning curve was one of the hardest things I have ever done in terms of learning,' he has said. 'I had to change from writing about economics for people who understood economics to writing about economics for people who really did not care a hoot, but you had to interest them in it because it was important to them.'

When the newspaper ran into rocky times, Lee left for a job with Riada Stockbrokers, but journalism beckoned him back when RTÉ offered him a job on its *Marketplace* programme in 1991. This turned out to be another challenge. 'TV was even harder than print because you have people's attention for a mere fifteen minutes, or one minute and forty-five seconds. Every week I had to present three minutes of the history of the Irish economy – really difficult for somebody like me.' After three seasons on *Marketplace*, Lee moved to the newsroom, and in the years that followed he was a regular fixture on RTÉ's nightly news. He became a household name in 1998 when a story he worked on sparked one of the country's most high-profile libel trials.

In January of that year, Lee and Charlie Bird, RTÉ's chief news correspondent, reported that National Irish Bank had defrauded customers, opened bogus accounts and knowingly facilitated the targeting of high-net-worth customers for the purpose of tax evasion. Between NIB's defensive strategies and the libel action taken by one of its former employees, Fianna Fáil TD Beverly Cooper Flynn, who sold bogus non-resident accounts, Lee and Bird's work triggered a High Court investigation and Supreme Court challenges. The ensuing High Court inspectors' report was damning of NIB. Flynn later lost her libel action.

The year after the NIB scandal, Lee made a name for himself again when he described as 'Thatcherite' Charlie McCreevy's third giveaway budget, which made it financially more attractive for both partners in a marriage to take paid employment. His comments in the hours after the budget had been announced played a huge part in the subsequent 'tax individualisation' controversy which followed it, one of the most embarrassing setbacks of McCreevy's career.

Since then, Lee has erupted into righteous indignation on a regular basis, demonstrating he has a social conscience and claiming that economic policy should serve the people and not the other way around.

For all his concern about the health of the economy, four years ago Lee was in danger of going into recession himself when he lost two-and-a-half stone after being struck down by a mystery illness which was later diagnosed as Chronic Urticaria – a condition which made him ultra-sensitive to certain foods.

'I thought I was never going to be able to eat anything again. I still have to be careful about what I take, although it's impossible to be sure what's in anything or how I will react.' One imagines that was a particular worry when he travelled to China earlier this year to film an acclaimed and thought-provoking series for RTÉ.

Because of his approach to his job, Lee does have a habit of rubbing people up the wrong way, even Bertie Ahern. Frustrated at having lost his chance to become Taoiseach in 1994, Ahern was asked to speak on RTÉ, but first had to sit through Lee commenting favourably on what the new Minister for Finance, Ruairí Quinn, was doing. 'Wouldja listen to him!' Ahern is reported to have raged through gritted teeth. 'Wouldja just listen to him!'

Lee's friends say that what keeps his fire burning is his concern for a public often flummoxed by the financial gobbledygook churned out by banks.

'I know that a lot of financial products can damage people because they don't know what they are taking and they don't know what they are getting into.'

Now that his time has come, you can be sure we're going to be hearing a lot more from George Lee. Earlier this year, it was reported he had been paid an advance of €100,000 for a book on the rise and decline of the Celtic Tiger which publishers promise will explain 'how a decade of easy gains and soaring expectations seduced people into unrealistic notions of what they are worth and what they are due'.

It sounds like the perfect marriage of book and author.

✦   ✦   ✦

Conor McMorrow

The Wayne O'Donoghue interview

In 2006 Wayne O'Donoghue was sentenced to four years for killing his eleven-year-old neighbour, Robert Holohan. McMorrow obtained this exclusive first interview with Wayne in prison.

30 April 2006

Security is tight. An electronic metal door slides open. Visitors pass through an airport-style metal detector. Then, more heavy metal doors and iron gates. The eerie silence of the prison corridor is interrupted by the sound of footsteps and the rattle of keys.

From a window, Padraig Nally, the man who was sentenced to six years for the manslaughter of the Traveller John Ward last year, can be seen working in the prison garden. A prison officer points in the direction of the visiting room.

Inside, the most talked about twenty-one-year-old in the country can be seen through the glass panel door.

Wayne O'Donoghue smiles as he introduces himself. The face of the student that was splashed across every newspaper in the country is not as recognisable now. He has grown a beard. His hair is a little shorter than it was during last December's trial and he has put on weight. The weight gain has been propelled by his medication – anti-depressants that help him cope with the events of the last sixteen months.

He is wearing a navy fleece top, as he has been out working in the prison garden where he spends most of his day. It passes the time. Wayne O'Donoghue lives his life between his cell and the prison garden. But no matter where he is, his mind is constantly focused on one day – 4 January 2005.

'I never stop thinking about what happened. I think about it 24/7. I just keep thinking why did this happen to me? Why did it happen to Robert? It was just a normal day like any other day. I had spent the morning studying for college and I had been visiting my girl-friend earlier as well.

'When Robert came to the house it happened. It all happened so quickly. He threw a handful of pebbles at my car and one of them hit me on the back of the neck. That's when it happened. It was over in seconds.'

At O'Donoghue's trial, the court heard how he caught Robert Holohan in an armlock, put his hand to the boy's throat and the young boy died from asphyxia due to neck compression. The former engineering student thinks constantly about those seconds when Robert Holohan's life ended and his own life changed irrevocably.

'I think about the Holohan family a lot, as they have lost Robert out of all this,' explained O'Donoghue. 'I cannot say how sorry I am for everything that has happened to them. I think that by getting a four-year sentence, I was treated fairly by the courts, but this is not a four-year sentence, this is a life sentence. I will feel sorry for what I did until the day I die. It will always be on my mind.'

O'Donoghue described how Ballyedmond, like rural townlands across the country, is one of those places where children of all ages mix together, as there may not be people of their own age living nearby.

'All of the kids in Ballyedmond were very close. We all hung around together like any other rural area in the country,' said O'Donoghue. 'My brothers and myself were very close to the Holohans. Majella would often ask me to look after Robert for a few hours because she knew she could trust me. We had been friends for about four or five years, although we were probably not as friendly in the last year, as I had got a car and I was always away in the car in town or at my girlfriend's house. Robert had taken up horse-riding so he was doing that a lot as well, so we didn't see as much of each other in the last year.'

Looking back on 4 January 2005, O'Donoghue points out that he was not even meant to be at home on the day. 'The only reason I was back at the house was because one of my brothers had bought an exercise bike and he wanted me to collect it and bring it home for him.'

After collecting the exercise bike in Midleton, O'Donoghue decided to stay at the house, and that is when Robert Holohan called to the O'Donoghue house. While Robert's death happened in seconds, it is what occurred after his death that has been the subject of most media and public comment, particularly after his mother made her victim impact statement in Ennis at O'Donoghue's sentencing hearing.

During his trial in Cork last December, O'Donoghue's barrister, Blaise O'Carroll, described how O'Donoghue and Robert Holohan had 'an extremely beautiful relationship' which led O'Donoghue to build a tree house for the young boy and play hurling with him as well as drive him into Midleton for ice creams and DVDs. It was in the context of 'this special relationship' that O'Donoghue panicked when he realised he had killed Robert.

'Had I been thinking any way logically, I would have rang an ambulance or the gardaí, but panic set in,' said O'Donoghue. 'I dragged Robert into the house to the bathroom and tried to get him back. I laid him out on the floor in the bathroom and even though I didn't know what I was doing, I lifted his right hand to check for a pulse.'

It is understood that when O'Donoghue dropped Robert's hand onto the bath mat, a tiny trace of semen got onto the deceased's hand. The *Sunday Tribune* has learned that detailed forensic tests carried out by a group of DNA experts in the United Kingdom found that the trace of semen on the bath mat was not that of Wayne O'Donoghue.

By taking DNA samples from all the males in the O'Donoghue house, the experts found that the trace of semen came from another member of the O'Donoghue family and, crucially, not from Wayne. 'That semen was definitely not mine, and I couldn't believe when people started to say that there was anything else going on between us,' said O'Donoghue.

'I couldn't believe it when Majella Holohan got up and said that there was semen on Robert's body, during her victim impact statement.'

Sitting last week in the visitor room of the Midlands Prison, O'Donoghue said he understood Majella Holohan's motivation for making her victim impact statement, but vehemently refutes her allegations. 'I can see why Majella Holohan came out with what she said at the time, and I don't hold anything against her for what she said. I have no problem doing my time in here, but there is no way there was anything going on between Robert and myself.'

Refuting Majella Holohan's allegation that pictures were taken on Robert's mobile phone in Wayne's bedroom at 7.30 a.m., O'Donoghue said, 'When Robert got the picture phone working, he took a picture of a poster in my room in the afternoon. The time on his phone was not set properly and that is how it looked like he was in my room at 7.30 a.m.'

O'Donoghue also offered an explanation to Majella Holohan's question about her son's body being found without his shoes. 'When I was dragging Robert into the bathroom, one of his shoes came off. I ended up wrapping that in a plastic bag before I put the body into the boot of the car. When I got to Inch, his other shoe had come off. I was in such a state at the time that I must have been driving around the back roads to Inch at about 100 mph. The body would have been thrown about in the boot and that could be how the other shoe came off. If people think about where I dumped the body, they could see how much of a panic I was in.'

For nearly eight days, Robert's body lay in a ditch near Inch Strand. In that period, the young boy's disappearance was elevated from a local tragedy to a national concern. Wayne O'Donoghue assisted in the search for the eleven-year-old. He reassured the boy's mother that her son would be found. He also filled in a garda questionnaire and gave two witness statements to gardaí.

When asked about the way he participated in the search and concealed the truth, O'Donoghue said, 'I was in such a state of shock and panic throughout those days. I had not slept or anything. I can say that the night that I handed myself in, I had the best night's sleep I ever had in my life, as I hadn't slept in days. I knew that I had finally owned up and that it was off my chest.'

Twelve days after Robert was reported missing, O'Donoghue eventually told his father, Ray, that he had killed Robert. His father immediately contacted the gardaí. 'I just couldn't keep going on not telling anyone what had happened to Robert so I told my father.

There was no else in the world I was able to tell. I knew that he was the only person that would be able to take the news and know what to do. I told him everything and I broke down. He rang the gardaí and got them to come to the house so that I could make a statement and hand myself in.'

Ray O'Donoghue locked his son into a garden shed as he feared he might take his own life. 'He even checked my pockets, in case I had a knife, when I went to the toilet,' Wayne recalled. 'If I had not told him what happened, I would probably just have cut my throat with a knife as I was in such a state. I just couldn't keep it going.'

Members of O'Donoghue's immediate family visit every week in prison. But since the false allegations of paedophilia, many of his friends have stopped coming to see him. 'I can understand why they started to believe it when I was called a paedophile across the front of some of the papers. Before the allegations were made, I got hundreds of letters. Some of them were even from the wives of gardaí investigating the case saying that they believed what happened was an accident. I have not got as many letters since the allegations were made, but I still get some.'

He is still in a relationship with his longtime girlfriend. 'I am still going out with Rebecca and she comes to see me. She took a year out after doing her Leaving Certificate and now she is going to college in the UK,' said O'Donoghue.

There have been media reports that O'Donoghue has received death threats in prison. He has been made aware that he may be in danger. 'While some people have treated me differently in here after the trial and the allegations were made against me, I have friends in here.' When asked if he associates with any other prisoners at the midlands prison, O'Donoghue said that he knows Padraig Nally and sees him working in the prison garden most days. 'I spend most of my time working in the garden. In the evenings, I have a shower and spend time in my cell.'

Formerly an engineering student at Cork Institute of Technology, O'Donoghue has not furthered his education during his time in prison. 'While there are courses inside here that are offered to me, none of them really interest me.'

O'Donoghue believes in God and prays every night. 'A few years ago, I was like a lot of teenagers as I would not go to mass that often. When my grandmother died in 1998, I started praying every night and I still do. I have rosary beads in my cell and I say a few prayers every night.'

O'Donoghue was sentenced to four years in prison by Judge Paul Carney at the Ennis sitting of the Central Criminal Court in January. He had already served thirteen months of the sentence by that time and, while his case and the events of 4 January 2005 will always be with him, he is attempting to look towards life after his release.

'I am not really sure what I will do as I take each day one at a time in here, but I will probably go abroad for a few years,' O'Donoghue admitted. 'I might go to England or somewhere and see after that about coming back to Ireland.'

✦ ✦ ✦

Ethiopia time to lend a hand

The nightmare of the 1980s famine could be about to hit once again. The *Tribune* visited some of the worst-hit areas to see how agencies are dealing with a crisis in which six million children could die.

25 May 2008

Don't read this. It's about Ethiopia. Let it slip under your radar. Famine in Ethiopia was interesting back in the 1980s but Live Aid sorted all that out. Surely the money we all sent to the 'black babies' solved their problems twenty-five years ago. Surely all those babies grew up to learn from the mistakes of their parents. Surely they all know about birth control in Ethiopia by now. They don't. Ethiopia is facing widespread famine.

Millions of children are at risk of malnutrition and if the world does not take notice immediately, history will repeat itself. Failed rains, the subsequent drought, and the global food price crisis have triggered massive food shortages across Ethiopia. In recent days Unicef, the UN children's agency, warned that six million children in the country are at acute risk of malnutrition.

'I am deeply concerned about the food security situation in Ethiopia, and the consequent increasing numbers of malnourished children, as a result of the drought,' said John Holmes, the UN's Under Secretary for Humanitarian Affairs.

'We will need a rapid scaling up of resources, especially food and nutritional supplies, to make increased life-saving aid a reality. In addition the rising global costs of fuel and basic staples are posing hardship for Ethiopia's people – especially the poorest.'

Visiting Ethiopia last week, the *Sunday Tribune* witnessed children with distended stomachs and skeletal chests – the trademark signs of acute malnutrition. Tens of thousands of children need immediate specialist feeding just to survive. Crops will fail in the coming months. So the situation is expected to get worse. As the world's media are focused on the aftermath of natural disasters in China and Burma, Ethiopia has been forgotten.

The Ethiopian government has admitted there is a problem, and declared a localised emergency, but their appeals for aid have been deemed woefully inaccurate and unrealistic by international aid agencies. There is a consensus among the aid agencies that they are using band aids to fix a problem that needs life saving surgery.

Some 200 miles towards the Equator from the capital Addis Ababa, south of the town of Shashamane, which is the spiritual home of Rastafarianism, the *Sunday Tribune* arrived in the town of Awassa. There, the poverty becomes more and more evident. At night the town is completely dark. Much of Ethiopia's power supply is generated by hydro-electricity. The previous two rainy seasons have failed, causing the power shortages, but it is the water and food shortages that have caused most ills.

Just outside Awassa, the signs of the famine are much more obvious. It is easy to count the ribs on the scrawny farm animals as they amble around fields that are quickly transforming in colour from lush green to a putrid yellowish brown. There is no significant harvest due until September but the poor rains have already compromised that harvest long before it is due. As the people and farm animals look for food over the next few months they cannot rest assured that there is light at the end of the tunnel. There will be no bumper harvest in the autumn.

There is some rainfall but not enough. When it does rain people and farm animals gather around the same puddles and ponds of dirty water to drink it. With nothing else to eat, millions of Ethiopians, are barely surviving on 'enset', more commonly known as 'false banana'. The most important staple crop in the south of the country, it tolerates drought better than most crops and people are left with it as their only food. It does keep people alive but it has poor nutritional value and really only serves to prolong the process of malnutrition setting in.

At the Yirba Health Centre about an hour's drive from Awassa, fourteen-year-old Taricka Wote has just arrived with his father Wote Woyamo. Taricka is in dire need of urgent medical attention if he is to survive. He weighs 11.5 kg (1.8 stone) which is just half the expected weight for a child of his height. He is the same height as an Irish toddler, as malnutrition has stunted his cognitive development and physical growth.

Speaking through an interpreter, the skeletal teenager's father explained that his wife died four years ago from either TB or HIV. Living in frugal circumstances Woyamo, a subsistence farmer, has struggled to provide for his children from their meagre resources, and the recent crop failures have left them depending on false banana as their only food.

Medical staff at the stabilisation clinic say that Taricka is extremely lucky that his father brought him to the centre when he did. As well as being severely malnourished, staff believed he may also have TB. Although he is at death's door, the staff are confident they can treat him and he will survive. Taricka is just one of thousands of children that are showing up at clinics like the Yirba Health Centre. Mothers, who are struggling to survive themselves, carry sick children on foot for distances that can take over eight hours to walk.

TB is extremely common at the Belela Health Centre, a health worker explained, 'Usually children under five are vulnerable to malnutrition but because the situation is so bad here we are getting children of all ages with malnutrition.'

The World Health Organisation has funded a drive to treat children with TB but it is still extremely common. An aid worker, who has worked in Ethiopia for eight years, said he was shocked to see the condition of one girl at the Belela Health Centre. The girl has just arrived with her mother and her pain is easily visible as she weeps. Her neck has burst open with mucus and there is scarring all around her neck.

An aid worker explains, 'She obviously has pulmonary TB which has caused lymph nodes in her neck to swell up and burst. I have never seen a case as severe as that where her neck has burst open. She will have to be rushed to hospital immediately.'

Elsewhere in the Boricha area, women queue to have their children weighed and their height measured in a screening area at the Derara Health Centre. The reality is harsh. If the children are deemed malnourished, they get medical attention and food. If they are not malnourished they return home. The likelihood is that they will end up coming back in a few weeks, malnourished.

An aid worker at the clinic explained, 'Community volunteers place the children in a plastic container that hangs from a weighing scales and then they lay them on a bench where they measure the children's height. We have a very scientific way of monitoring the children. Each height has a median weight. If a child is less than 70 per cent of their median weight, they are deemed severely malnourished. If they are between 80 and 90 per cent of their median weight they are deemed mildly malnourished.'

Inside the health centre, medical staff assess the appetite of the children, they check the levels of edema or swelling of their bodies. After that they assess the children's appetites by seeing if they are able to eat and keep therapeutic foods called Compact BP100 and Plumpy'nut down.

Plumpy'nut, commonly known as 'Plumpy', is a high-protein and high-energy peanut-based paste that has been used as a famine relief food for children over the last eight years. It can be eaten without any preparation from its foil wrapper so parents can be given supplies of it, through an out-patient therapeutic (PT) programme, to take home with them for their malnourished children.

The global food crisis that has caused Irish consumers to pay more for their goods at the checkout is also affecting Ethiopia as the cost of therapeutic foods like Plumpy'nut has multiplied in recent months.

With drought and famine on one side and rising food prices on the other, Ethiopia is really suffering. Last week Paulette Jones of the World Food Programme (WFP) stated that the WFP needs to raise $147 million to tackle Ethiopia's needs. But other aid agencies claim the necessary money is not arriving as donors are concentrating on the situation in Burma and China.

As well as visiting medical centres, the *Sunday Tribune* also visited a number of family homes. It felt like going 200 years back in time. A lot of rural Ethiopians live in round mud huts with thatched roofs. It takes a few minutes for the visitor's eyes to adjust to the darkness of the hut after stepping inside. One twenty-eight-year-old father explained that he, his wife and their six kids share their dark hut home with their farm animals. The smell inside, where a wooden fence divides the area where the children and animals sleep, is nauseating.

The mother was not there when we visited as she had made the long walk to a food handout centre with some of her children. The children we did meet have already got distended stomachs as the family are surviving on false banana. This family is symbolic of millions of people in Ethiopia as they wake up in the morning with the sole aim of trying to stay alive until they go back to bed again at night.

Nothing is simple in Ethiopia. According to the local calendar the current year is 2000. They had millennium celebrations when their new year began on 11 September last year. Few of us knew that. Their millennium celebrations slipped under all of our radars.

We should be careful not to let their famine do the same.

✦ ✦ ✦

John Downes

'I am now my mom's kid,' says Tristan

In 2001, Indonesian baby Tristan was adopted by an Irish accountant and his Azerbaijni wife. Two years later they gave him back to an orphanage. Now Tristan is happily reunited with his birth mother.

18 April 2010

'I like it here; my mother is here ... I am my mom's kid.' The playful and inquisitive boy who greets the *Sunday Tribune* at his home in the port city of Tegal, Indonesia, is virtually unrecognisable from the two-year-old who used to cry uncontrollably in the orphanage to which he was sent by Joe and Lala Dowse in May 2003.

Now almost nine years old, the boy formerly known as Tristan Dowse still identifies himself by the first name that his adoptive parents gave him as a two-month-old child. But there is little doubt as to where his loyalties lie. In the years since he was reunited with his birth mother Suryani, they have rebuilt a relationship that was fractured as a result of his illegal adoption by the Irish accountant and his Azerbaijani wife.

Speaking in the local Javanese language, Tristan says he liked living with the Dowse family 'because I got to eat bread with butter and cheese every day'. He describes Joe Dowse as 'nice', but cannot say the same of his wife.

Suryani adds that Tristan used to tell her how the Dowses often took him to church, and to vacation in Bali on a plane. He had a closer relationship with Joe than with Lala, she says. His memories of his time in the orphanage are far less pleasant, however. Tristan does not speak about the 'bad experiences' of the past, his mother confides, 'unless you ask him'.

'The people there are not nice, they are sharp and mean. They hit my head with a jar or glass bottle when we made noise,' he says.

Suryani has never had any direct contact with Joe or Lala Dowse. But through one of their friends in Jakarta, who lives in their old house there, she sends greetings to them from time to time. Sometimes, she hears back from this friend that Joe sends his greetings back, asking how Tristan is doing. She doesn't hear from Lala, though.

The house that Joe and Lala Dowse bought, on foot of an Irish High Court order that they should support Tristan financially until he turns eighteen, stands out from the rest of the village of Debong Wetan. It has white ceramic floors and storage areas, unlike most of the houses in the town. The first floor also has a terrace, a living room, a kitchen and a bathroom, as well as a bedroom, which Tristan shares with his mother. On the second floor is another bedroom, and a terrace for hanging out some washing.

Suryani bought the house in July 2007 with the money she received from the Dowse family for Tristan. Everything was arranged by a local notary, and the certificate for the land is under Tristan's name. The overall cost of buying and furnishing their home was around €10,500.

Before they moved to their new home, Tristan, his mother and his two older brothers Wahyu (16) and Agung (13) shared a house with her parents about three kilometres away. Suryani's mother still lives there with her other son and his family. The ability to buy their own home, which is a direct result of Judge John McMenamin's landmark 2006 High Court ruling, has meant a huge improvement in their lives.

Every month, without fail, she receives half the monthly money to which Tristan is entitled – €175 – into her local bank account directly from Ireland. She says this is enough to pay their daily expenses, with the remainder of the €350 a month paid by the Dowses invested by the court on Tristan's behalf. He will also receive a further lump sum of €25,000 from his former adoptive parents when he turns eighteen.

Tristan's school is free, but Suryani still has to pay for schoolbooks and other considerations such as food and clothing. As a single parent whose ex-husband does not contribute financially to the family, she struggles to make ends meet. Suryani spends her days taking care of the kids and making pillowcases and bed sheets with her home sewing machine, earning the equivalent of less than one euro a day for the twenty pieces she manages to make in that time.

Tristan is now in third grade of elementary school, and goes there from 7 a.m. until 11.30 a.m. each day. After school he attends a Koran reading play group until 2.30 p.m. every day, something which he says he enjoys. He says his favourite subject at school is maths.

Suryani brings Tristan to school herself, and picks him up on her red motorbike afterwards. His friends and family now call him Erwin, because his Indonesian name is Erwin Reynaldi. But on official papers, his name is still Tristan Joseph, reflecting what is written on his birth certificate and school reports.

Asked which name he prefers, he answers simply: 'Tristan, because that is my name.'

His mother says he is a healthy and happy child, who gets along very well with his neighbours and friends. His older brother, Agung, is always there to accompany him or watch him from a distance. If he has trouble with his kite he would come directly to Agung. Sometimes they argue and Tristan will cry just like a younger brother does.

But most of the time Tristan makes Agung and his mother laugh with his funny facial expressions. During the conversation, he shows a real interest in what is being discussed, and tries to add what information he can.

'I like it here; my mother is here. And my friends are here and my school and Koran reading play group too,' he says at one point, before heading outside to play in the rain.

Suryani would love Tristan to go to university in the future, maybe in Jakarta. She doesn't care what he studies, although she suggests he may be suitable to a mathematics based discipline such as engineering. Perhaps understandably for an eight-year-old boy, she says Tristan still has no idea about what he wants to become. It is hard for her not to worry about what Tristan will decide to do when he turns eighteen and receives the remainder of the monies due to him as part of the High Court judgement.

Her concern is that his head will be turned by the money, and he will forget about her. 'I am also confused about the status of Erwin [Tristan] now, because they said that Erwin is a foreigner so that's why he is still supported by the Irish government,' she says. 'I am worried that Erwin will be deported when he reaches the age of eighteen.'

But she says she is not angry with the Dowses anymore and is grateful to have her son back in her life. Instead, she reserves much of her anger for a shadowy Indonesian baby smuggler named Rosdiana, who has since been convicted for her crimes.

'I am angry at Rosdiana, the woman who "helped" me pay my hospital bill after giving birth to Erwin. Because she promised me that she and her daughter would take care of Erwin and not sell him to other people. So I would be able to come see him later. If I knew that she was in the kid trade syndicate, then I would never have given Erwin away to her.'

When Tristan first came back to live with his mother he was always afraid of being left behind by Suryani. But he adapted quickly to his new life, and spoke the Javanese language tinged with the local dialect within a few weeks. His mother says he is no longer afraid of strangers. But every time he is naughty, Suryani only has to ask him if he wants to go back to the orphanage and he will stop his bad behaviour right away.

She remains fearful of the risk that he will be kidnapped due to the financial support he receives from the Dowses, which is a significant sum of money by Indonesian standards. It is a situation which was not helped when a local newspaper ran a front page story a few years ago describing him as the 'millionaire kid'.

Thankfully, nothing has happened to him to date and he has had no threats of kidnapping. But the fear is still there, and she always keeps a particular eye on him, explaining why she brings him to and from school herself. If he goes out of the house, she sometimes directly follows him too, just to find out where he is.

Towards the end of our interview with Tristan, we ask if he would ever like to visit Ireland one day.

'No, I don't want to go to Ireland. Because I'm afraid I won't understand it if people are talking to me,' he says matter of factly.

He falls silent when we ask him if he understands what happened with the Dowse family, answering simply: 'I am my mom's kid.'

He shakes his head when asked if he ever wants to meet his one-time parents Joe or Lala Dowse again. Unusually for such an outgoing and friendly young boy, he continues to remain sullen and silent when asked why not ...

JOE DOWSE:

Wicklow-born accountant Joe Dowse was working for the well-known firm KPMG in Baku, Azerbaijan when he first met his wife Lala. The pair married there on 18 June 2000. A few months prior to their wedding, in September 1999, the couple had moved to Indonesia to further Joe's career. While there, he engaged in voluntary work with local orphanages.

Unable to conceive a child of their own, they took steps in 2000 to adopt a child in Indonesia. Having decided to adopt Tristan, they brought him to their family home where he lived from August 2001 until May 2003. But both Joe and Lala claimed the adoption simply did not work out, contending that Tristan did not react or bond with them.

They eventually sought and were granted permission by the Indonesian courts to hand him over to an Indonesian couple, while the couple planned to return to Azerbaijan. But he was in fact placed in the unlicensed Emmanuel Orphanage in Bogor, South Jakarta in May 2003.

In April 2004 Joe Dowse wrote to the Irish Adoption Board seeking to have Tristan's name removed from the register of foreign adoptions. In March 2005 the couple also applied to the Indonesian authorities to formally revoke the adoption order of 2003.

In the only interview Joe Dowse gave at the time, he said the pair 'came to a painful realisation that the adoption wasn't working out, an extremely difficult and painful realisation to make.'

LALA DOWSE:

'(We) are delighted to announce the adoption of Tristan into the Dowse family. Tristan was born on 26 June 2001 and is a healthy

little boy who has now taken up full time residence effective yesterday. We are thrilled and would like to thank everyone who helped
and supported us throughout the whole process.'

So wrote the Azerbaijan-born doctor, Lala Dowse and her husband Joe in an email reportedly sent to his family and friends not
long after they adopted Tristan. Less than two years later, they gave
up the toddler and effectively abandoned him in an orphanage. He
was a few weeks short of his second birthday at the time.

In their application to the Irish High Court, the Dowses claimed
that he became disturbed in the presence of Lala. They said they
had sought the assistance of a psychologist, who advised them that
the long-term adoption of Tristan was not in his best interests.

Coincidentally, Lala had also become pregnant and gave birth to
a baby girl on 29 May 2002. She already had a daughter, Tata. In an
April 2004 letter to the Irish Adoption Board, solicitors instructed
by Lala and Joe Dowse stated that her pregnancy and the subsequent birth had 'interfered' with the adoption and the bonding with
Tristan.

TRISTAN DOWSE:

The boy, given the name Tristan by Joe and Lala Dowse, was
born on 26 June 2001 and adopted by them in August 2001, when
he was two months old. At the time, the married couple were living in Indonesia and had tried unsuccessfully to conceive a child of
their own for some time. After they decided they no longer wanted
him, Tristan was placed into an orphanage in Bogor in May 2003. He
spoke only English, was one of only two children under five there,
and reportedly cried uncontrollably.

Although he settled into the private orphanage and formed
friendships with older children, in May 2005 the Indonesian authorities decided to move Tristan to a larger state-run orphanage for
Muslim children which segregated the children according to age.

But the High Court here was told that by July 2005 'Tristan was
described as being hurt, confused and somewhat bewildered'.

Things began to look up for the boy after an RTÉ documentary
found his birth mother, Suryani, and they were reunited later that

year. Suryani explained that she had been pressurised and deceived into giving up her son by a baby broker named Rosdiana and a nurse at the maternity unit where she gave birth. Investigations by the Indonesian authorities found she was not paid for the adoption.

Eventually, after a lengthy reunion process, Suryani was allowed to take her son home to the port city of Tegal, about 350 km from Jakarta. Tristan is now known as Erwin Reynaldi. Rosdiana was subsequently convicted of her crimes and sentenced to nine years in prison. Her daughter Reta, who took part in the illegal adoption of Tristan and up to eighty other babies, also received an eight-year sentence.

WHAT THE HIGH COURT SAID:

Tristan's case caused major public concern in Ireland and around the world when details of his situation emerged. In July 2005, the Attorney General commenced proceedings on behalf of Tristan, as an Irish citizen. As part of these proceedings, he sought a declaration that the Dowses had failed in their duty of care for and support of Tristan, and sought orders that they should do so.

But Joe and his wife took a counter action that August seeking to have his name removed from the register of foreign adoptions. The hearing of both applications together took place in camera, as they involved a child. However, Judge John McMenamin ruled that much of the judgment should be made public.

In his High Court ruling delivered in January 2006, McMenamin acceded to the Dowse's application. But he made clear that since Tristan had been reunited with his natural mother, compelling the Dowses to take care of him outside Indonesia was not an option.

As a result, he ordered that the boy receive a €20,000 lump sum, a monthly payment of €350 until he is eighteen – half of which will be invested for him by the High Court – and then a further lump sum of €25,000 when he reaches maturity.

Under the ruling, Tristan's mother, Suryani is his guardian while he retains his Irish citizenship and he is a ward of the High Court. He also retains succession rights to any estate of Mr and Mrs Dowse.

✦ ✦ ✦

SHANE COLEMAN

Obituary: Charles J Haughey (1925-2006)

18 June 2006

It was a Saturday night in the Main Hall of the RDS in the mid-1980s. The audience, which had been worked into a frenzy of excitement, was standing, dancing on the chairs. But the subject of its worship was not U2, Bruce Springsteen or one of the other international rock acts that periodically lifted the gloom in the recession-hit Ireland of that era.

Incredible as it may seem in today's politically apathetic climate, the adoration was directed exclusively towards a politician. However, this was no ordinary politician, but one Charles J Haughey ... the dominant and most controversial figure in Irish politics in the second half of the twentieth century.

Haughey was out of government. The disgrace of the GUBU era was still fresh in the memory, as was his Houdini-style survival in a series of incredibly bitter leadership challenges. The slightly aging figure standing at the podium had served two terms as Taoiseach, but without any tangible success to show for it.

Yet the reception Haughey was receiving was akin to a returning Messiah. The strains of 'Rise and Follow Charlie' filled the hall and the swaying masses made clear their unbridled passion for their leader. Jack Lynch before him and Bertie Ahern after him may have enjoyed wider popularity, but neither man ever attracted such devotion from the Fianna Fáil masses.

Haughey revelled in the moment. A chieftain being acknowledged by 'his people'. For that was how he saw himself. He may have been a Republican, but certainly not in the French egalitarian sense. Not for him the traditional de Valera/Fianna Fáil values of austerity and simplicity. He had a taste for French cuisine, fine wine, expensive clothes, and high art, buying a fine house and hunting with hounds.

The contradictions in Haughey's persona, and in his legacy, are too numerous to ignore: the fire-in-the-belly Republican from Donnycarney; the darling of the working classes who lived like a lord of the manor; the brilliant minister who was seized by indecision on becoming Taoiseach; the politician who gave us the infamous Talbot workers deal as well as the incredible success story that is the IFSC; the wrecker of the economy in the early 1980s turned saviour seven years later; the 'teapot diplomat' who had been at the centre of the Arms Trial and subsequently opposed the Anglo-Irish Agreement; the super-confident, at times arrogant, whizz-kid who felt the need to surround himself with the trappings of an aristocrat.

He was an intellectual snob, who despised the bourgeois values of businessmen he regarded as boring, dull and uncultured, but who relied on hand-outs from them to fund his opulent lifestyle. He was the politician who told the country that we were living 'way beyond our means' at a time when he was himself up to his neck in debt. He regarded himself as a man of destiny yet within hours of becoming Taoiseach, he was willing to tolerate a twenty-nine-year-old upstart demanding: 'Tell me the truth. How much do you f**king owe?' He was the most divisive politician since de Valera, a leader who managed to skillfully run a coalition government with his arch nemesis.

Despite, or maybe because of these contradictions, his influence over four decades of the Irish State's existence was enormous. Even now, a decade-and-a-half after his resignation, he casts a long shadow over Irish politics.

In his resignation speech, he quoted Othello ... 'I have done the state some service and they know it, no more of that' ... but to his many critics, Haughey was more an Iago than Othello.

As far back as 1960, Gerry Boland forecast that Haughey would one day 'drag down the party in the mire'. Boland's fears were shared by others. It was an open secret in the party that other senior figures, most notably the hugely respected founding fathers, Frank Aiken and Seán MacEntee, were seriously worried about his growing influence.

Yet such views did nothing to delay a meteoric rise within the

MARK CONDREN

Cork, 2006

THE SUSPECT: Ian Bailey poses for photos in a lane near his home in Schull, Co. Cork. Bailey is the self-confessed main suspect in the murder of French woman Sophie Toscan du Plantier, who was found dead outside her West Cork home in December 1996.

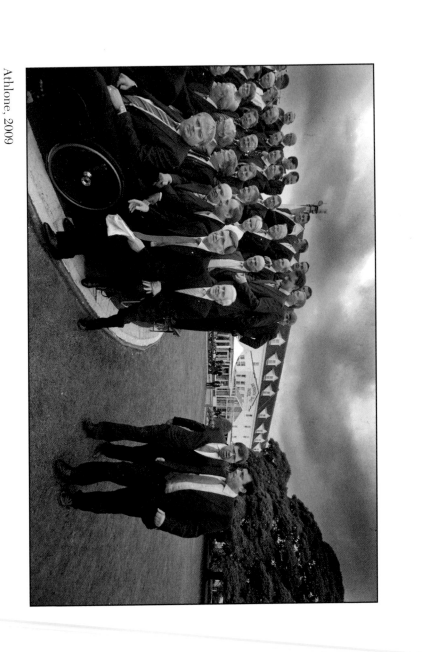

Athlone, 2009

SNAP HAPPY?: The two Brians – Cowen and Lenihan – arrive for the 'family photo' at the Fianna Fáil parliamentary party think-in in September 2009.

Dublin, 2007

ONLY CHOKING: RTÉ presenters Pat Kenny and Ryan Tubridy at the launch of the State broadcaster's autumn schedule.

India, 2008

ASHES TO ASHES: The funeral pyre of Dilip Sharma, a legendary folk singer, in the Guwahati region of India. In keeping with Hindu custom, Sharma's body was laid out face down, with his head facing north. Logs were placed on his head and ankles so his body would stay flat. Four coins were then tossed on the flames to finance a voyage to heaven.

Dublin, 2006

SHELF LIFE: Writer Colm Tóibín in the study of his Dublin home.

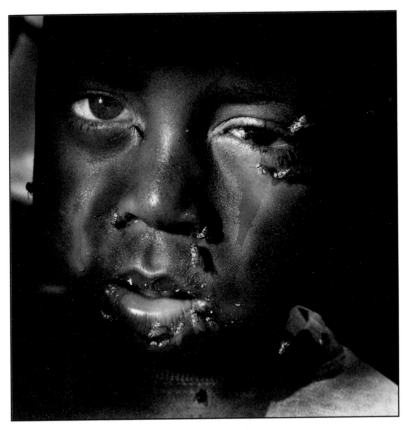

Ethiopia, 2008

HUNGER: A malnourished child attends the GOAL-run Derara
Health Centre in southern Ethiopia.

Cavan, 2004

GRIEF: Jamie Farrelly Maughan's sister, Rebecca, and mother, Josephine Farrelly, at Jamie's funeral in Cavan town in July 2004. The body of the fourteen-year-old had been found in the garden of a vacant house yards from her mother's home, six days after her disappearance. An inquest later ruled that Jamie had died of an ecstasy overdose.

Wicklow, 2009

THE CRUEL SEA: The wrecks of the fishing trawlers *Maggie B* and *Pere Charles* lie in Arklow harbour. The trawlers, which sank in March 2006 and January 2007, claiming the lives of seven fishermen, were originally brought to Arklow in 2007 for a one-month survey. Four years later they remain as a poignant, if controversial, reminder of the tragedies.

Dublin, 2009

DECKED: The scene on Dublin's O'Connell Street moments after a Luas tram collided with a bus. Scores of people were injured, including three seriously, in the accident. The driver of the Luas, who had to be cut from the wreckage, was later charged in connection with the incident.

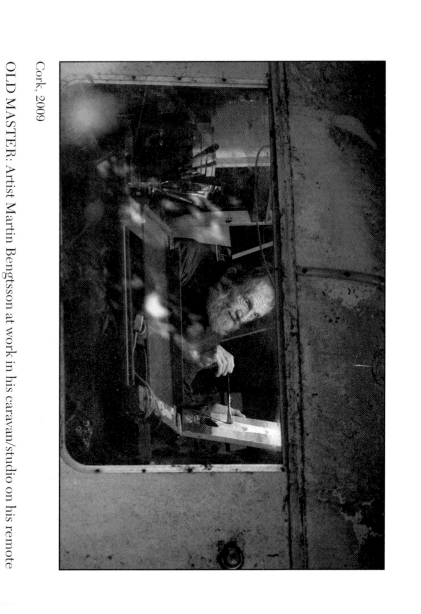

Cork, 2009

OLD MASTER: Artist Martin Bengtsson at work in his caravan/studio on his remote farm in Co. Cork. A former spy, bodyguard, stuntman and self-confessed forger of paintings, Bengtsson was attempting to fund the raising of the *Asgard II*, which sank off the coast of France in 2008, by auctioning his painting of the famous ship.

Rathcoole, 2010

LAID TO REST: The body of Toyosi Shitta-bey, a fifteen-year-old Nigerian boy who was stabbed to death in Tyrrelstown, Dublin, is laid to rest at the Muslim burial ground in Rathcoole Cemetery. Two brothers were charged with Toyosi's murder. Five months after his death, his family were forced to move home following racist death threats.

Dublin, 2010

DOUBLE TROUBLE: Former Taoiseach Bertie Ahern relaxes beneath a portrait of himself at St Luke's, his constituency office, in Drumcondra.

Dublin, 2007

PYRRHIC VICTORY: The family of Rachel Callally celebrate outside the Four Courts after her husband, Joe O'Reilly, was found guilty of her murder.

Haiti, 2010

CRUCIFIXION SCENE: A man prays in front of a crucifix, which was all that remained of a church in Port-au-Prince after the earthquake that devastated Haiti in January 2010.

Carlow, 2009

LIFE AT A GALLOP: Willie Mullins training one of his horses.

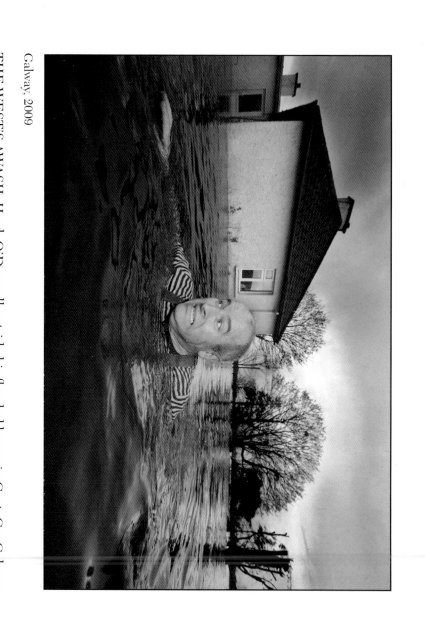

Galway, 2009

THE WEST'S AWASH: Hugh O'Donnell outside his flooded house in Gort, Co. Galway. The previous week his family, including his eighty-seven-year-old mother, had to be airlifted to safety from the rising waters that swamped their home. The flooding in November 2009, which was widespread in the south and west of the country, was the worst on record.

party. He had qualified as an accountant and set up the firm of Haughey Boland in 1951 with his old school friend Harry Boland. But Haughey's real ambitions were clearly political. He was elected to the Dáil in 1957 and was promoted in 1960 by the Taoiseach, his father-in-law, Seán Lemass, to parliamentary secretary. In the same year, he acquired a house in Grangemore in Raheny, on forty-five acres of land.

The following year, Haughey was elevated to the cabinet as justice minister. He quickly made an impression, introducing legislation such as the Succession Act, which protected the inheritance rights of wives, and the Extradition Act. He also drew up a ten-point programme in his first month of office, highlighting the crushing of the IRA as a primary objective. The Special Criminal Court was reactivated and in less than a year the IRA called off its campaign.

Haughey was a young man in a hurry. The powerful secretary of the Department of Justice, Peter Berry, later wrote that 'while he was in Justice, Haughey was a dynamic minister. He was a joy to work with and the longer he stayed, the better he got.'

But the top civil servant also recalled a less attractive side to Haughey's personality. When Berry objected to a blatantly political promotion in the immigration service, Haughey flung the departmental file at him and the papers were strewn across the floor of the minister's office.

While Haughey's next portfolio was less successful – as agriculture minister, he became involved in a series of controversies with the powerful farmers' lobby – his flamboyant lifestyle ensured that his profile continued to soar. Around this time, Conor Cruise O'Brien, later to become an arch political opponent, wrote of him: 'Haughey's general style of living was remote from the traditional Republican and de Valera austerities. He had made a great deal of money and he obviously enjoyed spending it, in a dashing eighteenth century style, of which horses were conspicuous symbols. He was a small man and, when dismounted, he strutted rather. His admirers thought he resembled the Emperor Napoleon, some of whose better known mannerisms he cultivated. He patronised, and that is the right word, the arts. He was an aristocrat in the proper sense of the word: not a nobleman or even a gentleman, but one who believed in the right of the best people to rule, and that he himself was the best of the best people. He was at any rate better, or at least more intelligent and interesting, than most of his colleagues. He was considered a competent minister, and spoke in parliament with bored but conclusive authority. There were enough rumours about him to form a legend of sorts.'

Haughey added to the legend by socialising with cabinet colleagues such as Donagh O'Malley and Brian Lenihan, becoming, in the memorable words of Tim Pat Coogan, 'the epitome of the men in the mohair suits'.

Stories about their drinking exploits in the Fianna Fáil haunt of Groome's Hotel were legion. They also frequented the upmarket Russell Hotel, where Haughey socialised with financiers and builders.

By the mid-1960s, Haughey was a candidate for the leadership of Fianna Fáil. However, amid fears that the party would split between Haughey and Colley factions, Haughey made a tactical decision to withdraw from the 1966 leadership contest and backed Jack Lynch. In return, Lynch made him finance minister. The country was in the middle of an economic boom, allowing Haughey scope for some imaginative reforms. He introduced free travel, subsidised electricity for OAPs and endeared himself to the arty set by abolishing income tax for artistic work.

He also introduced a special provision in the 1969 Finance Act that opponents would claim provided a direct financial benefit to himself. In the general election of that year, Haughey's wealth, long a subject of fascination, became a big issue. The *Evening Herald* revealed that the minister had sold his home at Grangemore to well-known property developer Matt Gallagher for over £200,000 and bought the Abbeville estate, the former summer home for lord lieutenants in Ireland, partly designed by James Gandon, and its 250 acres for £140,000. Haughey's line of defence – one he was to stick to when questions were raised about the origin of his wealth, right up to the setting-up of the tribunals in Dublin Castle – was to object 'to my private affairs being used in this way. It is a private matter between myself and the purchaser.'

But Fine Gael's Gerald Sweetman claimed that Haughey had

benefited from legislation he had introduced himself, amending part of the 1965 Finance Act so that he did not have to pay tax on the profits. Haughey was left in the clear when, after he referred the matter to the Revenue Commissioners, they reported that 'no liability to income tax or surtax would have arisen' even if the act had not been amended.

At around this time, Fianna Fáil was also facing criticism over what were believed to be growing links between politics and business, best epitomised by Taca, the fundraising organisation of 500 businessmen who attended monthly dinners at the Gresham Hotel and, in return for contributions to the party, were given special access to ministers.

Although traditionalists in the party also attended Taca dinners, Haughey, who organised the first dinner, was the politician most associated with it. Kevin Boland later recalled that first dinner attended by all the cabinet.

'We were all organised by Haughey and sent to different tables around the room. The extraordinary thing about my table was that everybody at it was in some way or other connected with the construction industry.' Inevitably, Taca provided plenty of ammunition to opposition TDs who questioned the ethos of the organisation.

There were also persistent rumours about a link between Haughey and property developer John Byrne, who had built O'Connell Bridge House, which was then leased by the government.

The sense of unease about Fianna Fáil's changing values was not confined to the opposition. In 1967, Haughey's rival George Colley urged those attending an Ogra Fianna Fáil conference in Galway not to be dispirited 'if some people in high places appear to have low standards'. Despite Colley's denials, the comment was widely regarded as a reference to Haughey.

But Fianna Fáil and Haughey were soon to be facing into a crisis far more serious than questions about the appropriateness of the links between ministers and the building industry.

For the first forty years of its existence, Fianna Fáil only had to deal in abstract with what Kevin Boland described as 'the fundamental reason for the existence of the political party to which we all belonged' (i.e. the ending of partition).

The outbreak of the Troubles in the North would bring an end to this cosy situation and threaten the very existence of the party.

Haughey had never been seen as a particularly hardline Republican, in the mould of Boland or Neil Blaney. It had not gone unnoted within the party that his Fianna Fáil lineage was non-existent ... his father had been a Free State army officer. However, his father and mother had come from Swatragh in Co. Derry, and the plight of northern Nationalists was a regular dinnertime conversation in the Haughey household when the future Taoiseach was growing up. On VE Day in 1945, a young Haughey, a student in UCD at the time, had burned a Union Jack outside Trinity College.

Yet it was still a shock to many when it emerged that Haughey was one of the hawks in a cabinet divided over what to do about the deteriorating situation in the North during 1969. Haughey was put in charge of a £100,000 fund to relieve distress for the Nationalist population in the North. But the evidence available suggests that Haughey and Blaney were following their own Northern strategy. Haughey summoned army intelligence officers and IRA leaders to meet him, and even invited British ambassador Gilchrist to Abbeville to discuss the future of the North. At that meeting in early October, Haughey told the ambassador there was nothing he would not sacrifice, including the position of the Catholic Church and neutrality, if the British would give a secret commitment to move towards Irish unity. He offered NATO bases on Irish soil as part of the deal.

Matters came to a head in May 1970 with the sensational sacking by Lynch of Haughey and Blaney from the cabinet. The two men were brought before the courts and charged with attempting to import arms. The meteoric rise had come to a shuddering halt.

Acquitted of the charges, Haughey make vague challenging noises in the direction of his party leader but it quickly became apparent that Lynch was in total control of Fianna Fáil.

While Blaney and Boland left Fianna Fáil, Haughey swallowed hard and stayed. He knew he would never be Taoiseach if he left the party, but the medicine was particularly unpalatable.

Not only did he have to suffer the indignity of backing Lynch, but Haughey had to vote confidence in former cabinet colleague

Jim Gibbons, whose testimony at the arms trial had flatly contra-
dicted his own.

As well as eating humble pie, Haughey had to stomach hundreds
of chicken-and-chip meals as he set about his own rehabilitation by
travelling the length and breadth of the country talking to any group
in Fianna Fáil willing to invite him. He was accompanied on these
trips by PJ Mara, who was to become one of his closest political con-
fidants and a legendary government press secretary to Haughey's
governments.

It was hard work, but the slog paid off, building on the huge
reservoir of support for him in the grassroots of the organisation.
Although he had always denied the gun-running charges, the arms
trial only added to the whiff of sulphur around him and appealed to
many in the party who remained steadfastly anti-partition.

By 1975, Lynch bowed to the inevitable and returned Haughey
to the front bench. Two years later, Fianna Fáil was back in government with a twenty-seat majority and, seven years after being
fired from cabinet, Haughey was back as a minister – this time in
Health. In his new job, Haughey added to his populist image by
distributing free toothbrushes to every child in the country. He also
introduced the Family Planning Bill that allowed married people
to buy contraceptives with a prescription, memorably describing it
as 'an Irish solution to an Irish problem'.

However, Haughey never lost sight of the bigger prize. Despite,
or maybe because of, the large Dáil majority, Lynch started to lose his
grip on the party. The party establishment was firmly behind George
Colley to succeed Lynch who, it was widely known, intended to step
down. If Colley had the insiders in his camp, Haughey was relying
on newer, younger and hungry TDs outside the centre of power –
the likes of Ray MacSharry, Albert Reynolds, Padraig Flynn, Seán
Doherty, Charlie McCreevy and Bertie Ahern.

There was a feeling among some sections of the party that Fianna
Fáil under Lynch had drifted from its Republican roots and they
saw Haughey as the man to return them there. In December 1979
Lynch announced his resignation as Taoiseach and Fianna Fáil
leader. Unlike thirteen years earlier, there would be no compromise
candidate. It was a straight fight. Colley against Haughey: The old

guard against the young Turks.

The entire cabinet bar Haughey and Michael O'Kennedy supported Colley, but it wasn't enough. To the horror of the Colley camp, Haughey won the day by forty-four votes to thirty-eight. The party was hugely divided.

It was that knowledge of the bitterness and division in Fianna Fáil that would colour the speech made by opposition leader Garret FitzGerald on the day of Haughey's nomination for Taoiseach. FitzGerald would be sharply criticised for referring to Haughey's 'flawed pedigree' in a speech that was witnessed by Haughey's elderly mother sitting in the visitors' gallery.

But the savaging by FitzGerald wasn't the most pressing issue for Haughey at that time. We now know that his personal finances were deep in the red, and with AIB pressing for Haughey's £1-million-plus debt to be repaid, it required urgent intervention.

While Haughey would later claim that his devoted friend and accountant Des Traynor had handled his financial affairs, it subsequently emerged that Patrick Gallagher was told by Haughey days after his election that he needed £750,000 to clear his debts. With help from wealthy benefactors, Haughey's financial problems eased for a time.

The same could not be said for the public finances. After an impressive start, when Haughey told the nation in a televised broadcast that it was living way beyond its means, the new Taoiseach bottled out of making the tough decisions required. He caved in to vested interests and massively increased exchequer borrowing.

Haughey did achieve some early successes on the North. He refused to accept a purely internal solution, and in his famous bout of 'teapot' diplomacy with Margaret Thatcher, he persuaded the British to discuss the North in the context of the totality of relations between Ireland and Britain.

But he then infuriated Thatcher by overhyping the breakthrough, implying that changes in the constitutional status of the North were on the way. To make matters worse, Haughey stood almost alone in the EEC by taking an anti-British stance over the Falklands War in 1982.

And, while this played well with the FF grassroots, it was a diplomatic disaster and ended any chance of further progress on the North.

In the general election of 1981, Haughey was facing a Fine Gael revitalised under FitzGerald. Despite taking a populist line on taxation, spending and Northern Ireland, Haughey lost power. Fianna Fáil's performance was more than credible, winning 45.5 per cent of the first preference vote, but the loss of two traditional FF seats to H-Block candidates put an end to Haughey's chance of winning the day.

However, by January of 1982, the Fine Gael-Labour government had collapsed and the ensuing general election produced another inconclusive result.

Thanks to the votes of the Workers Party and Tony Gregory – with whom Haughey had personally negotiated the controversial 'Gregory Deal' – Haughey was back as Taoiseach and felt sufficiently emboldened not to offer the position of Tánaiste to Colley.

However, the failure to win an overall majority gave Haughey's many opponents within Fianna Fáil fresh ammunition. While moves to put Des O'Malley forward as an alternative candidate for Taoiseach after the election came to nothing, in October Charlie McCreevy, frustrated at Haughey's performance on the economy, put down a motion of no confidence. McCreevy's unilateral action caught the rest of the anti-Haughey wing wholly unprepared. And, with Haughey insisting on an 'open roll call', only twenty-two parliamentary party members voted against their leader.

1982 is now best remembered as the year of 'GUBU'. When the most-wanted man in the country, Malcolm Macarthur, was apprehended in the home of the Attorney General (who was unaware that Macarthur was a fugitive), Haughey described the strange series of events as 'grotesque, unbelievable, bizarre and unprecedented' to which Conor Cruise O'Brien applied the acronym 'GUBU'.

But it would not be until Haughey's government collapsed that a fuller picture would emerge of what was going on in that government. Ironically, it was Haughey's belated attempt to address the country's economic crisis that precipitated a general election. The Workers' Party and Gregory withdrew their support over 'The Way Forward', a Fianna Fáil document which envisaged major cuts in public spending.

Fine Gael and Labour swept back into government in the following general election, with Fine Gael coming within five seats of Fianna Fáil. But Haughey's problems were only beginning. His leadership would be tested yet again when revelations emerged that the phones of two leading political journalists had been tapped.

Seán Doherty, who was a controversial justice minister during the GUBU government, took the fall for the phone taps, but there was enormous pressure on Haughey and it appeared that finally his enemies in the party would be able to overthrow him. However, the tragic death of Clem Coughlan in a car accident led the crucial party meeting to be postponed. A fierce lobbying campaign by his supporters in the days following saw Haughey once again defy the odds and scrape through.

The leadership contests had taken their toll on everyone. The party organisation reacted almost hysterically to every challenge and there were stories of threats, intimidation and inducements. The pressure on everyone was enormous, with a number of Fianna Fáil TDs suffering physical collapse under the strain. One story from the time speaks volumes of the atmosphere within the party. A couple of days after Martin O'Donoghue was dropped from the cabinet, he received a special delivery at his home. When he and his wife opened the parcel, they found two dead ducks inside along with a short message from Haughey.

'Shot on my estate this morning.' O'Donoghue regarded this as both a bad joke and a menacing gesture.

Longtime ally Albert Reynolds recently recounted that he went to Haughey's office after the heaves to tell him face to face that he couldn't count on his support from then on. But it was also the end of the line for many of his critics in the party, who understandably yearned for a return to normal politics.

By February 1985, with the expulsion of Des O'Malley from the organisation for refusing the vote with the party against the government's Family Planning Bill, Haughey was finally in complete control of Fianna Fáil.

Typically, Haughey took a wholly opportunistic approach to opposition politics, opposing the government's divorce referendum and the historic Anglo-Irish Agreement, while also strongly criticising

the Fine Gael/Labour coalition's (admittedly limited) efforts to res-
cue the economy. With the economy in the grip of the worst reces-
sion since the 1950s, the coalition's popularity plummeted and
Haughey at last seemed destined to win that elusive overall major-
ity at the fourth time of asking. The only cloud on the horizon was
O'Malley's decision to create a new political party, the Progressive
Democrats, where he was joined by high-profile Fianna Fáil figures
Mary Harney, Bobby Molloy and Pearse Wyse.

In the general election, Fianna Fáil attacked the government for
spending cuts, running posters declaring that 'Health cuts hurt the
old, the sick and the handicapped.' Fine Gael had a bad election,
losing nineteen seats, but the PDs' surprise success in getting fourteen TDs elected meant that, once again, Fianna Fáil fell just short
of an overall majority, with Haughey needing the casting vote of the
Ceann Comhairle to be elected Taoiseach in the Dáil.

Yet, despite being three seats short of a majority, it proved to be
Haughey's best period in office. Seven years after talking the talk on
rescuing the country's finances, Haughey finally began to walk the
walk.

With Ray MacSharry as finance minister and Alan Dukes' Fine
Gael lending support in the Dáil for tough economic policies, budget
cuts were introduced in all government departments. The positive
impact on the economy and public confidence was almost immediate. There is little doubt that the basis for the future Celtic Tiger
was laid during the last three years of the 1980s. Haughey's other
major success from that time was his backing of the International
Financial Services Centre (IFSC), which despite the many sceptics,
has proved a massive success.

Haughey ran his cabinets in a brutally efficient manner, in stark
contrast to the all-day agonising of FitzGerald's term of office. He
bluntly told ministers he was not interested in hearing their problems, only their solutions.

Whatever about his relationship with his ministers, Haughey's
tough line on the economy was going down well with the electorate, with opinion polls continually showing Fianna Fáil over fifty
per cent in the opinion polls. In late April 1989 Haughey returned
from a trip in Japan to the news that the government was about to be

defeated in a Dáil vote. Lured by the prospect of an overall majority, he decided to call an election for 15 June. It was a political gamble and it backfired spectacularly. In a campaign dominated by cutbacks in health, Fianna Fáil ended up losing four seats.

When the new Dáil sat, it was the first time in history a nominee for Taoiseach failed to achieve a majority when a vote was taken.

In order to stay in power, Haughey now had to sacrifice one of Fianna Fáil's core values – that it would never go into coalition. To the horror of party diehards, he did just that, agreeing a deal with the PDs, led by Des O'Malley. Haughey's absolute control of the party, which he had enjoyed since surviving the final heave against him six years earlier, started to slip from this point. If the 1989 general election was bad for Haughey, the presidential election of the following year was arguably worse. The Tánaiste, Brian Lenihan, was the Fianna Fáil candidate and he looked a shoo-in early on. However, during the campaign, controversy erupted over calls made to Áras an Uachtaráin in 1982 by Fianna Fáil, on the night that the FG/Labour coalition collapsed, urging president Paddy Hillery not to dissolve the Dáil. Lenihan gave conflicting accounts, denying on television that he had been involved in the phone calls, but saying the opposite in an interview with postgraduate student, Jim Duffy.

With the PDs demanding action, Haughey was forced to sack his old ally from the cabinet, a decision that disgusted many in Fianna Fáil. Mary Robinson, who had been running an impressive campaign anyway, went on to win the election. Even at the time, it seemed clear that Haughey's time was drawing to a close. Ireland was changing dramatically. Haughey's appeal was on the wane and Robinson successfully tapped into a major mood for change.

A series of business scandals, which led to claims of a 'Golden Circle', increased the pressure on Haughey, and there was near open revolt in the party by the autumn of 1991. Haughey won a no-confidence motion put down by Seán Power, and sacked Reynolds and Flynn from his government. It later emerged that a week after this no-confidence vote, supermarket magnate Ben Dunne famously handed Haughey bank drafts worth £210,000, prompting the immortal 'thanks, big fella', line from the Taoiseach.

Haughey's political victory was short-lived. In early 1992, Seán Doherty went on RTÉ TV's *Nighthawks* programme and told the nation that Haughey had known and authorised the phone tapping of the early 1980s.

Haughey denied this, but with the PDs insisting they could not stay in government with him, he signalled his intention to retire. He stood down as Taoiseach on 11 February, when he was succeeded by Albert Reynolds, and retired completely from politics at the general election the following December.

It looked as if Haughey could look forward to a quiet, dignified retirement, enjoying the usual mellowing of public opinion towards departed public figures. However, the dark secret of his personal finances finally came into the public domain. The revelations about his extravagant private life – the £16,000 a year spent on Charvet shirts, the expensive dinners at top restaurants funded by party money and the many millions he had received from various benefactors and businessmen would change the public perception of him forever. The adoration of the masses at ard fheiseanna was replaced by protesters lobbing coins at him during his appearance at the Moriarty Tribunal.

His reputation was further damaged by his initial attempts at the McCracken tribunal to bluster through, suggesting that Des Traynor had handled his finances – that he had been too busy running the affairs of the nation to worry about such things.

While charges of obstructing the work of that tribunal were suspended indefinitely on the grounds that he could not get a fair trial, in the court of public opinion Haughey was tried and found guilty.

Some of Haughey's advocates have suggested that history may well judge him more kindly. Certainly it would be unfair to overlook his many achievements, not least his belated role in laying the foundations for the current prosperity.

Undoubtedly he was a politician of enormous intelligence, imagination and vision. Imagine what he might have done, for example, with the billions of euro in surpluses created by the exchequer in recent years. But it's also impossible not to dwell on the lost opportunity. Garret FitzGerald said Haughey had the potential to become one of the best taoisigh the country ever had. However, his preoccupation with wealth and power clouded his judgement.

What is undeniable is that in the five general elections he contested as Fianna Fáil leader, Haughey won between 44 per cent and 48 per cent of the popular vote – a figure his successors have never come close to.

His flaws and strengths said more about Ireland in the second half of the 20th century than we might wish to acknowledge. There is an old Irish saying on a person's passing: 'Ní bheidh a leithéad arís ann'.

Never does it seem more true than in the case of Charles James Haughey.

✦ ✦ ✦

1988: the year the Celtic Tiger earned its stripes

8 June 2008

It was the worst of times. Anyone under the age of thirty-five would struggle to appreciate just how bad things were in Ireland in 1988. Economically the country was a basket case. The national debt was so enormous and crippling that most of the money raised in taxes simply went on interest payments. Unemployment was at 18.5 per cent. Each year, 30,000 of the nation's young people were opting to or being forced to move abroad. One government minister said at the time that 'we can't all live on a small island'.

It was like the miserable 1950s, but worse, because of what was happening in the North. So many horrendous things happened during the three decades of the Troubles that it's impossible to pick out a low point. But March 1988 certainly seemed like a nadir at the time. The series of connected incidents – the shooting of three IRA volunteers in Gibraltar, the attacks on their funerals by Michael Stone and the subsequent killings of two British army corporals – that occurred during one two-week period, led many people to believe that the North was on the brink of meltdown.

For the vast majority of people back then, it seemed the violence would go on for ever.

Few of us wanted to admit it at the time, but we were living in a failed state. It was probably just as well for national morale that we didn't know then about the corruption that was going on at senior levels of government. All in all, the country needed a lift and, oh boy, was it about to get one.

Amidst all the gloom, 12 June 1988 shines through like a beacon. It was our JFK moment, but in reverse. It was the day we started to believe, even if we couldn't fully take in what the giant scoreboard in the Neckar Stadion in Stuttgart was telling us: 'England 0: Rep. Ireland 1'.

Lady luck for possibly the first time ever had favoured an Irish football team. As writer Dermot Bolger puts it, 'In the old days when you followed Ireland, you may not have found Jesus in Dalymount Park, but you certainly heard a lot about him.' But, finally after the heartbreak of disallowed goals and dodgy refereeing decisions in places such as Paris, Sofia and (most notoriously) Brussels, fortune had finally favoured us.

The team had qualified for its first ever major tournament finals courtesy of a late goal by Gary Mackay, who was playing for an already eliminated Scottish team against a Bulgarian side that had only needed to draw at home to qualify. And the gods continued to shine on Jack Charlton's team during that epic encounter with England. After Ray Houghton headed Ireland into the lead in the sixth minute, the old enemy had enough gilt-edged chances to win the game comfortably. But, somehow, they failed to convert any.

The tension throughout the game was unbearable. Historian and broadcaster Diarmaid Ferriter was just sixteen at the time and recalls watching the match in a friend's house with a big group of pals. 'We were just waiting for the ref to blow the whistle [to end the game]. We didn't care about the style of the Irish team, we just wanted him to blow the whistle.'

'I was just finished fifth year. It was the start of the summer holidays. It was really hot weather. Ireland had just beaten England. It can't really get much better,' he says.

What sticks in the memory of author and commentator David McWilliams is the tricolours on the cars in Dublin immediately after the game. Back then the tricolour was a rare sight, other than on state buildings. 'I never saw them [on cars] before. We were thinking,

"Where did you get them?"'

After watching the game with an 'unfeasible amount of cans' in a friend's house in Monkstown, McWilliams and his friends – who had just finished their final exams in college – went on a 'massive pub crawl from Monkstown to Dun Laoghaire'. He remembers sitting outside Goggins pub in Monkstown a few hours after the game. 'We were all pinching ourselves and singing the name of Kenny Sansom [the England full-back whose mis-kick had led to the Houghton goal] over and over again.'

Dermot Bolger, a diehard fan of the Irish team, had a ticket for all the group games in Euro '88, but couldn't travel for the English match because his publishing company had a book launch that day.

He watched the match in a house in Phibsborough's Connaught Street, across the road from the spiritual home of Irish football, Dalymount Park. It was there, thirty-one years earlier, that England had broken Irish hearts with a last minute equaliser by John Atyeo in a World Cup qualifier.

Bolger remembers, after the game ended, meeting an elderly man who he knew well as a great talker and raconteur. But on that day, the man uttered only four words to him: 'I can die happy.'

It was said after Atyeo's late goal in Dalyer in 1957 that you could hear the silence as far away as O'Connell Street. But on 12 June 1988, the silence in the city centre was broken by a cacophony of car horns that greeted Ireland's victory. The then Lord Mayor of Dublin, Carmencita Hederman, was walking back to the Mansion House from an official engagement and she knew Ireland had won when she heard the beeping.

The euphoria of the homecoming stunned the entire squad as hundreds of thousands turned out to greet their heroes on their procession through the city centre.

Hederman broke off her holidays in Connemara to be there to host the civil reception and regards it as one of the highlights of her spell as Lord Mayor. 'It gave everyone a great lift and a great boost.' She recalls in particular the 'wonderful rapport Jack Charlton had with his team. They were one big happy family.' Delirious, even. Ray Houghton delighted the crowd in Parnell Square by chanting, to the tune of the 'Camptown Races', 'Who put the ball in the England net?

I did, I did.' It was heady stuff.

So much so that in retrospect it is tempting to trace many of the wonderful things that have happened since in this country back to that epic encounter in Stuttgart. Was the Celtic Tiger, as some have contended, conceived in those magical couple of weeks of Euro '88? Was it the beginning, as others have claimed, of a new post-Nationalist era?

Ferriter is sceptical about such theories. But he acknowledges that anything that gave people something to unite around was a good thing. 'The 1980s was a very divisive decade. There were so many elections and referenda. So yes, it certainly made an impact in that it gave people something they could unite around,' he says, adding that the country at that point was on the cusp of change.

It is a point taken up by Eamon Dunphy. He doesn't think the victory over England was a catalyst for change, rather another sign that Ireland, and Irish people, could cut it on the international stage. 'It coincided with a time when we were becoming much more confident vis-à-vis England. And this was reflected through our EU membership principally but also by the success of U2 and *My Left Foot* at the Oscars,' Dunphy says.

'It was a bleak time on the surface economically. People were emigrating. But there were green shoots of cultural significance. U2, *My Left Foot*, that match against England were part of a pattern of emerging confidence and competence. Irish soccer was no longer a shambles ... It [the match against England] was a brick in the wall, not a catalyst – one of the signs that we could do things.'

For Bill O'Herlihy, a new generation of Irish people 'walked taller' and realised they were 'as good as anybody.'

'It was an exciting time,' the popular broadcaster says. 'Between that and Italia '90, football identified us as a confident nation for the first time in a long time.'

Bolger and McWilliams both focus on the impact the game had on the definition of Irishness. 'In many ways, our view of the world was that of little Irelanders,' says McWilliams. 'But when Ray Houghton put the ball in the back of the English net, did you care that he was Scottish? That team opened up the meaning of Irishness. If Andy Townsend could captain Ireland, [in Italia '90], we're not just little Irelanders.'

Bolger also believes it resulted in a broader definition of Irishness. It struck him that the fans following the Irish team in Germany had arrived from across Britain and mainland Europe. And, of the first eleven players that day against England – six grew up in Britain.

'It was a great gathering of the Irish diaspora,' Bolger says. Coming from a large family where most of his uncles and aunts emigrated, he realised 'this team represented my extended family. The Aldridges and the Houghtons were playing for my uncles and aunties; people who had been written out of Irish history ... The sense of narrow Irish nationalism took a dive.'

Bolger wrote a play based on those Irish supporters who were returning to life as emigrants after Ireland's exit to the Dutch (*In High Germany* is to return in the Bewley's Café Theatre on Grafton Street later this summer). 'A lot of those fans were going back to factories in Eindhoven or Hamburg to resume life. When you have emigrated, you don't quite belong in the country [you left] but they belonged on the terraces,' he says.

Ireland has changed so much in the intervening years. The Troubles are no more. The people in the factories of Eindhoven and Hamburg have returned home and been joined by hundreds of thousands of immigrants from Eastern Europe, Africa and Asia. We are one of the richest nations in the world.

Football has also changed. The Irish team has had its downs, as well as ups, since Euro '88. But the days when qualification was a distant dream are certainly no more. The euphoria of Euro '88 was surpassed two years later in Italy when the whole country literally came to a standstill. Soccer was by then a national game, no longer restricted to its traditional heartlands. It became fashionable, which it certainly wasn't when Ireland played its final qualifier for Euro '88 in a half empty Lansdowne Road.

Success, in the words of Bolger, 'brought in a weird section of people who used the word "footie", which sends a shiver down my spine.' Those of us who wept at the continuous near misses in the 1970s and 1980s had to come to terms with the fact that we were no longer part of an elite group after 12 June 1988. It was the day everything changed.

Martin Frawley

Fast food and TV breaks: how the war over pay is being waged

There's a lot more to national wage talks than meets the eye.

14 September 2008

Takeaway food is a highly potent weapon in the armoury of national pay negotiators, which has been deployed in the past to undermine the morale of the opposing camp.With negotiations dragging on into the small hours of the morning – as has been happening all week at Government Buildings – tiring the other side into submission is frequently the best and often the only option open.

Late into the night, just when you think the other side is going to cave in, there is nothing more dispiriting than to see another tray of takeaways being carried down the corridor. It is a sign of intent that they are determined to hold out, said one veteran national pay negotiator.

Major sporting events can also have a huge bearing, with talks being mysteriously adjourned and resumed ninety minutes later. In 1994, when Ireland's exploits at the World Cup clashed with national pay talks, extra TVs were brought into Government Buildings.

In late July, it was the August bank holiday and the approaching holidays that served to concentrate the minds of the negotiators. By midnight on Friday 1 August, Taoiseach Brian Cowen was strolling around Government Buildings with Tánaiste Mary Coughlan.

The third, absent member of the triumvirate of national pay nego-tiators, Finance Minister Brian Lenihan, had a dental appointment.

In separate rooms inside Government Buildings, union and employers may well have been dreaming of dental appointments to get them out of pay negotiations that had been dragging on for months and were hours away from a well-choreographed 'breakdown'. Some of the union leaders were hearing about the employers' offer from news bulletins even though the employers' representatives were down the hall.

One myth about pay talks is that the employers and the unions actually face each other across the table. They don't. Instead they are camped in separate rooms with Dermot McCarthy, the secretary general of the Department of the Taoiseach, shuttling between rooms and positions in an attempt to cut a deal. Of course, an 'accidental' meeting in the toilets or a back corridor can result in a sudden breakthrough.

With the bank holiday deadline approaching, tempers began to fray among the unions, with some arguing that they should take the 5 per cent over twenty-one months on offer in order to preserve partnership and their continued influence at national level. Others argued that they would be massacred by their members if they brought back that offer. It was becoming a matter of self preservation.

By 3 a.m. on Saturday, McCarthy, a highly experienced facilitator, rang Cowen, who was still in the building, to say a deal was not on. Cowen made a courtesy call to each party, thanked them for their efforts, told them to go away and 'reflect' and come back refreshed in September. And they did.

There was never any question of Cowen intervening with a compromise proposal. For a Taoiseach to successfully intervene and save the country from financial ruin, a deal has to have already been agreed or as good as agreed. This is how 'dramatic eleventh hour interventions work' at national pay talks. They are meticulously rehearsed.

Cowen's predecessor, Bertie Ahern, was a master at knowing precisely when and how to intervene. A couple of national agreements ago, with the employers and unions seemingly deadlocked on pay, Ahern let it be known that he expected a deal to be done before he left for a state visit to Mexico. On his way to the airport, Ahern dropped into the talks and left a piece of paper on the table with a single figure – the proposed pay increase – written on it and proceeded on his way.

The next day, with the Taoiseach photographed pressing the flesh in Mexico, a deal was done and we all slept soundly in our beds.

Of course, the deal was cut many days before Ahern's intervention but the subterfuge suited everybody. While it boosted Ahern's image as 'Mr Consensus', it also acted as a face-saver for the unions and the employers. If the deal they brought back did not go down well with the members, they could say that the deal was forced upon them by the Taoiseach and that they felt morally obliged to comply 'in the national interest'.

The reality in these long and tedious pay negotiations is that while buckets of midnight oil are burnt, in most cases a deal or at the very least the outlines of a deal, have been agreed before the talks open.

So much of the sabre-rattling outside Government Buildings is for the optics, as union and employer leaders demonstrate the sterling work they are doing on their members' behalf. 'I don't like going into any pay negotiations not knowing what I am going to get,' said one senior trade union leader.

Ahern was the master of being all things to everyone. He never took decisions until he absolutely had to. The effect of that was that he didn't antagonise people unless he absolutely had to.

'Ahern never gets upset, never fights with you,' said one senior union leader, who has been at Government Buildings all week.

'He might mean to say 'no' but he would never say it like that. Then again he might say 'yes' and you wouldn't know it was 'yes'. And it worked,' recalled Peter McLoone, general secretary of the public service union, Impact, in the book *Saving the Future* on national agreements.

Visiting politicians, union and employer leaders who come over here to look at Ireland's partnership system are amazed at how it seems to be built and maintained on personal relationships between the so-called warring parties.

'All the key players know each other very well and know what each needs. While that would be frowned upon in other countries, here the familiarity and friendship has kept partnership alive,' said one senior negotiator.

Former ICTU president Phil Flynn – a key player in the partnership process – recalls how Ahern resolved a bitter industrial dispute involving a vehement anti-Fianna Fáil trade union leader, over a pint in Kennedy's pub in Drumcondra.

Cowen's approach is more distant, although all employer and union leaders agree that he has been no less determined to cut a deal. It's just that he wouldn't lose as much sleep as Ahern if it collapsed.

The current talks are the longest on record, having formally started in the third week in April, although they have been interrupted by a change of Taoiseach, the Lisbon fiasco and the rapidly declining economic situation.

Even if a deal is reached this week, the parties could be back again in early spring to negotiate the next agreement. When it was put to one of the business leaders that in such a scenario they may as well hang on in Government buildings, he replied, 'I think I'd rather kill myself.'

ALI BRACKEN

I have to tell people about the type of person my son really was

'People are judging Shane Clancy on the last hour of his life,'
his father Patrick says. 'But that's not the Shane I know and love.'

4 October 2009

On Sunday morning seven weeks ago, Patrick Clancy got a knock at his front door that changed the course of his life. He was greeted by two gardaí standing on his front doorstep. Invited inside, it soon became clear they had come to deliver bad news. His son Shane's car had been discovered early that morning outside a house in Bray where a young man had been fatally stabbed and two others had been injured. The gardaí believed his son was responsible. 'It was as if their words fell to the floor. I said, 'If you're looking for him, you're wasting your time.' I knew immediately that my son would not be able to inflict that on other people and still be alive; I knew he could not live with himself.'

His paternal intuition was right. The twenty-two-year-old Trinity student was lying dead in the back garden of Sebastian Creane's family home in Cuala Grove, Bray. Gardaí had yet to discover his body, but Shane had turned the knife on himself after fatally stabbing Sebastian and injuring his ex-girlfriend Jennifer Hannigan and Sebastian's older brother Dylan in a knife attack.

'It's not the Shane I know and love. He wouldn't hurt a fly. He was a pacifist. I know in my heart and soul it was Shane's hand that took a life – but it wasn't his mind. I do not know how he got to that point. He spent twenty-two years on this planet as a wonderful, loving person. But people are now judging him on the last hour of his life.'

The gardaí asked Patrick to try and phone his son that morning but it went straight to voicemail. 'I don't blame the gardaí for not finding his body immediately. I'd like to thank the two gardaí who called to my house that day for how they handled it, and all the gardaí involved in the investigation. In the next few days, it was hard to take in the circumstances of what happened. It goes against everything my son stood for.'

Shane's personality was light years away from what happened on that fateful night in Bray. In the seven weeks since his death, Shane's father has been trying to reconcile in his mind how the well-adjusted young man he helped raise could be capable of such mindless violence. Patrick is acutely aware of the sense of loss and pain the Creane family are experiencing as a result of his son's actions. 'The last thing I want to do is upset the Creane family. Loss is loss. There are no words. I can't give them back their son; I wish I could. But I owe my son this much. I have to tell people about the type of person my son really was.'

Shane had no history of mental illness and lived life to the full. He was entering in his final year at Trinity College, studying Irish and Biblical and Theological Studies. He lived in an apartment in Dalkey and had cousins and an uncle living nearby. He regularly saw his father, who lives in neighbouring Dún Laoghaire, and his mother Leonie, who lives in Redcross, Co. Wicklow, with her second husband Tony and their three children.

Shane was a young man with a busy life. He didn't smoke or drink and had a large circle of friends and interests; he was passionate about the Irish language, keeping fit and travelling. 'To describe what he did as out of character is an understatement. He was a happy, independent young man. To know him was to love him,' adds his father. Patrick remembers his son as someone who was always reaching out to help others. When he was ten or eleven, his father brought Shane and his two younger brothers Liam (now twenty) and Jake (now eight) to a pound shop.

'I gave each of them a pound and the three of them ran in to spend it. When the two younger boys were paying for what they bought I asked Shane what he was buying. He pointed to a homeless man outside. He'd given him the money instead of spending it on himself. That was Shane.'

On his twenty-first birthday, held in the Club pub in Dalkey, where he worked, Shane left a collection box for St Vincent de Paul for his guests to make a contribution rather than bring a gift. Last Christmas and the Christmas before, Shane phoned his father to say he'd be late up to visit him. 'He was feeding the homeless in Stradbrook. The kind things he'd do wasn't something he'd tell people about. He'd be embarrassed if he could hear me talking about him now. He was a gentleman.'

What kind of a big brother was he? 'He was the best,' says Liam, with a simple shrug of his shoulders. 'Always there for everyone.'

Patrick knew his son was feeling low over the break-up of his relationship with Jennifer Hannigan. Shane had ended the three-year romance but never got over it. By the time he'd decided he wanted to reconcile with Jennifer, she had moved on and had begun dating Sebastian Creane. The pair were both students at the Dún Laoghaire Institute of Art, Design and Technology. Shane was due to travel to Calcutta during the summer to do aid work but pulled out. 'He told me he didn't feel up to it. He went to Thailand and Australia instead – one of his cousin's lives in Thailand so he visited him. The last time I saw him was a few days before he went. I asked him if Jen was going with him and he told me they broke up. "Do you mind if I don't talk about it?" he said. I said, "Of course." He went to try and clear his head, to sort himself out. He was twenty-two and broken-hearted. When you're that age, you think it's the end of world. Himself and Jen were a lovely couple; she's a lovely girl. They were very happy whenever I saw them together. He was besotted with her and she was besotted with him,' he recalls. 'I think she knows what happened that night wasn't really him.'

Patrick was worried enough about his son to ring his nephew in Thailand to enquire about how he was getting on. 'He said Shane was still a bit down but seemed better than when he first arrived. He was reading Barack Obama's autobiography. Obama was a hero of his, so was Ché Guevara. And Superman; he loved Superman.'

But when Shane returned from his trip, he was still suffering. His father didn't get a chance to see his son when he returned from his travels. During college term, Shane would call up to his dad's for dinner every Monday and Wednesday but during summertime, he'd see him less frequently But Shane did see his mother Leonie and confided in her about how he couldn't seem to get over his depression. Then he went to the doctor with his mother. The GP prescribed Citrol, a brand of the antidepressant citalopram.

Shane was taking it for about a week when he took the remaining three weeks' supply in one day, possibly an attempt at suicide. He told his mother what had happened. Two days later, she took her son to another GP. It was explained to the second doctor that Shane had taken a high dosage of Citrol two days previously. The GP prescribed Cipramil, another brand of citalopram.

As this GP was aware Shane had misused antidepressants two days previously, it was instructed on the three-week prescription that the chemist should only supply Shane with one week of the drug at a time, according to his father. But when Shane went to fill the second prescription, the chemist asked him if he wanted to get the three-week prescription filled at once, and Shane said yes. It was Friday 14 August. His family believe Shane took another high dosage of antidepressants the next day. In the early hours of 16 August, Shane Clancy carried out his attack.

'Shane was the type of person who was always careful about taking pills. If he had a Lemsip, he'd phone me to ask if he could take paracetamol as well a few hours later. I don't know if he was attempting suicide when he took three weeks' worth of antidepressants in one day. I might never know,' says his father.

'I don't want to be seen as pointing the finger at the doctors or the chemist, but surely if it said to only give him one week's supply at a time, the chemist should have followed that instruction.'

Patrick believes no one should be put on antidepressants unless they're already undergoing counselling and that St John's Wort, the herbal treatment for depression, should still be available without prescription. 'I think some people do need antidepressants. But the number of young people who are taking them is frightening and they seem to be very easy to get, as you know.'

In the aftermath of the tragedy in Bray, the *Sunday Tribune* visited five GPs and reported feeling depressed. Four of the five prescribed antidepressant medication. The purpose of this investigation was to establish how easy it would be to obtain a prescription for antidepressants under false pretences and highlight that people looking for help have a wait of several weeks or months for counselling in the public service.

'I think every parent should ask their GP where they stand on antidepressants and in what circumstances they would prescribe them to their children. We all need to look at the relationship between doctors and pharmaceutical companies. Shane put a high dosage of chemicals into his body and I've no doubt he reacted to that. Some people take antidepressants and they don't agree with them. The consequences of that can be horrific.'

A joint inquest into the death of Shane Clancy and Sebastian Creane in the coming months could provide some answers for the two grieving families. It is possible that the two GPs who prescribed antidepressants, as well as the chemist, may be called to give evidence as to his state of mind.

'It's easy to dramatise what happened. But we have to look at the bigger picture and ask why,' says Patrick. 'I hope that out of Shane and Sebastian's death something constructive can happen. We all never think things like this can happen to us. I did too until I got that knock on my door.'

✦ ✦ ✦

Did the media create a monster?

Overnight, rapist Larry Murphy became the most feared man in Ireland, and Larry-watching became a national sport. Did media coverage of his release from jail reflect the public mood, or create it?

15 August 2010

The angry mob outside the hostel in Coolock were united in misplaced anger and fear. 'Get him out,' they chanted. But Larry Murphy wasn't there, nor had he ever been. Gardaí were called to control and calm the crowd of about sixty people. Eventually, the mob was placated and the possibility of violence was narrowly averted. Overnight, Larry Murphy had become the most feared man in Ireland. The scene outside Priorswood House in Coolock, a halfway house for ex-prisoners, was a truly extraordinary ending to a truly astonishing day.

Larry Murphy mania began early on Thursday morning. Reporters and photographers began to assemble at 5 a.m. in the hopes of catching a glimpse of Ireland's most infamous rapist. Journalists had been hanging around outside the prison on and off all week because of the slim chance that Murphy could slip out early. Despite the early hour, the press corps were in high spirits. No-one had even glimpsed the forty-five-year-old carpenter in the ten-and-a-half years since he was convicted of the horrific rape and attempted murder of a Carlow businesswoman.

The release of Larry Murphy from prison was always going to be a big story, the main reason being that he is the suspect in the disappearance of three other women in Leinster. Also, the brutality of his crime suggested to gardaí that it wasn't the first time he had carried out an attack of this nature. As Ireland's only suspected serial killer, the Baltinglass native is a legitimate object of fascination to the media and the general public.

The fact that he steadfastly refused to have any rehabilitative therapy for sex offenders while in jail is of major concern. It suggests this man has no remorse and does not want to address whatever psychological problems drove him to carry out such a violent crime. People are afraid he might do it again.

But fear over Larry Murphy's release took on a life of its own last week and it is still not clear how this story will end. Many gardaí privately believe Murphy will be driven to suicide by the relentlessness of the media coverage.

Adding to the excitement among journalists outside Arbour Hill on Thursday was the fact that no-one knew how he would exit the prison. Would the prison service smuggle him out in a van? Would the gardaí whisk him away in an unmarked car? Journalists began making bets about what time he would emerge.

At about 9.30 a.m., news trickled out that Murphy would make his first public appearance in a decade at around 10.15 a.m. A taxi had been booked to pick him up. He was not going to be hidden by the prison service, gardaí or anyone else. He would walk out the door of Arbour Hill prison and face the music outside. Many ex-cons are greeted warmly by family and friends. Murphy had a large group of media instead. The gardaí had sensibly erected a barrier to keep the press back.

As the door opened, the heave to get a glimpse of him was immediate. Larry Murphy was everything we expected and more. Wearing an Adidas cap and black sunglasses, he strode out confidently. What seemed to be the beginning of a smirk was visible at the corners of his mouth. But didn't he have plenty to smile about? He was a free man. Murphy strode purposefully towards the waiting taxi. He looked fit and healthy in a black hoodie with gold NY lettering, runners and jeans.

'Do you think he's going to New York and he's sending us a message?' one hack speculated moments later. 'No, sex offenders aren't allowed into America,' another replied.

Murphy had put on some weight, but his physique appeared well-toned from exercise. Out of boredom, many inmates work out regularly. Since Murphy didn't feel it necessary to try rehabilitation, he spent his days working in the carpentry workshop and exercising.

He had been told there was a crowd waiting for him. He had had ten years to look forward to his freedom and must have imagined every day what the moment would feel like when he walked out the prison gates. If he was perturbed by the scrum, he didn't show it. But he didn't hang around either. He ignored the questions shouted by the media and jumped into the waiting taxi.

A handful of angry spectators were also present. They shouted 'rapist', 'beast' and 'you f**king bastard' as he was spirited away. One woman said she'd come because she just wanted to see what Murphy looked like ten years on.

The media were relatively happy. Everyone got their photograph. A few words from the now mythical man would have been great, of course. But journalists knew this was unlikely. Larry Murphy has never explained to anyone, not his family or gardaí, why he did what he did to that young woman that winter's night in February 2000. Never has so much been written about a man whom journalists know so very little about. Aside from his well-documented crime, we know nothing about what makes Larry Murphy tick. This makes him all the more fascinating.

The taxi quickly drove away from the prison. Imagine the

conversation between the driver and the Wicklow native. That driver had a story to tell that every journalist in the country was dying to hear. He broke his silence in the *Star* yesterday but did not go into detail about the journey.

Murphy surely expected to be followed and the media did not disappoint. Three photojournalists on high-powered motorbikes were in immediate pursuit as the taxi made off towards Phoenix Park. Gardaí in unmarked cars and motorbikes also followed, as did many more photographers and reporters in cars. Adding to the drama was the garda helicopter circling overhead. Murphy might be free, but he would not be allowed to enjoy his freedom. The chase was on.

Murphy's next move, though, surprised everyone. He did not seem to be a man with a plan – strange, considering he had had nothing but time to prepare his release. After driving around aimlessly for a while, he asked the driver to take him to Coolock garda station. He wasn't happy.

Inside the station, he complained that journalists and photographers were following him. His complaint was noted but as it was a civil matter there was nothing gardaí could do. Murphy wasn't in any rush to leave the garda station, possibly discussing with officers what his next move would be or getting security advice.

'Who is Larry Murphy's only friend?' asked a senior garda source. 'The gardaí, that's who.'

He eventually emerged and got back into the taxi. The chase was on again. Many people expected him to go straight to Dublin airport and get the first plane out. Journalists armed with their passports were on standby at the airport ready to fly out to wherever he went, fingers crossed that he'd choose somewhere exotic and sunny. But it wasn't to be.

'He has a driver's licence and a passport. If I was Larry Murphy the first thing I would have done is get out of town. But he didn't,' added the garda source. 'If he does intend to leave the country, he has to give us an exact address. He can't just tell us he's going to Spain. So it's possible that's delaying him. He would have to make arrangements to book in somewhere or we won't let him go. We then pass on that address to the authorities in whatever European country he could head to. Don't think he wouldn't be closely watched abroad. If a sex offender of his calibre from Spain came to Ireland, best believe he would be watched closely. The only difference would be the media attention would be far less, which is why leaving might be an attractive idea for Murphy.'

Despite Murphy's protest to the gardaí, the photographers on motorbikes were not to be deterred. The excitement was palpable. The radio bulletins kept everyone informed. Larry-watching had suddenly become a sport. Where would he go next?

'Come on, why don't you just tell us where he's going?,' one photographer asked a garda. 'Where's the fun in that?,' came the quick-fire response.

The taxi began to make its way into the city centre, still hotly pursued. Then somehow, inexplicably, Murphy did the unimaginable: he managed to get away – not from the gardaí, but from his much more bothersome pursuers, the press. He alighted from the taxi at about 1 p.m. near Grafton Street and headed towards St Stephen's Green. At the time of writing, the gardaí knew exactly where Larry Murphy was staying. It would take more than twenty-four hours for the media to catch up with him again.

This was the most high-profile release of a prisoner since Wayne O'Donoghue got out after three years for killing Cork schoolboy Robert Holohan. In many ways, interest in Murphy could last a lot longer than interest in O'Donoghue. The main reason for this is that Larry Murphy, unlike Wayne O'Donoghue, is at high risk of reoffending.

The media frenzy over Larry Murphy is unprecedented. The only other prisoner who might receive such attention if he were let out is Malcolm MacArthur. The infamous GUBU murderer has been in jail for twenty years and there is no sign of him being released.

The media had prepared well in advance for Larry Murphy's reintroduction to society. In the months before his release, stories about the rapist began to appear. The *Sunday Tribune*, along with every other national newspaper, has written extensively about him. The story has also been well covered on TV and radio.

Some media outlets are more obsessed with Larry Murphy than others, with entire teams of reporters working solely on the story. Before his release, every possible angle was covered. And since he got out of Arbour Hill, Murphy has become a national obsession. But is the coverage documenting the public mood or creating it?

O'Leary Analytics, which monitors and analyses online media in Ireland, has researched the press handling of the Larry Murphy story.

'Some coverage has been criticised as hysterical, sensational and promoting panic. Journalists and editors have claimed that they are merely responding to and reflecting the interest and attitude of the public to Murphy's release, but our research proves this to be untrue,' media analyst Stephen O'Leary told the *Sunday Tribune*.

'By comparing the references to Larry Murphy in the news media with those in social media, including Twitter, Facebook, YouTube and blogs, it is clear the traditional media is driving the public interest in the case rather than reacting to it. Before the press reporting of Murphy's imminent release on Wednesday, there had been fewer than twenty references to him in social media during August. In the twenty-four hours after the story hit the headlines, Larry Murphy was mentioned in social media more than 250 times. This demonstrates that there was a massive increase in the public's interest in the case after the media began to report it, rather than the press having responded to massive public concern,' he said.

It was undoubtedly the story of the week, rendering the Ivor Callely expenses scandal virtually unimportant in comparison.

'Certain elements of the media have protested that they simply reflected the public's interest in the frenzy surrounding Larry Murphy's release. But our research shows the media created that interest, fed it and exploited it,' added O'Leary. 'Before the press began stoking it up, there was almost no awareness that Larry Murphy was going to be released. There was, therefore, no fear, no panic, no interest among the public at large. Editors cannot argue that some of the more excessive coverage simply reflects the attitude of readers, listeners or viewers. The truth is journalists have created the interest which they now claim to have an obligation to serve.'

It seemed as if some newspapers were covering nothing but the Larry Murphy story last week. Criticism of some of the coverage began in earnest on Friday.

The *Daily Star* covered the story extensively. Thursday's front page headline read: 'DANGER. Rape beast Murphy due out today – and every woman should memorise this evil face.' On Friday, the *Star* printed a poster for its readers of Larry Murphy, presumably so people could cut it out and hang it up on their wall, something usually reserved for celebrity idols. *Star* editor Ger Colleran has been happy to justify his paper's stance.

'The reason we printed the poster is because Larry Murphy is a clear and present danger. He was about to murder that woman and disappear her until he was caught by chance. It was a random assault. It could be someone's wife or daughter,' he told the *Sunday Tribune*. 'By printing the poster, we were making the point that this person is still a danger and people should remember his face.'

Colleran said his paper's extensive coverage of the story wasn't a cynical attempt to increase circulation but a genuine reaction to public hysteria.

Several tabloid newspapers also published a hotline number for their readers to ring if they spot Larry Murphy, who by now must be the most recognisable man in Ireland. Another newspaper was giving away a free Larry Murphy book this weekend.

The Sun raised some eyebrows when it put up posters of Larry Murphy all over Wicklow, warning people to 'keep away' from the dangerous rapist. The paper's editor, Mick McNiffe, defended the move on Today FM's *The Last Word* programme on Thursday. McNiffe told presenter Anton Savage that it was not his newspaper's intention to encourage vigilantism or to put Larry Murphy or anyone else in danger. Almost the opposite was true, he said, since his newspaper was advising people to keep away from the rapist rather than attack him.

There are countless reasons why Larry Murphy's release from prison is a valid story that has generated so much publicity. Aside from the violence of his abduction, rape and attempted murder of the Carlow woman, and the fact that he's a suspected serial killer, other factors have also been at play. His brother Tom has spoken to several newspapers, RTÉ and TV3 about how he wants nothing to do with his brother and he will not be welcome in his home. This has helped keep the story alive.

It has also sparked important debate about whether remission should be available to all inmates and about electronic tagging. In some countries one of the conditions of the release of a rapist from prison is that they must have had therapy. But, in the main, a lot of the coverage has focused on the fear.

'People know a story like this will sell. A lot of the stories in the papers are focusing on the fear element in all of this. It's hard to know where this story can go next, aside from if he leaves the country,' said O'Leary of O'Leary Analytics. 'I cannot imagine that this level of publicity can be maintained.'

Brian Trench, head of the School of Communications at DCU, believes the Larry Murphy story fascinates the media because it has so many elements to it.

'A lot of the coverage is focused on anger, anxiety, fear and terror. This is not a tabloid versus broadsheet issue. It's being covered widely by the press. There is certainly an appetite for this kind of stuff. It ensures an audience and readership,' he said.

'The tabloid press have been more preoccupied with this story. While there are important issues, like monitoring of sex offenders and rehabilitation being raised, it seems to me that a lot of the information about the story is coming from unattributed sources and some unverifiable statements are being made. It is all 'garda sources' and 'prison sources'. There has certainly been an unhelpful level of speculation around Larry Murphy.'

Naturally, the media have focused on the shocking details of Murphy's attack on the Carlow woman. But Trench said constantly repeating the facts of her abduction and rape adds to the fear that is being created about Larry Murphy.

'It's hard to see what public purpose is being served. There is a self-fulfilling prophecy when newspapers keep saying, 'public fear is rising over the release of Larry Murphy'. It is telling people they need to be afraid. There has been a lot of drama built up around this.'

Trench believes people have an appetite for stories that generate fear. 'Perversely, we like to feel anxious. This story is playing out its natural cycle. While we almost enjoy the fear, at the same time we are hoping that by the weekend there will be some kind of conclusion to it,' he said. 'Some of the things that have been printed have been proven not to be true. Larry Murphy is an exceptional type of case; there are not very many like him. It is too simple to just describe him as 'evil incarnate' and not explore why. We know so little about what makes sex offenders tick.'

In the summertime, particularly August, there is a dearth of newsworthy stories to focus on, since the Dáil and the courts are not in session. During this 'silly season', stories that wouldn't usually be printed suddenly appear for want of other news. The massive media coverage of Murphy is partly because of this, according to Trench.

The impact of all this publicity on Larry Murphy's victim must be immense. While the Carlow woman has moved on from the horror inflicted on her that night in 2000, all her feelings about the incident have been dragged up again. She has consistently refused to talk to the press in the past ten years about her abduction and rape.

Other victims of the Larry Murphy fallout include his family. His estranged wife and two sons are no doubt feeling emotional about his release. So much so, in fact, that they left their home for a few days recently to get away from the constant stream of journalists calling to the door.

'It would certainly make our job easier if this wasn't such a big story,' said a garda. 'He is being absolutely hounded by the press, hunted like an animal. That's a bad situation for Larry Murphy. The last thing we need is a high-risk sex offender being really stressed out. That brings with it its own dangers.'

When Larry Murphy was spotted on Friday evening at Heuston Station and then later at Kevin Street garda station, the public, and the media seemed to breathe a collective sigh of relief. Simply knowing where he was had acquired major significance. But it remains to be seen whether Murphy can again give the media the slip. The danger with this is that hounding someone as potentially dangerous as Murphy can force them underground.

'No-one has to worry. He might be able to give the press the slip but he cannot give the gardaí the slip; the general public can be assured of that,' added the garda source. 'But how long can he put up with this? Larry Murphy must be feeling so much pressure right now. He must be at boiling point.'

ARTS

JOHN BOYNE

Shorts column

John Boyne is the author of seven novels, including *The Absolutist* and *The House of Special Purpose*, and two for children, including *The Boy in the Striped Pyjamas*. A collection of fifty short short stories appeared in The *Sunday Tribune* during 2006/07.

Gazebo

7 January 2007

It was almost ten years since Maggie had last sat by the bay windows, overlooking the garden, and her eyes moved slowly as she surveyed the damage that her husband's whore had done to it since replacing her in a bloodless coup, shortly after her fiftieth birthday. The laburnum had been trimmed back to almost nothing, while the pale blue gillyflower had withered and died. Worst of all, however, was the disappearance of the aspidistra that she had nurtured from a cutting gathered in the Himalayas during her honeymoon.

'Tea,' said Susan, appearing beside her suddenly with a cup and saucer and placing it by her left hand, her good hand, the hand that still worked. 'I thought it might cheer you up.' Maggie stared at it with contempt before looking away; it would spill down her blouse and scald her if she tried to drink it; a simultaneously thoughtful and thoughtless gesture.

Being here was an unwelcome stopgap but she had been offered no choice. The hospital had kept her for eight weeks after the stroke but they needed the bed. And so, until her daughter had time to prepare her flat, she was back in her husband's house for the first time since she had been forced out of it. The irony of it was that it had been Susan's idea. He had insisted she was nothing to do with him anymore but the whore had said that they owed her this at least.

'Aspidistra,' said Maggie, raising a cautious finger and pointing out the window. 'Where?' These days, her words came out like a series of grunts and spits and shattered sibilants and she tried to limit herself to the bare essentials. A noun, a verb when necessary, an adjective if she had the energy. She who had once recited the whole of *Paradise Lost*, word perfect and without the text, on the stage of the Abbey Theatre. She who had called her husband every name she could think of when he told her what had been going on.

'Kids,' replied Susan, shaking her head. 'One night when we were asleep. They ripped it out by the roots and threw it on the roof of the gazebo, the little vandals.' Maggie watched her face, wondering how she had the temerity not to blush when she said the word 'we'. 'You brought that back from Singapore, didn't you?' she asked, leaning over her now as if she was a child.

'Himalayas,' said Maggie, grunting out the word; it didn't even sound like English to her.

'What was that?' asked Susan.

'Himalayas,' she repeated, and this time the four syllables ran into each other like a crash on a motorway. She stared at the younger woman, knowing that she still hadn't understood, but chose not to repeat herself again; instead, cold and resentful, she turned back to the peace of the garden.

Gazebo. She couldn't even imagine what would happen if she tried to pronounce that.

✦ ✦ ✦

Oil

21 October 2007

The car won't start and you walk around to the front, lift the bonnet and peer inside. You might as well be looking at a schematic for a rocket-ship for all the sense it makes to you, but still you touch things and hope that inspiration will strike. Your neighbour comes out and sees you standing there but you pretend you don't see him. He kissed your wife once at a party. You saw him do it. You lost your way trying to find a bathroom and there they were, kissing in a bedroom, her hand pushing his away from her breast. You did nothing about it because you didn't know what to do. It wasn't a movie, after all; it was a party.

'Problem?' he asks and you look across at him. He's not as tall as you. And he's not as good-looking either. He wears a cheap suit. Still, she kissed him. You tell him that the car won't start and he offers to take a look for you.

'Aren't you a botanist?' you ask, refusing to move.

'I understand cars,' he says, pushing you away and looking down at the oily black engine and all those things, those things you don't know the name of, that surround it. He strokes his chin for a moment and mutters something to himself before tightening a few caps and squeezing a couple of wires. 'Try her now,' he tells you.

You sit in the car and put the key in the engine. You have an important meeting in an hour. A lot of things could come from that meeting. A lot of very good things. But still, you hope that the car won't start.

'No luck,' you say, stepping back to the front.

'I thought I had her,' he tells you before looking down again and shaking his head.

'I can handle it from here,' you tell him.

'It's no problem,' he says. 'I understand cars.'

You watched them for longer than you should have and when she stopped pushing his hand away and let him touch her, you got hard and wanted to see what would happen next. It wasn't like being at a party after all; it was like watching a movie.

'Battery's dead,' he says finally. 'You leave your lights on all night? That'll do it every time.'

'Thanks for your help,' you say, slapping him once on the back of his white shirt as he turns away, a gesture of friendship, two buddies talking engines. He walks over to his own car, which is smaller than yours, the dark imprint of your hand, black and greasy, perfectly centred on the back of his white shirt, the fingers stretched wide, the middle finger pointing north.

✦ ✦ ✦

Friends

11 February 2007

The day I met Neil Armstrong I was already teetering on the edge of sanity from a life gone wrong. A week before, fearing that I might take a scissors to my throat, I confessed my secrets to a doctor, who went pale and said 'Jesus, Mary and Joseph' before writing a prescription. I didn't cut down on the gargle though and the two mixed badly. In fact, when I showed up in Tralee that morning I was more than a little unsteady on my feet and was starting to see triple.

A large crowd had gathered and when I asked a young girl what they were there for, she grew very abusive and accused me of molesting her. The situation was turning violent so I turned on my heels and before I knew it I was standing in front of a man who shook my hand and thanked me for coming out to see him. I hadn't a clue who he was but later that evening in the pub, I picked up the local paper only to see the two of us standing together, and a headline announcing that my new friend was none other than Neil Armstrong, the first man to walk on the moon.

'Can you believe it?' I asked the barman, who had once been a friend of mine but who had fallen out with me over a nag. 'I'm a celebrity.'

'You're an oul' bollix,' he suggested. 'You always were and you always will be.'

I retaliated and he hit me a slap.

The next morning I woke up in a hospital bed and a nurse, one of them foreign bits, told me I'd overdosed on my medication and collapsed on the street. She said she needed the name of my next of kin.

'I'm an unmarried man,' I explained. 'There was a woman, once, but she left me because of my ways.'

'Family then?' asked the nurse.

'No one. Not any more.'

'Well, we need a name,' she said with a shrug.

'I don't know what to tell you,' I said.

'Sir, I'm sorry, but we have to put someone down on the form. In case you die.'

That gave me a fright, but still nothing came to mind. I looked away from her and saw the local paper folded up on a chair.

'Neil Armstrong,' I told her then. 'We're not close, but –'

'He'll do,' she said, signing the form. All she wanted was to get away from me on account of my stink. I could smell it myself. I was rank.

'And I have photographic evidence of our relationship, should it be required.'

'It won't be,' she said. And for a moment or two, I felt happy. On account of my having a friend. Someone who would look out for me. Someone who would see that I was taken care of.

In case I died.

✦ ✦ ✦

Memory

17 December 2006

It was three months after William's death before Caroline could even think about clearing out his closets. His demise had been sudden and unexpected and she found herself fighting the urge towards depression on a daily basis. Their daughters, both grown-up and married now, had taken good care of her in the intervening time and one grandson in particular had outdone himself with his many kindnesses.

However it was another teenager, a boy called Joe who lived on the second floor of their building, who she asked to help her carry the bags of clothes downstairs for the Goodwill on the morning she decided that it was time and he had said he would be glad to help. She spent the first hour of the morning dividing William's clothes into two bundles – those to give away and those to keep, just in case. At some point during the second hour she realised that there was no 'just in case' left in her life and she swapped the idea of two bundles for more black bags.

When Joe arrived she hoped that he wouldn't notice her tear-stained cheeks or, if he did, he would have the sense to ignore them. To his credit, he simply glanced at the bags that surrounded them both and asked, 'These are all to go, right?'

'Yes,' she replied, hesitating, unsure whether she was actually ready to give them away yet after all. 'These are all to go. Just give me a moment, will you?' she added, disappearing into the kitchen to compose her thoughts.

When she stepped back into the bedroom a few minutes later, Joe had picked up her husband's old army jacket from the sofa and tried it on. William had worn it on almost every date they ever went on before they were married and had held on to it for nostalgic reasons; it was the kind of jacket that now, forty years later, kids were wearing again.

'I'm sorry,' said Joe, startled and embarrassed. 'I shouldn't have –'

'Please,' she said quietly, stepping towards him and staring at him for a moment. She put her hands out and felt his slender arms in the sleeves that had encircled her body so many times when she was a young woman. The jacket smelled of William still and she breathed him in. Unable to stop herself, she closed her eyes and leaned forward, her mouth finding Joe's quickly, her lips softening against his as they kissed, this old woman who'd been young once, this young boy who'd grow old sooner than he knew.

A moment later she stepped away from him and looked at the floor for a moment, resisting an urge to laugh. Instead, she turned her attention to the bags again. 'It will take at least three trips, I think,' she said, nodding her head. 'What do you think, Joe, will three do it? Can we do it in three?'

✦ ✦ ✦

CIARAN CARTY

Faster Pussycats

Quentin Tarantino's back. And, true to form, his new film is full of sexy women and fast cars.

9 September 2007

The temperature is topping thirty degrees even in the shade on the Martinez Beach in Cannes. Zoë Bell is so flimsily dressed she mightn't be dressed at all. The safest place to look is into her eyes, which isn't difficult.

Whenever things got really nasty in Quentin Tarantino's *Kill Bill*, she was the stunt double for Uma Thurman, the 'bride' in pursuit of vengeance for the killing of her husband on their wedding day. She impressed Tarantino so much that he asked her to turn to acting in *Death Proof*, his exuberant tribute to gory slasher movies of the 1970s. 'What if I'm terrible?' she said. 'You're not going to be terrible because I don't make bad decisions,' he told her.

She shrugs, the thin strap of her silk chemise almost slipping off her shoulder. 'So what could I say?' she asks me. 'OK, I told him, I'm going to be amazing.'

Amazing she is, clinging to the hood of a car travelling at 100 mph in a duel to the death with a psychopath – played by sinisterly appealing Kurt Russell – who stalks young girls, involving them in fatal crashes for his sexual gratification.

'The really fun thing about *Death Proof* is that it changes so much,' says Rosario Dawson, who makes Zoë seem almost overdressed and talks even faster than Tarantino. She plays one of a bevy of female characters who get to kick ass. 'My character is a little shy; she's not as promiscuous as the other girls, but then she has a sudden turn. It's interesting to see a character turn into a person she never would have imagined being able to see in the mirror.

Although *Reservoir Dogs* gained Tarantino a foul-mouthed macho reputation, his movies invariably feature tough sexy women, whether Uma Thurman in *Pulp Fiction* and *Kill Bill* or Pam Grier in *Jackie Brown*. Perhaps it comes from being brought up with his sister by a single mom, Connie, or his childhood addiction of the 1970s exploitation movies that pioneered black women superheroes. 'I have male friends, ' he says, 'but I'm fascinated by the dynamic of a bunch of girls who hang out together, like a posse. A lot of my characters come from that.'

Tracie Thoms butts in. 'We were having a conversation one night, and I was going, "I'm just saying, I'm just saying,"' she says.

'And Quentin laughed. A week later, we shot a scene outside a store and my line was, "I'm just saying". That's what's great about him. If something comes up, he goes with it.'

Although famous for an infectious enthusiasm on the set, Tarantino has his down moments. 'Maybe in the course of a long shoot I might have a couple of days when I'm a grumpy bastard,' he says. 'There's this crazy movie people have never seen called *Hollywood Man* by Jack Starrett. It's about the making of a motorcycle movie. They're on location and they're having a production meeting in the kitchen of a motel that they're staying at, and the director is being told the bike is not working, the stunt's going to cost too much, and this that and the other, and at one point he goes, "That's it, I've had it, I've f**king had it." I watched that movie after *Kill Bill* and I laughed so damn hard. I was like, that is the perfect, perfect expression for a director to say, because that's what it is. You've had it.'

It happened to Tarantino twice on *Kill Bill*. 'I just got sick of making this f**king movie. I got sick of getting up so f**king early every morning, working so goddamn hard. I got sick of not having a life other than this one f**king thing for a year. I just got f**king sick of it. I got sick of answering f**king questions. Now, here's the thing. At a certain point you realise, Aw, poor Quentin, you get to live your dream, you get to be an artist. Aw, isn't life terrible. That makes you snap out of it.'

It happened again later, shooting a night scene with Zoë.

'I'd told her she had to start thinking like an actress. It's not just jumping through a window to get stunt money. She's not a void here, she's playing my f**king character. So she wasn't used to that. She's very unpretentious. She kind of chuckled a bit but realised I was serious. So she tried to do it. She started really getting it. I'm playing a character. If I put on that costume, I am the bride.

'Now during that night we were shooting the scene where the bride is on the motorcycle with the helmet. I'm in my little "f**k this" mood. People are scared of me. Somebody comes up. Umh, Zoë needs to talk to you. So I walk over. She's sitting there in her yellow jump suit. I go, Zoë, you want to talk to me, what about? She goes, well you know, I'm scared to do the scene, you know, actor-wise, is there anything you want me to know, anything you want me to think about? Oh, she's thinking this way now. She's an actress. Even though there's a helmet on her face and we can't see her face, she wants to be thinking what I want her to be thinking. And suddenly I wasn't grumpy any more.'

Like John Travolta talking about a Big Mac in *Pulp Fiction*, Tarantino can't open his mouth without going into a riff about something. More than anything else it's what makes his movies so gripping – not the sex, or the cursing or the violence, but the talk. 'My whole thing is dialogue – that's what I do,' he says, sitting with me on the beach, his open-necked black shirt flapping outside his trousers.

Born in Knoxville Tennessee in 1963, but brought to LA by his mom when he was two, he grew up on television and movies. He got his name Quentin from a Faulkner novel she was reading, *The Sound And The Fury.* He watched *Carnal Knowledge* with her when he was five. When Art Garfunkel tried to talk Candice Bergen into bed, saying 'Let's do it,' he piped up, 'What's he wanna do, Mom?' He has an IQ of 160, but dropped out of high school at sixteen to be an usher in a porn cinema and then a video clerk at $4 an hour. The video store became a film school where, between acting classes, he wrote *True Romance* and *Natural Born Killers*. 'In every movie I've ever done I've been criticised for having long boring dialogue sequences, with the exception of *Kill Bill Vol 1* where they kept complaining I didn't have any dialogue,' he says.

'You can't be a fan of mine if you don't like my dialogue. Where

I'm coming from it's the same thing as going to a Tennessee Williams play or a David Hare play and saying, what's all that f**king dialogue? Am I a playwright? No. But I could be. *Reservoir Dogs* could be a play. Actually when I was writing the first half of *Death Proof*, I was thinking if I want to go where I want to go with this I could make it a play, a kind of exploitation Eugene O'Neill play.'

Death Proof started out combined with his buddy Robert Rodriquez's zombie romp *Planet Terror* as the second part of a three-hour double-bill homage called *Grindhouse*, the nickname for flea-pit cinemas that screened 1970s over-the-top exploitation flicks. Although *Grindhouse* got rave reviews, it flopped at the US box-office. 'People didn't want to see two movies at once,' he says. 'It seems so obvious now, but the whole industry was shocked it didn't do well.'

Outside the US, it was always intended to release fuller versions of the two movies separately. 'I'd to cut *Death Proof* not only down to the bone but past the bone to make it work for *Grindhouse*,' he says, 'because otherwise you'd run out of patience waiting for the car chase.' Everything shown in the car chase actually happened. No computer effects were used. 'CGI car chases to me don't mean shit,' he says. 'After watching 1970s car chases like *Bullitt* where they actually did it, how can you be impressed by a facsimile of a computer? It's the fact that they did it that was so good.'

Although Tarantino's movies are spattered with movie references, he uses them as a vocabulary to create something completely different. 'If all I did was quote, I doubt they'd be having me to Cannes for sixteen years,' he says. 'I have no problem taking things from anybody and using them. I love these genres but I always have a different agenda. I'm using the trappings but mixing their coat of many colours. Every film is a genre movie or a subgenre movie. Bergman achieved a kind of sub-genre to himself. So is doing an adaptation of a Henry James novel more valid than doing a *Women In Prison*? It's different, but is it more valid?'

✦   ✦   ✦

The rough guide to Frank

The newest member of the Hennessy Hall of Fame discusses life,
love, work – and why he'll never find the challenge he needs
at the Abbey or the Gate.

22 April 2007

When Frank McGuinness was sixteen years old a dismiss-
ive teacher changed his life. 'I won't say it was the making of me, because that would be giving credit to a man
who set out to destroy me,' he says, 'but if I survived that bollocks,
I'll survive other bollocks.'

He'd just got his Intermediate Certificate. The teacher wanted
him to do science. 'But we had a terrible science teacher and I knew
I wouldn't get the honour I needed to get a scholarship to go to college,' he says. Nobody in his immediate background in Buncrana
had ever gone to university. All the women worked in the local shirt
factory. 'If your father had a job, you were middle class,' he recalls.

'So I said I wanted to do history because I thought I could do
it well enough to get an honour. He looked at me and said, "You'll
never get to university". I remember saying nothing but inside I
said, "Well I'll do it and I'll do it without you." And I did it. And that's
been my motto. I rarely give up. In fact, I never give up. You have
to have that side to you. On many occasions perhaps I should have
given up. But I didn't. Absolute ruthlessness may not always be the
best policy. However, it's the only one I know. I have to follow my
heart, no matter what.'

His determination won him a place at University College Dublin,
then a job as a lecturer at the New University of Ulster in Coleraine
where he met his lifelong partner, Philip Tilling, fifteen years his
elder. Patrick Mason recognised his raw talent in *The Factory Girls*,
a play he wrote for a workshop in Galway in 1980 about women
shirt workers in Buncrana standing up to their employers. It was
accepted by the Abbey Theatre, and directed by Mason, as were his
next two plays, *Baglady* and *Observe The Sons Of Ulster Marching
Towards The Somme*, which won him the *London Evening Standard*
Award for Most Promising Playwright.

Mason also directed *Innocence*, which caused uproar at the Gate Theatre with its explicit re-imagining of a day in Caravaggio's life.

'Patrick is an incredible force,' says McGuinness. 'We're still friends, which is not common in theatre. We have survived each other, although we're not easy men by any stretch of the imagination, and eminently capable of killing each other. I put great store on his love and friendship and I'm immensely proud of his achievements.'

Earlier this year, London's Almeida Theatre premiered McGuinness's thirteenth play, *There Came a Gypsy Riding*, to plaudits from Michael Billington and other leading critics, while a new production of his Brecht translation *The Caucasian Chalk Circle* is on at the National Theatre. On Tuesday he joined Dermot Bolger, Patrick McCabe, Joe O'Connor and Colum McCann as a member of the Hennessy Hall of Fame, an award marking the achievement of major writers whose first work was published in *New Irish Writing*.

'I was twenty,' he says. 'I'd started writing at UCD but couldn't get into the student magazines. Then *New Irish Writing* published a poem about the death of my grandfather. And that really was the beginning of it. I knew what I wanted to do, although something in me knew that poetry was not going to be the medium. I remember I was paid £3.50, which in 1974 bought two steak dinners and a glass of wine.'

We're sitting at a wooden table in the blue-walled cottage on Booterstown Avenue, a twenty-five-minute walk from UCD where he lectures in literature. All his writing is done on this table. The room opens out onto a patio and narrow garden of trees and bushes, an oasis of quiet. I drink coffee from a Nicholas Mosse mug with the face of a cat given to him by his niece Selina. 'She loves cats, and so do I,' he says. 'They're like small children. The grief when they die is appalling.' I try an organic chocolate cookie. 'I got them for Philip, but he's not here.'

The couple celebrate their thirtieth anniversary next year. 'It's been a flash, really,' he says. I remark that I've been forty-five years with my wife and we're still discovering each other: maybe relationships need mystery to survive. 'It's the same with me and Philip,' he laughs. 'There has to be some unknown.'

Although his 2002 play *Gates of Gold* deals with the love of two men who have been together a long time, it was inspired not by his life but by Micheál MacLiammoir and Hilton Edwards. He invariably draws on life but only to reimagine it. 'If the facts lie, they are my lies,' he says. He gestures to an armchair piled with books on Guy Fawkes. 'I did a play for the Royal Shakespeare Company called *Speaking Like Magpies* about the Gunpowder Plot, of which I knew nothing other than it didn't work, that Guy Fawkes was not the ringleader and I knew that James I was probably gay. That was the extent of my knowledge. So I read those books and then just threw them aside and wrote as if from scratch, as I always do. I have this anti-historical gene. I cannot see a fact without turning it on its head.

'I loved Micheál MacLiammoir and Hilton Edwards too much to do a documentary on them. I wanted to spin a strange haunted story, something exotic, dangerous and dark that they would have appreciated and staged.'

He never met MacLiammoir, but saw him perform his one-man show in the art deco bar of Lough Swilly Hotel in Buncrana. 'It was one of those great nights. People were mesmerised by him. He was so disciplined, so absolutely focused. An extraordinary quiet spread across the place when he talked about Wilde. I was eighteen and I'll never forget it.'

While there were no books in his home in Buncrana, he steeped himself in Greek mythology and Shakespeare and modern drama courtesy of the BBC. 'It became my encyclopaedia. Those were the glory days of British television with a whole new generation of anti-imperialists ruling the roost. They put enormous emphasis on broadening the horizons. I had this cosmopolitan education in the wilds of the Inishowen peninsula. We were lucky as well because we had Derry only fourteen miles away, where we could go to the ABC and see films without the censors crapping on them.

'When I was fifteen or sixteen I saw *Midnight Cowboy* uncut – my god, the shock of that.' He was traumatised by the move to student digs in Dublin, just up the road from where he now lives. 'I'd never been out of my home alone. I was so homesick I refused to warm to the city; but of course, unknown to myself, it was really becoming my territory.'

The first play he saw at the Abbey was Brian Friel's *The Gentle Island* in 1971. 'It was ahead of its time in terms of sexual politics and sexuality,' he says. Several of the cast would later have roles in his emergence as a major playwright. Playing the little boy was David Herlihy, who subsequently portrayed Dido in *Carthaginians*, an elegy to the dead of Bloody Sunday. Maureen Toal would become his 'glorious muse' in a tour de force *Baglady* monologue.

Bosco Hogan created the role of the loyalist volunteer Pyper, whose comrades were annihilated in the trenches but return to haunt him in *Observe The Sons of Ulster*.

'I'd probably run a mile if I met them in the streets of Belfast but they wouldn't go away. They were eight young men full of energy and full of purpose there in the room in my head, coming out. They were good company for a while. They were in New York a couple of years ago. I went to visit them on their travels. I can talk very rationally about it now but when it was happening I certainly wasn't thinking rationally about it. I just went for it.

'That's what we were encouraged to do in the early 1980s when Patrick Mason and Joe Dowling and Seán McCarthy were out to get fresh blood into the theatre, writers like Bernard Farrell, Graham Reid and Neil Donnelly. They moved hell and high water to make the Abbey what it should be, putting money into new productions and into young writers' pockets. Not much but it was great, believe me. When the Abbey neglects this, it is in decline.'

McGuinness has never lost this sense of daring. He has been a wonderfully subversive influence in Irish theatre, confronting political and sexual taboos with a poetic intensity that has undermined deep-rooted prejudices, not just with his original plays but in translations of classics. He enters into a creative dialogue with Ibsen, Chekhov, Lorca and Brecht undaunted by the fact that he's never been to Norway, Russia, Germany or Spain, nor speaks a word of any of the languages. 'They come to me,' he says. His is a theatre of imagined worlds, not literal reality. 'I loathe being predictable to myself even when I'm clearly mining a territory I've looked at before. I want to do something different with it. That's part of the joy of it. I've no notion where things are going, absolutely no notion.'

There Came A Gypsy Riding, set in Connemara, is about suicide, a theme he will soon return to with a BBC screenplay *A Short
Stay in Switzerland*. 'I think one of the terrible consequences of
suicide is that it confronts everyone else with the possibility that
they might do the same,' he says.

'There was a terrible tragedy in my own family. My cousin took
his life, unexpectedly. I didn't want to exploit that, so he's radically
transformed into a much younger man, a teenager. But there's no
doubt that that event is the core of the play. I didn't want to examine
the boy's decision, I wanted to look at its effect on his family. I'm not
going to say it's a happy ending. It's not, by any stretch of the imagination. But it's an ending where there's life afterwards. And that's as
much as you can take from it.'

McGuinness doesn't do sentimentality. 'There's too much
Donegal ice in me for that. We're a very hard people. I'd like to think
I'm a very violent mix of the rough and the courteous. That's what I
like about the landscape of Donegal, its spectacular harshness with
occasional signs of pleasantness. Not too much pleasantness, but
enough to make it endurable. That's what my work tries to do.'

There are no plans for an Irish production of *There Came a Gypsy
Riding*. 'It's a long time since I've had anything new in Dublin. I've
theatres I can go to in London. It means I'm not dependent on anyone here. I'm not dependent on their commissions or on their good
will. I don't need to lick arse.

'It's terribly dangerous to have a single outlet or a single working relationship. For everybody concerned, it can only end in tears.
I wish the Abbey and the Gate all the best, but I think they would
understand me when I say I have to go elsewhere at times to get the
challenges and the shaking up that I need.'

✦ ✦ ✦

Una Mullally

Planet of the Apes

The buzz around Fight Like Apes is building to a roar. The *Tribune* joined them on the road to observe the monkey business up close.

21 September 2008

Glastonbury, June:

Fight Like Apes' bass player, the tall-and-skinny-with-an-afro-on-top Tom, stands victorious in front of the drum kit as his bandmates disappear to the wings following a storming set on the BBC 6 Music Stage. He holds a bottle of Buckfast aloft like a raucous prince might a sword, surveying a battlefield of conquered enemies.

Backstage, while loading her keyboard into the back of a van, lead singer MayKay hugs it momentarily and calls 'hold me' to no-one in particular with hysterical humour. In the dissipating audience on the other side, journalists and industry people wander back to the press bar rather stunned, while a BBC radio reporter gathers vox pops on the gig – generally breathlessly excited appraisals of many people's new favourite band.

This is the world of FLApes, a band three-quarters Dublin, one-quarter Kildare, who have been touring the UK almost every day since February, making inroads in an indie music industry where the only way to do it is play live, play live, play live. It's working.

Oxegen, Punchestown, July:

The 2FM New Band tent is heaving, partly with the curious, looking to see the band everyone is talking about. As the Apes enter to a deafening roar, there are tears of delight in the eyes of their PR team. No-one now, not even them, can believe the rise of a band not even two years old, still to release an album. On that stage, like every stage, they kill it.

Afterwards, the keyboardist, Pockets, addled by adrenalin after what was probably the crucial gig of their just-happening careers, stomps towards the dressing room, sweeping back his Worzel Gummidge-meets-Robert-Smith hair, saying, 'Let's go drink some vodka.' He readies the refreshments with the excited shakes of a housewife who has just been told her husband has been in an as-yet-unspecified accident.

Someone offers the mohawked drummer, Adrian, a drink and a cigarette, to which he replies, smiling, 'I don't do either.' A short while later, Fight Like Apes begin to, well, fight like apes – all camaraderie, of course, wrestling, jumping about, trying to work off the impossible energy of what just happened. Other bands pass by, staring at the antics. The buzz around FLApes of possibilities, magic and talent is almost audible. Since Glastonbury, Jonathan Ross, Zane Lowe and other influential BBC DJs have been playing their tunes. It's all happening.

Birmingham, August:

In an airport car park, MayKay bundles herself out of the van wearing a pyjama ensemble and a half-on eye-mask. This week, the band is in the *NME* for the first time, under a headline that says 'Everybody's talking about Fight Like Apes.' It's a big deal. Irish indie bands are generally ignored entirely by the British music press. Outside of the mainstream, there hasn't been a success story since Ash or JJ72. 'Well, now that "everyone's talking about us", you think they'd write about us more,' says Pockets wryly, as everyone settles down in the van to watch an episode of *King of the Hill*. As it happens, the *NME* does just that. The next week, they will be in a list of bands not to miss during the upcoming Reading and Leeds festivals. The week after that, the *NME* will make them No. 2 in a list of 'hopes for the future'.

The next day, Green Man Festival, Wales:

After an evening of drinking vodka, wine, whiskey and beer on a fire escape outside their hotel and on top of their van (although MayKay and Adrian both went to bed rather early), the band arrive at a boutique festival in a valley in Wales. MayKay is annoyed that she mightn't be able to swear in her songs as BBC Radio One wants to record the gig. 'They always do this,' she strops, 'if I knew they were going to use it [the recording] straight away, I would be OK, but I don't.' When they go on stage, she swears in every song that has swears. BBC Radio One probably isn't pleased. Before they went on, she hung back behind the stage backdrop. She's wearing American Apparel disco hot pants. She doesn't like going out on stage until the last minute, rather cutely scared that she'll look like 'an eejit' wandering around in sparkly shorts before the music kicks in.

She needn't really worry. Everyone who has seen MayKay play, worked with her, photographed her, will tell you the same thing. The woman is a star. But this band is not one person. MayKay may hold the visual key to Fight Like Apes' image, but their sound and attitude is very much a sum of its parts. They address each other as 'friend' and 'pal'. And although Adrian doesn't drink – something that can often be an alienating setback in rock and roll – he still gels, with the rest of the members nicknaming him 'side-stage-drian', such is his interest in watching bands that play after them at festivals from the side of the stage.

The day after that, Carlisle:

The Apes are faffing around their dressing room, about to go on stage to a rather intimidating crowd of Kasabian fans. It's a downsized tour for Kasabian, one of the most popular bands in Britain today, but the venue still holds about 2,000 people. 'Are Kasabian a big band?' asks Tom innocently, when they wander into the colossal hall for the first time earlier that day.

It's this lack of stopping to think, coupled with a constant motion in touring – just yesterday, they began a sold-out UK tour with The Ting Tings – that has been a blessing to the Apes. MayKay says other Irish bands sit down and examine everything, dissect it, over-think it, whereas she and her bandmates just do it. 'What has happened with us since the band started, is when big things come up, a million little things come up as well, so we don't have time to get worried or panic about anything bigger. For example, Glastonbury – we gigged all the way up to Glastonbury, so we never really thought about Glastonbury until the day. It's the same thing with the album. It's done now,' she says, frankly.

They are scarred by the road. Knackered, but having a blast. When they get home for a couple of days' break, after a few hours, they end up in Pockets' house. They can't stay away from each other. They admit to having become institutionalised by touring, leading to endless conversations like this:

Tom: 'You'd miss an aul' truck stop, wouldn't you, when you're at home? Not specific or anything, just the idea of them.'

Pockets: 'I'd like to leave my house and be able to go across and have a good selection. Maybe win some cash prizes.'

Tom: 'No. You've got too much choice at home.'

MayKay: 'I'm sorry, I definitely don't miss truck stops. Do you ever just find yourself sitting at a truck stop and eating or something and being like, "I was here before. Don't know when, don't care when, never gonna find out." Oh my God.'

Tom: 'You should buy a paper.'

MayKay: 'Buy a paper?'

Tom: 'Yeah, then don't be in a truck stop, because you just zone out.'

MayKay: 'I've never seen you read a paper.'

Tom: 'You've never seen me read a paper?'

MayKay: 'I've never seen you read a paper in a truck stop.'

Tom: 'I read papers in truck stops, yeah.'

MayKay: 'Anyway! I don't know if reading in a truck stop makes me like them any more.'

Tom: 'It makes me like them.'

MayKay: 'Well, that's good. You've found a method. I have not yet. I'm sure I will.'

As for the music? It's odd genius (Pockets describes it self-deprecatingly thus: 'Hook, verse, hook, verse, end of song. The end. That's it. Run it through a distortion pedal.') Obsessions with 1990s popular culture, an incredible talent for catching a melody, then another one, then another one, and ending up with a pop song that has fifty times as much catchiness as anything near it. Feminist, occasionally violent lyrics; almost cartoon-like, and full of strange fantasy. The result is near-perfect pop befitting of a culture where pop doesn't exist anymore; music that's simultaneously assaulting and comforting, stupid and remarkably intelligent.

There's a seven-second song called *Megameanie* on their forthcoming album, as well as what's probably one of the most beautiful post-breakup songs ever written, *Snore Bore Whore*, which runs over five minutes and contains among other things a sample from the narration of newscaster George Putnam on the 1965 anti-pornography propaganda film *Perversion For Profit*, primal screeches from MayKay and beautiful keyboard parts. It's the song that reinforces the fact that, despite their appearance, anti-coolness, and tendency to bang pots together on stage, they are truly remarkable songwriters.

After playing a few practical jokes that involve soaking each other in the dressing room showers and chucking chairs about, they bounce on stage. Confronted by skinheads hugging their girlfriends, waiting for the blokey Oasis-aphiles Kasabian to come on stage and not these weirdos from Ireland, it could all go horribly wrong. Does it? Of course not. They're that good, you see. Do you not know that yet?

Modern Nursery Rhymes: a lyrical journey into the heart of Fight Like Apes

Knucklehead

Hold up stay fresh / Don't let that
beast consume you yet / You're
looking like a rack of lamb / And
you're talking like a caravan / So, no pressure, no
pressure / You're spending tea time with / Fran
Drescher, Fran Drescher / From that awful TV
show ...

Do You Karate?

And he hides behind the guise / Of making life a big surprise / Until you realise / He doesn't even know you like stars

Snore Bore Whore

It's getting better / I sleep well again and now / And I saw my successor yesterday/ And I smiled 'cause she looks like a cow / But none of that matters / 'Cause she's been your cow for a while / So none of that matters / 'Cause there's something she does that makes you smile

Jake Summers

Hey! You! What's your face? / I've got a pocket full of fist / You got a stupid face / Hey! You! Know your place / You're like Kentucky Fried Chicken / But without the taste / Hey! You! Get some grace / You know you're Driving Miss Daisy all over the place / Hey! You! You're taking up space / And you're a f**king disappointment to the human race

Recyclable Ass

I'd love if my ex-boyfriends / Would stop getting with new girlfriends / And stay single forever / Just in case I change my mind / Woo-ta-ya, that one's a home-wrecker / Woo-ta-ta, looks like Woody Woodpecker / Woo-ta, just let me know and when / So I can take you off my list, you recyclable men

TOM DUNNE

Unlike me, my kecks were up for the crack

3 October 2010

Week number two of my new fitness regime and it's already gone pear-shaped. Week one – buying runners – went well, but week two – wearing them – went horribly wrong. I made the mistake of bringing them to a gym. I'd forgotten what a testosterone-fuelled pit the whole shower area can be. And I'd also packed my sports bag in the dark, selecting from the underwear drawer an item that would have further effeminised a lady boy.

I'd have been safer wearing my wife's underwear, particularly as the other men present seemed to be a group of body-building bouncers from various eastern European countries, many of whom could well have been war criminals. 'Don't hurt me, I work in the media' cut no ice here. Nor indeed did the words 'mercy', 'help' or 'hello, sailor'.

The real mistake I made was thinking I could buy my own underwear. This is a fallacy of mine linked to a belief I still vaguely have that I am an independent person who can survive in the world without adult supervision. Wiser heads than mine believe shopping for underwear is beyond most men, and they are right. 'Leave it to your wife,' they say, but I am nothing if not old-fashioned.

I thought I knew what I was doing. 'How hard can it be to find white kecks with a red waistband?' I asked myself? But it's not that easy in real life. The underwear boxes are vaguely homoerotic and I'm not sure it would reflect well on you to linger over them. I spotted the ones I thought I needed and was just about to pounce when I saw similar ones with a more fetching gold-coloured band. 'Ah,' I thought, 'live a little. What harm can it do?'

The answer was quite a lot. They weren't the same. The back, an area for which I think the word 'generous' should be used at all times, was more akin to a G-string than a comfortable seating area. The front had been designed during a cotton shortage but made up in dynamic uplift, support and pinpoint definition what it lacked in common decency. 'Don't ever wear them out,' my wife told me solemnly, 'unless you intend to leave me.'

I couldn't bring them back. That would have involved me holding them up in front of a beautiful young sales assistant and telling her, 'I'm not this type of man.' And that would have exposed me to the possibility of her looking at the box and saying, 'No, you aren't.' I thought of trying to offload them onto a friend but my wife argued it would be too public a questioning of his sexuality. 'He'll come out when he's ready,' she told me. So they languished in a drawer until they ended up in my sports bag. I realised the mistake as I sat naked and wet after the shower. Naked and wet and among a group of men who lift weights four hours a day, drink weird protein things and have 'packages' that would disappoint a hamster.

So I took the only option: Commando. Yeah, I know. What must they think of me? Still, they didn't get my name and will remember me only as the 'Commando' guy who can dry himself really, really fast! No, honestly, really, really, really fast.

✦　✦　✦

Now, what will I wear in the afterlife?

10 October 2010

Did you know that the follow-up question to 'Is there anybody there?', much loved amid mystic circles, is actually 'wearing anything nice?' I didn't either, but it is. Dead people wear clothes and only right too. It was one thing for the young boy in *The Sixth Sense* to see dead people, but if he'd also been exposed to his aunt Gertrude – naked as the day they found her body in the coal shed – well, even Bruce Willis would have blushed.

It was a psychic that told me. Now psychics, cleverly, maintain that in reading terms I am dead to them. 'You are dead to me,' they say, eyeing me suspiciously. 'I feel no energy from you, nothing,' they add. My wife says the same, but they also hint that my deceased kin on the other side are in no rush to contact me anyway. Even she doesn't do that.

This psychic, like the *Sixth Sense* boy, also saw dead people when he was a child. 'Were you not terrified?' I asked him. 'No,' he told me, 'you see, for a long time I didn't realise they were dead. They were so normal to me.'

I wondered aloud, 'Had they clothes on?' He seemed surprised, 'Of course, of course they had clothes on.'

He thought I was wondering if the ladies might be in the naughty naked nude. But I wasn't, really. It's just, you would have thought, when the mystery of death is at last revealed and the veil between this world and the next is lifted, you wouldn't have to worry anymore about being caught wearing the jumper your mother gave you.

Be just our luck, wouldn't it? To be badly dressed for eternity.

He was losing me now. I was thinking random thoughts? If we have clothes do we have to have presses? Who irons? Do colours still fade? – when I suddenly heard him telling me that he is often asked to help in missing-person cases.

Then the words 'car key' appeared mysteriously in my mind. I hadn't seen my car key in two days. Operative word here is 'key', not 'keys'. I lost the spare ages ago. The garage had told me I could only order a new one if I had the log book. The log book was locked in the car. I started screaming the words 'where are my keys?' in my mind and asked him if there was anything he wanted to tell me.

His answer was so vague that even now I struggle to remember a single word of it. It was like a James Blunt B-side. Initially it seemed to be going nowhere but then suddenly it petered out. It was like a ghost itself. He may have answered my question but I just can't be sure. I might have imagined he answered it, or dreamt it.

In the absence of the car key I asked him if my producer should get engaged. He became very serious: There was a very dramatic pause for effect. 'No,' he said, 'no, I'm sorry, tell her "no".'

She isn't dating or even planning to.

We found my keys under a curtain, bedroom variety as opposed to netherworld.

They'd just been on the dark side for a bit.

Moving to the raw beat of the lesbian witches

17 October 2010

The vegetable man – as in he who sells vegetables – has gone all Lewis Carroll on me. I had thought the day's headline – 'Taxes to rise' – deserved a mention, but when I did, he eyed it derisively and raising his eyes to the beautiful sunny day said cryptically: 'Why assume that's any more real than any of this?' This, from a man who knows his onions, seemed like a fair point.

I tripped lightly from the park resolving not to buy any more papers. As An Emotional Fish once sang: 'That's the trouble with reality, it's taken far too seriously,' and I hadn't really taken reality seriously since the 'incident' on a Something Happens tour in 1995. The one with the lesbian witches.

Ah yes, the lesbian witches! We'd been touring a while, you see, and the distinction between a bit odd and utterly barking had been wearing thin. Boston, where we were playing, was Salem, Massachusetts territory and a support band made up of witches was par for the course. The fact that they were also lesbians made it mildly more original but Boston's *Buy and Sell* magazine was full of second-hand gear from previously failed similar bands. The lesbian witch market was a notoriously competitive one. The dressing room was below the stage, so while they played, and we read poetry and discussed manly things, we couldn't help but hear their set.

Forty minutes in it took on murderous intent. The vocals had given way to insane Apache-like whooping and the onstage dancing seemed to have an American Indian war party quality to it. It felt like the ceiling would soon come in on us. What was happening on stage we wondered?

Our best guess was that it was some kind of Indian massacre. The most likely scenario was that a member of the audience was being burned alive on stage as the band danced around him naked. There were other theories but this seemed the least far fetched. It was time to investigate. It wasn't quite what we'd expected. They had just all gone a bit mad, jumping up and down and running around. You'd find more choreography in a bouncy castle. It was very intense so we stood side stage, sipping beer and trying to share the intensity.

Then we noticed the drummer. She had taken her top off. We gulped beer in unison. We were just the main band come to offer the support act a little morale uplift. We certainly weren't four lads from Dublin come to look at the topless drummer. Topless female drummers were commonplace to us, our demeanour suggested.

She was remarkable. Her torso made Christian Bale look flabby. There literally wasn't an inch of excess flesh and as she flayed that kit into submission we stood enthralled. Nothing north of the border moved an inch, literally nothing!

I handed her a towel as she left the stage. 'Great gig,' I said. 'Thanks, man,' she replied. I've thought about the way she said 'man' ever since. I don't think it was an insult. As she dried herself off the reality/unreality debate ignited briefly in my head. I was going to enquire what sticks she used but thought better of it. Ah, we band of brothers.

✦   ✦   ✦

When did we become so damned good looking?

21 November 2010

'No mud ducks!' we used to say. We were unsure where it came from but it was written on the dressing room door to encourage only models and aspiring soap stars to enter. It must have worked. We were left safely unmolested for our entire time in music. I thought I was finished with that phrase. Until I saw the ladies of PricewaterhouseCoopers!

Keen to be as PC as the next man, I banged the table. 'What kind of narrow-minded, sexist beasts would rate female co-workers on a scale of one to ten,' I cried. 'Oh, those sleazy bean-counters.' I pointed the story out to our accountant, Doreen (an eleven, easily!), and our foreign affairs correspondent, Maureen (a twelve, possibly a thirteen, some days even a fourteen!).

But then the strangest thing about the story struck me: All of the girls in the PwC story were beautiful. Eleven random Irish people, all stunning: what are the chances? There were no exceptions. They were eerily similar in looks, with a whiff of The Stepford Wives about them, but you couldn't argue with the attractiveness. The phrase 'No mud ducks,' just fell from my lips.

The following day, another photo adorned many papers. This time it was the girls, and one boy, of TCD. It was yet another 'Faux Nude Calendar to Raise Funds for Charity'. It too was notable for an absence of mud ducks. There wasn't one amongst them. 'This country is in a mud duck crisis,' I thought, 'and once we had so many.'

And didn't we just. Not many people know this but the 1983 UCD calendar, then simply called 'Semi Naked Hairy Students' was withdrawn due to a lack of same. Only two students could be found that wouldn't frighten the children and the idea of a two-month calendar simply wouldn't wash, much like its subjects. The follow up, 'Hairy Lads in Wool', was also cancelled while 'Hairy Girls in Sweaters' was a surprise hit in Denmark. It was the era of gender uncertainty. The engineer handbook of 1985 gave the class breakdown as 120 male, twenty female (definitely) and sixty students about whose gender the college authorities commented that they 'wouldn't like to say'.

So what's happened? When did Ireland become beautiful? Somewhere along the way, improved diet, foreign travel, changes in the gene pool or exposure to *Beverly Hills 90210* seems to have made us a beautiful race of people. Children born after 1988 would seem to bear no comparison to the misshapen, malnourished and wizen creatures that brought them into this world.

This will have repercussions for those of us born prior to 1980. As the years pass and the new beautiful ones are in the ascendency, 'mud ducks' born before the beauty miracle will become rarer and rarer. People will travel from over the world to see us. We'll be lucky if we aren't exhibited in zoos.

'Look,' the tourists will say, 'you can almost see the famine in their eyes.' I had experience of this once in Davis, California. We played there. The audience were unspeakably beautiful. Young, fit, tanned and toned, they looked at the stage with a mixture of pity and awe. Mostly pity though, which is not a great card to play when trying to seduce someone. Useful in marriage, however.

✦   ✦   ✦

Paul Lynch

Film reviews

2012

15 November 2009

2*012,* the new blockbuster from Roland Emmerich, is something of a disaster. But what else is new? You would think we had enough doomsday already, what with a global economic recession, never mind Hollywood being intent right now on remaking all your favourite 1980s movies. But Emmerich can't help himself. This is the guy who zapped the planet with extra-terrestrials in *Independence Day,* shook us almost to death with *Godzilla*, then fridge-freezered us en masse in *The Day After Tomorrow*. Now he's moving the ground beneath our feet. *2012* begins in 2009 as the sun begins emitting dangerous radiation and picks up in 2012 when the earth's core melts magnificently.

Stuck in the middle of this oncoming cataclysm is a sprawling ensemble cast running for their life. There's Chiwetel Ejiofor's Adrian Helmsley, a level-headed scientist who predicts the disaster. There's Danny Glover as the US president, and he's exactly how you would imagine Obama in three years' time: cranky and crumpled like an old suit. There's Woody Harrelson's quirky turn as prophet of doom Charlie Frost. While centre stage is John Cusack's Jackson Curtis, a crap novelist, limousine driver and ex-husband of Kate (Amanda Peet). His job is not just to save his kids, get rid of the ex-wife's annoying surgeon boyfriend, reunite his nuclear family and somehow get his family to the secret location where the world's governments have built mysterious 'ships' to save an elect few [this is a thinly-disguised recession movie: the world is collapsing, the plutocrats are out to save themselves, good luck if you're an ordinary punter]. But he also has to tread a fine balance between solemn and cheesey.

Emmerich, meanwhile, goes to work with the Easi-Singles like a man making school lunches. Kate's beau (Thomas McCarthy) stands in a supermarket aisle. 'I feel there is something coming between us,' he tells her. There certainly is. A giant crack appears right between them which then tears the supermarket into a canyon. Then we watch a spoof Arnold Schwarzenegger tell California: 'It seems to me that the worst is over.' Thirty seconds later, California pretty much ceases to exist. Giant earthquakes toss the state into the sea, solving in one shake California's spiraling budget deficit. The inhabitants of 2012 are screaming. In the stalls, the audience is screaming laughing.

2012 careers with the campy tone of a 1970s disaster movie. I'm happy to get into the spirit, slurping on its hokum with only the occasional gulp of disbelief – for Emmerich cannot surprise you with his silliness. But for all his earthquakes, neither can he move you. Not once do you get a wobble in the gut, a stir of adrenalin, a rush of feeling for a character. It's mass destruction on a comic-book scale. Worse, whatever direction our hero travels in, the dismantling of the earth follows conveniently just inches behind. All that's left for you to do is figure out who among the film's many Russian characters will be killed off by our disaster-meister. (Answer: pretty much all of them). Our American heroes are never in doubt.

2012 is the kind of disaster movie where everybody has to keep telling you it is the end of the world. Now, you would assume most people who go to feed on this kind of falderal know exactly what they're in for. But Emmerich has absolutely no trust in his audience. Old bums are wheeled out wielding The End Is Nigh slogans. The US president tells us, 'The world as we know it will soon come to an end.' Soon, everybody's mouthing it, with dialogue being delivered on screen as if it were written in bold underline with exclamation marks. ('You need to read this! You need to read this now!!!' says one). All this leads us to believe Emmerich doubts his ability to communicate the importance of what's happening on screen. So he dials in the music on high alert. Or, failing that, he has a character comment on the patently obvious. From an aeroplane, Hawaii looks like a melted Terry's Chocolate Orange. 'Thiz iz not good,' a soon-to-be-killed-off Russian tells us. Really? How so?

I put much of this down to the fact Emmerich believes you won't pick up on his telling details because you're so busy being wowed by his special effects. And the CGI is impressive. On a scale of one to ten, it goes to eleven. Having discarded any interest in human interplay, the Stuttgart native opts for global blitzkrieg. He demolishes Rio de Janeiro's Christ the Redeemer statue. He rolls a decapitated St Peter's Basilica around the screen like it was the Pope's salt shaker. He drops an aircraft carrier onto the White House. He sinks whole cities into the sea. He must have been a terror as a toddler.

You start to wonder, too, what someone like James Cameron could do with this kind of CGI muscle. But the thought is quickly squashed as Emmerich moves whole continents at finger snap. I imagine it was hell in the effects studio:

'I'm afraid, Mr Emmerich, we can't make the global destruction any bigger.'

'Say vhat? It must be bigger!!'

'But Mr Emmerich, the computer is on the brink of a meltdown. And anyway, we've already blown everything up.'

'Vhat! Vhat! But I vhant to blow up ze world again, again!! NOW!'

Running out of things to blow up, Roland Emmerich's next movie will have to be set in outer space.

✦ ✦ ✦

His and Hers

20 July 2010

Here's a film they could have called *Magnolia*. *His and Hers*, Ken Wardrop's multi-ensemble documentary, is shot in ordinary homes around the midlands of Ireland and that damned and drab wall colour is everywhere. It gambols up gables, crouches behind couches, bestrides blandly beside blinds. Then there are the bolder houses. The houses of reckless abandon. There are living-room walls laid out like sick patients slapped in iodine; walls the colour of slippery snot or Saturday night hurl. The houses of the Irish become unexpected characters, lurking behind the heads of Irish mammies who spend much of the film talking about their sons. Listen to the walls exclaiming boldly behind them: you gave birth to us too! We too are your children!

Ken Wardrop is certainly an original. And *His and Hers* is the blossoming of a directorial voice. His first full feature is a formally-conceived documentary beaded together in bite sizes. A parade of seventy or so females, from children to grannies, discuss in beautifully framed, snappy stories the men in their lives. We watch the women. We imagine the men, though never see them. A picture of life emerges.

The film's eighty-minute lifespan grows old with its protagonists. Like that devastating sequence in the Pixar cartoon *Up*, the one that made you and me cry, where the cuddly couple grew old together in a quick series of knotted ties, Wardrop's film is a document of the passing of time. A child crawls through a doorway and another emerges older on the other side. Young faces grow knowing then harden from living. Long hair sneaks up from shoulders until it sits short and eventually grey on shriveling faces. Men die and all we see are their empty chairs. The women live on alone. Some of them have sons for comfort.

Don't expect anybody to say anything mean about anyone. Little girls talk affectionately about annoying daddies. They become young ladies and talk of daddy is soon forgotten. The men in their lives now are their young fellas. The young fellas become their fiancés, their fiancés their husbands, their husbands fathers to their children, these fathers companions in later life when the children leave. Later, they become the ghosts that stalk the house when they die.

A gentle humour and sweetness bubbles throughout. 'I had to give him a tenner to get him to sleep,' says one mammy of her young son. 'I took it back when he fell asleep.' And then there's the mollycoddling mother who tells us that when her smothered boy gets older, 'he's going to mind me'. Let's see how he feels about that in ten years. Males are all kinds of everything: carefree and careless sons; daddies who dink about with footballs, or drill their daughters to drink their milk, or who teach them to drive. There are husbands that cook meticulous curries but leave collateral damage in the kitchen. There's the joker who has built a pond in his garden and hangs a life-ring outside it. And there's the fat man who fancies a younger woman and cheats greedily on his wife. (Sorry, wrong film.)

Where *Up* could move you to tears, Wardrop, you begin to suspect, doesn't want any of that kind of thing at all. 'The small things are the big things,' says one woman, speaking of her dead husband. And Wardrop advances with his eye fixed on the mundane. The just-cleaned-for-the-camera houses reflect a false neatness in the film's form. Stories are just too tidy; every tale is nice. Men are bizarrely trouble-free. The film does its best to insulate us from any of the difficult undercurrents of life that it is the job of the artist to expose and explore. Without those shadings, the film is in danger of being twee.

There is a poignancy, though, that creeps in and it is worn in the frayed faces of the elder aged. This achieves its greatest depth in scenes with Wardrop's own mother – a woman whose entire frame drips with sorrow. We saw her before in Wardrop's terrific first short, *Undressing My Mother*, and perhaps there is a natural advantage, for her story is more keenly felt than all the others.

Wardrop displays a real interest in real people and their stories. But I can't help but feel he is assuming the role less of a documentarian probing real stories, than that of a stereotypical mammy: he wants to see the best in everybody.

The cinematographers, Kate McCullough and Michael Lavelle, overcome a major obstacle: how to make the anodyne architecture of Irish homes interesting. They frame rooms like postcards and create careful symmetry by splitting rooms in half. The camera peeks like a small child through doorways or watches from the Irish mammy's viewpoint of the kitchen window. Their images revel in the familiar. But they create something spiritual out of the mundane.

✦ ✦ ✦

Broken Embraces

30 August 2009

I t would be unfair to say that Penélope Cruz stars in *Broken Embraces*, the great new film from the Spanish master Pedro Almodóvar. Better, perhaps, to say she supernovas her way through it: Cruz emits a white-hot blast of radiation that would outshine a galaxy of other stars. Her eyes glitter with a soul straining under passion. When she parts her mouth, she shows teeth that glisten like fresh water pearls. She wears red velvet high heels that punctuate the screen like exclamation marks; a red dress that would outflame passion. In *Broken Embraces*, Almodóvar shows us why Cruz is the great sensualist actress of our age, capturing her in ways no other director has. He drinks her in deep.

The film is a noir-tinged story about sexual obsession and high passion. And it is also, perhaps, Almodóvar's most ambitious film – something you look upon as you would one of Picasso's Cubist faces, observable from many angles. The centre of the picture is Harry Caine (Lluís Homar), an intriguing blind writer who used to direct films under his real name of Mateo Blanco. And the story veers out in multiple perspectives from there.

Harry, we learn, lost his sight years ago. Or did he? It does look like a fantastic ruse: in one scene, he appears to be looking through the keyhole of a door. And then there is the leggy stunner he seduces after she takes his arm to cross the road: the sex scene that follows is one of gentle amusement – the camera tracks craftily behind the back of a bouncing couch till we get to the woman's painted toenails curling over the top. Mateo seems to know exactly what he is doing.

A bag of cut-up photographs in his drawer suggests he is blind, too, to the past. That is until the past comes looking for him. A knock at his door reveals Ray X (Rubén Ochandiano), a wannabe director who transforms hilariously, when the film takes us back in time, to a super-camp limp-wrist. And the past takes us to Cruz's Lena, who we meet back in 1994 – an upmarket call girl and aspiring actress.

French filmmakers, so in thrall to the love triangle, look like anaemic amateurs beside the love polygon Almodóvar cooks up. Ray X has a dangerous crush on Harry, now called Mateo. Mateo's scowling assistant Judith (Blanca Portillo) clucks over him like a hen and looks at him sidelong with unrequited longing. While Mateo develops a passion for Lena, who lives with her jealous old husband, the powerful businessman Ernesto Martel (José Luis Gómez), a live-action version of Montgomery Burns.

As the entanglements ensue, there is much to savour. There's Almodóvar's playfulness, and the humour that bubbles gently to the surface. There's the warmth he shows to his characters – one scene, on a street that involves Lena's elderly parents, is achingly tender. And then there's Almodóvar's ability, abetted by his long-time composer Alberto Iglesias, to effortlessly switch tones.

Cruz's blazing high heels nod to the films of Douglas Sirk, similar terrain to Almodóvar's high passion and studied female characters. Though unlike the lopsided world of his earlier film *Volver*, Almodóvar has let men into this universe. That red dress screams femme fatale. The music turns smoky. A scene opens with a shot of a pop-art print of a revolver and the camera trains slowly down its barrel as if danger is about to come shooting out of it. There are shades of Hitchcock and classic noir, while duplicity and obsession snake about the shadows. And when Mateo falls for Lena, he's suddenly wearing a blood-red shirt, as if she has spilled on him the hot blood of her love.

There is something very autobiographical in the way Almodóvar explores his passion here for making movies. Certainly this is a celebration of acting and role-playing and of our love affairs with great actresses. In one scene during Mateo's movie, Lena, his lead actress, stands in a kitchen cutting tomatoes, while he whispers directions over her head. The moment is funny because it slices through the artifice of making movies. And yet *Broken Embraces* is all about capturing that unique magic that occurs on screen when a movie really works, with playful nods to Almodóvar's own early work.

Cruz is magisterial, an actress playing an actress. She transforms from office grey to a red ruse. Auditioning for Mateo, she's a wide-eyed Hepburn; a platinum-wigged Monroe. When she has to make love to her ancient husband, she turns grey out of disgust. Then she puts on her make-up and emerges beaming. Mateo sees her as his muse and they make love hungrily. Almodóvar does too. But he makes love to his actress with the camera.

There is always at work here an elegant see-saw between sense and sensibility; raw passion and intellectual rigour. You do feel, though, the film straining under the weight of Almodóvar's desire to make the parts fit and his determination to drive it home. The movie loses its glide but it gains something else – a spirituality, if you will.

You think of a film like Tarantino's *Inglourious Basterds*, so infused with movie love yet riding along on a glossy surface with nothing beneath. Almodóvar's surfaces are beautiful – take the scene where Lena makes love to Ernesto: a whispering sea, crinkling white sheets and their bodies ghosting underneath. Yet beneath those sheets is a woman grappling with momentous decisions. Underneath, too, *Broken Embraces* twists with feelings and ideas about the nature of film-making that can barely be expressed. For dedicated fans of cinema, these are immense pleasures to be had.

✦   ✦   ✦

Wall-E

28 July 2008

Wheeling myself out of the new robot cartoon *Wall-E*, my rusted eyelids re-oiled with glee and my enthusiasm for Hollywood recharged to optimum power, I was struck by a thought: Harrison Ford, Will Smith, Edward Norton, Robert Downey Jr and James McAvoy have been out-classed this summer by a robot that can't even talk, let alone preen, pout or pull a face.

Wall-E is the new animation from those clever clogs at Pixar and it is a film for the ages – a masterwork of visual, almost silent, poetry and a gentle love story between two robots set on earth and in space. It sets out to restore our faith in reckless humans who cause nothing but disaster, but it had the unlikely effect instead of restoring my faith in machines. For *Wall-E* does something not one of Hollywood's live-action blockbusters has done this summer: it moves us. Not that low rumble you feel in your backside from the sonic assault of something blowing up on-screen, but that rare thing nowadays: a tug of the emotions. Those A-listers look like unfeeling androids beside Wall-E, whose eyes are shaped like metal tear-drops and who has but a few metal prongs for hands.

But none of this would come as a surprise to Wall-E. In his world, set in the distant future, humans have long lost the ability to look after their own planet, let alone manufacture heart-rending entertainment. Wall-E (Waste Allocation Load Lifter Earth-Class) is the last robot on earth. He was built 700 years ago as a trash compactor because earth was being consumed by mountains of rubbish. This was before humans gave up on the planet and jetted forever into space. All these years later, he diligently keeps going at his work. For what is a lonely robot supposed to do?

Wall-E has a boxy torso, but is resiliently quick on his tracks, and his wide-spaced eyes are not unlike that other great flat-head of the cinema, E.T. And Wall-E is just as wholesome: he is so unfettered by anything other than a desire to do good, it is impossible not to take him into your heart. Yet if he could talk, instead of beep, he would tell you all he wants is a heap of junk to squash in his chest cavity and for someone to squeeze his little robot heart.

This comes in due time with a white droid called Eve who is sent to earth by space-shipped humans to rummage for plant life. And Wall-E, in the kind of reckless but gallant bravery beknown to love-lorn men throughout the ages, follows her back into space. Their love affair develops in a flurry of electronic beeps and a magical pas de deux in space that involves the use of zero gravity and a fire extinguisher. The moment would make Nijinsky look like he had flat feet.

And amid the techno hair-chase that ensues, one can detect a gentle homage to Kubrick's 2001: A Space Odyssey. But the real nod here is to Charlie Chaplin: were it not for snippets of human talk, Wall-E could be a great silent film. This is not something you see at the movies very much, though recently Paul Thomas Anderson had a masterful and silent fifteen-minute opening sequence to There Will Be Blood. There are few films where you could turn the sound down and understand what is going on: telling a story visually without the crutch of dialogue is the calling card of cinematic greatness. But to do it with robots who cannot talk and have limited facial gestures? Wow.

Director Andrew Stanton, who made *Finding Nemo*, achieves in *Wall-E* something of the pathos of Chaplin's tramp, a hapless yet poetic physicality and that low-slung dignity. How poignant is the sight of this lone robot caterpillaring through the rust and dust of toppled cities, collecting rubbish, which he compacts into giant trash skyscrapers like monuments to mankind's once towering status? Or the sight of him gently rocking himself to sleep?

When he's not building junk cities, he collects human trash, searching them for signs of what made us human: an old bra, an engagement ring, a Rubik's cube. Here is a robot whose curiosity unknowingly keeps alive the last vestiges of humanity. He watches a clip from an aged VCR recording of the 1969 musical *Hello, Dolly!* and Wall-E learns something that can't be learned from the detritus of human objects – what it is to touch another person, what it is to feel. He sees how humans used to love one another and Stanton later uses this to stunning effect.

The director of *Wall-E* insists he had nothing in mind other than a love story. I wonder who he's trying to kid? The lives of his space-trapped humans are controlled by a dystopian corporation. They are fat and indolent: space has crippled them with bone-loss; and they are only able to travel strapped into hovering armchairs with mini TVs wired inches from their face. Watching this it is hard not to think of the present, when *Wall-E* is more likely to be watched on micro-screen iPods, or at home on TV, with the complete loss of awe and scale you can only find in the cinema. And underneath all the whizz and bop of a future imagined is the tone of an elegy: that we are destroying our planet and destroying ourselves.

With their previous film *Ratatouille*, Pixar set the bar very high. Here, they take the limitations of the family animation and launch them into space. In 700 years' time, when the remnants of our culture are being excavated and studied by historians for clues as to what we were like, I hope a little piece of *Wall-E* survives.

✦ ✦ ✦

EITHNE TYNAN

Radio reviews

Nautical nitwits

Fianna Fáil set sail for the high seas of absurdity.

23 January 2011

The 'Not a Heave in the Classic Sense' tour rolled into town last week, and what a blast it was for Heave Heads. There were bootlegs, T-shirts and dancing bears, and you were never more than five minutes away from a radio interview with group leader Micheál Garcia Martin.

The tour was tugging a parade of metaphors behind it (to which I've just added another. Curses). Best of all was the one from finance minister Brian Lenihan, who described himself on the *News at One* as being too busy in the 'engine room' to have time to think about a coup.

So you've got the finance minister as black-faced urchin, shovelling coal below decks ('More steam please, Mr Lenihan!'). You've got Brian Cowen in the wheelhouse, loaded to the gunwales, singing, 'If you'll give me some grog, I'll sing you a song. Way, Hey, Blow the Man Down.' The Greens are on the poop deck as usual, talking about where best to position their solitary deckchair (aka the Climate Change Bill). That leaves only one actor to play Roger the Cabin Boy, so it has to be Micheál Martin.

Martin did so many radio interviews on Monday that listeners will have begun to suspect cloning. After all, it wouldn't have been that hard to get a clone to do some of these interviews. You just programme it to say 'not a heave in the classic sense' and 'fire in the belly' over and over. On Newstalk's *Breakfast*, he introduced a few inept metaphors, but none of them stuck, certainly not once they had been outdone by the vastly superior Captain Pugwash series. He could have 'walked off the pitch', he said. There was talk of 'sacrificial lambs' and the usual economic 'tsunami' stuff. At one point Ivan Yates even went so far as to liken the Taoiseach to 'a pinball'. But in the end all parties pulled themselves together and settled on a nautical course.

Lamenting the fact that Brian Cowen had been more reactive than proactive, Martin said 'there comes a time when you have to push the boat out and be commanding the air space'. Shiver me timbers, tis not a ship at all, tis a seaplane. No wonder they can't agree.

Later in the morning, Martin appeared on *The Tubridy Show* (2FM). Some of his colleagues may have been wondering why he bothered, with one TD quoted in the *Irish Times* as saying that not many Fianna Fáil deputies listen to *The Tubridy Show*, but Martin would probably find that hard to believe, considering how many Fianna Fáil TDs are on Ryan Tubridy's Christmas card list.

Tubridy advised Micheál Martin to resign if Brian Cowen won the confidence motion. 'I think it's untenable for you to remain in cabinet with no confidence in the Taoiseach,' he counselled. Give it a rest, Tubridy, will you? Avast!

Then, weirdly, he began asking Martin about the death of his daughter, a line of questioning that seemed ill-timed, unreasonable, even cruel. Soon we saw the reason for it.

'I was wondering, as a father myself, how you would pick yourself up after that. Because I know that I wouldn't ... I would have to disappear, probably for a long time,' said Tubridy, relishing the chance to talk about Tubridy.

Micheál Martin said he didn't think the questions were appropriate but offered to talk about it another time. He was very gracious about it. I'd have keel-hauled Tubridy, the scurvy son of a biscuit-eater.

Then, on Tuesday's *News at One*, Brian Lenihan was accused of having spotted the iceberg long ago. Various backbenchers had seen the finance minister snooping around amid ships with a spyglass, despite his protestations about being in the engine room the whole time.

'I'm certainly getting plenty of muck on my hands but it's very important that I work in that engine room,' said Lenihan. His first duty is to the country, etc etc. Under no circumstances should personal ambition prevail over the interests of the country and so on. I tell you, sanctimonious wasn't in it with him: Master Bates promotes his mission of self-love.

✦   ✦   ✦

It's easy like Sunday morning, only at rush hour

8 March 2009

'On this drivetime show, we not only give you talk, we give you music,' announced Tom McGurk on his first programme for 4FM. Now whose idea was that, I wonder? The people behind 4FM, the new multi-city radio station aimed at older listeners, must never listen to the radio themselves if they honestly think there isn't enough Tina Turner on it already. They also clearly believe there's a vast 'demographic' of listeners who like nothing better than a bit of Elton John in the middle of a serious interview. Presumably these listeners also ask for a side of ice-cream with their salmon or beef, and draw little cartoons in the margins of their tax returns.

There are some serious things that can reasonably be interrupted by music – funeral masses come to mind – but current affairs is not one of them. RTÉ tried the same thing years ago on *Tonight with Vincent Browne* (a minute's silence please) and it was just as idiotic as it sounds. Browne would break off from filleting some petrified public servant for a recording of *Kathleen Mavourneen*, and no-one knew where they were.

At any rate, McGurk's musical interludes, combined with his own softly-softly approach, meant that his interview on Monday with Taoiseach Brian Cowen was more like *Desert Island Discs* than *Drivetime*. Think Sunday morning instead of rush hour.

In case you've been finding lately, reader, that you're getting just a teensy-weensy bit sick of the sight and sound of Brian Cowen and the rest of the whole godforsaken lot of them, we won't retrace the whole interview here. But there were one or two highlights worth revisiting for comedy's sake (since laughter, unlike music, is entirely acceptable in the midst of current affairs).

McGurk thanked the Taoiseach for coming in, and squeezed in a plug, speculating that Cowen's presence was a signal that he wanted 'to recognise that 4FM, despite all the economic devastation, is up there and is going to succeed'.

The Taoiseach responded with the following stream of conscious-ness, as if bent on forging, in the smithy of his soul, the uncreated conscience of his race: 'I think it's a great indication of just the sort of people, the can-do attitude that we need in this country to be honest, and the faith that people have in the project and the concept that they've devised and that they've worked on ... if I may say so a very strong presentation team which shows I think a great degree of confidence in the professionalism of those who have, uh, worked so hard to bring this day about.'

Cowen also used his new favourite quote, lambasting those com-mentators who say the economy was never anything more than 'a building site with a flagpole on top'. Love that. He'll never get rid of that one now.

McGurk wanted to know if the Taoiseach was hurt by the accusa-tion that he had lost his leadership. He also asked if he was being kept awake. I'm not joking. 'Are you sleeping well? Do you sleep well?' he inquired, much as you might ask a feeble relative in hospi-tal. (Mind you, if you are visiting someone in hospital, it's more ger-mane to ask: 'Have you seen anyone yet who is in any way remotely connected, even if only by marriage, to your consultant?')

For the record, Cowen was not hurt, and is sleeping, but he sud-denly went all surfer dude on us. 'A lot of politics is about psychol-ogy,' he said. 'People have to get their heads to where we're actually at.' Like, far out, totally. The Cowenmeister. El Cowenerino.

Even some DJs have been getting away from playing music these days, on the grounds that audiences seem to prefer giddy chat to exhausted hits. Witness Tom Dunne, erstwhile host of one of the few respectable music programmes on mainstream radio, and now host of yet another brainless forum for listeners' texts.

Having said that, last Tuesday your correspondent became new all-time bestest friends with Tom Dunne, after listening to his feisty defence of air travel, and of cars. After all, this green hegemony is all very well, but it can only go so far, and you can keep your sanctimonious hands off my Alfa.

Dunne was interviewing Alex Hochuli, founder of Modern Movement, an organisation set up recently to counter the arguments (mostly environmental) against aviation. It's high time, before taxation boots us all out of the sky and the rich have it to themselves again.

Predictably enough, the interview was followed by a stream of texts, with one listener asking won't someone please think of the children. Dunne replied that he is thinking of the children, that he wants his children to inherit a planet they can fly around in. Air high five.

✦ ✦ ✦

Flaws of science: bang goes RTÉ's interest in physics

14 September 2008

It was billed as Big Bang Day, and turned out to be Tiny Blip Day. However, we did learn something from the CERN experiment, and that is that physicists are a different species altogether. Delayed gratification isn't in it with them.

Consider that famous experiment at Stanford, when a group of four-year-olds were given a marshmallow and told they could have another one if they waited twenty minutes before eating the first. Those four-year-olds who ate the marshmallow at once, reasoning with a pragmatism beyond their years that they might be dead in twenty minutes, would never have become CERN physicists.

Four-year-old future physicists would exchange their marshmallow for a giant doughnut and instead of eating it they would conduct invisible experiments on it, and cry with happiness when the results were displayed for a fraction of a second on a computer screen.

Morning Ireland spoke with Leo Enright just before the event, and he was as excited as usual. But even though we've come to expect Leo Enright to be right there at the nucleus of any scientific event, he wasn't in Switzerland but in Dublin. 'I'm at the science gallery at

Trinity College,' he said, and then went on to satisfy the two main preoccupations of the national broadcaster: first, does the story have an Irish connection?; second, is there any way to link it to the M50?

'Ireland has a very, very strong history of involvement in particle physics,' Enright declared. 'You'll remember, of course, that it was an Irishman who split the atom – the wonderful, wonderful Ernest Walton.' And we all stood taller and hummed a bar of *A Nation Once Again*.

Cathal Mac Coille wanted to know when things were going to get interesting. He may have had his suspicions already about the pace at which things get interesting in physics. 'It's already interesting,' said Enright. That was when he brought in the M50, to give us something to relate to, don't you know.

'If you put 500 cars at one end of the M50 and 500 cars at the other end and collided them at the toll bridge in Lucan, at 100 km/h, the energy released would be roughly the same as the energy that's going to be released by these tiny bunches of protons colliding with another,' said Enright. Mac Coille may have mused that it would take a lot less than thirty years and €6 billion to crash 1,000 cars on the M50, and it would make a better story for *Morning Ireland*.

Meanwhile, Andrew Marr was in the CERN control room for the BBC World Service, all set to report live on the big moment. 'We're still waiting,' he said. Then he said, 'Here we go.' Then he said, 'Here we go again.' Then he was advised it would be another forty-eight seconds, which he struggled valiantly to fill, and at last the tiny blip happened.

'Yes!' exclaimed Marr. 'Yes, they've done it! That is a relief. A wonderful moment to see that flash on the screen.'

I suppose he couldn't help being swept along by the thing. Cathal Mac Coille wasn't, though. Back in the *Morning Ireland* studio, having played a clip of the blip, he was persisting with the question as to when exactly this will get interesting.

'It's absolutely thrilling,' Ronan McNulty of UCD told him, 'but it's going to be a while before enough data comes out of that, before we can actually say something. It's not like the moon launch where you go ten, nine, eight and off we go.'

So that's it then. Sit tight. Have a marshmallow.

Who does Joe Duffy think he is ... Bertie Ahern?

28 September 2008

I t's been a strenuous week down here in The Country. There was the bungalow to be repainted, the cow dung to be scraped off the generic family saloon and six cakes of brown soda to be baked in preparation for the Dubliners' visit.

Practically every radio programme vacated the capital this week and visited the National Ploughing Championships, the better to patronise rural-dwellers at close range.

Once outside Dublin, they found there was little to talk about. On Monday's *Mooney Show*, Brenda O'Donoghue invited the nation to consider whether or not she should leave her wellies at home for the trip. This was a lucky intervention by O'Donoghue, as we had grown weary of our four usual concerns – the weather, tractors, the old days and the recession – and needed something else to think about. Bless her.

The following day, she was good enough to remind us of this national dilemma. 'First of all, Derek,' she roared, causing the walls of the RTÉ tent to flap alarmingly despite the lack of a breeze, 'I asked the question yesterday on the show, should I ditch the wellies? And I have! I've no wellies on!'

One listener tried to spark up interest in the price of combine harvesters. A bystander informed us they cost about €180,000. Everyone was quietly aghast that farmers have that much money but no one would say it so far from Montrose. *Farm Week*'s Damien O'Reilly exclaimed that there are tractors that cost a quarter of a million.

'They have everything in them, Derek,' he said.

'Like what, Damien?,' asked Mooney.

O'Reilly paused for a moment. 'Air conditioning, the whole lot ... CD players,' he said.

Possibly the only thing more boring than a live broadcast from the Ploughing Championships is other people's family history. And have you noticed that people who say they're interested in genealogy only ever want to talk about their ancestors? They don't give a toss about yours. To borrow from another axiom, genealogy is like farts: you can just about stand your own.

Nevertheless, *The Tubridy Show* made a big deal out of the family history of *Liveline*'s Joe Duffy on Monday, as he was to be featured in the TV programme *Who Do You Think You Are?* that evening.

Before we could get on to the enthralling subject of Duffy's great-grandpappy, though, we had to wait for him to get to the end of a sermon that was heavy with bitterness. Seemingly the programme's title had touched a nerve.

'I grew up with that and I still get it. I got it yesterday in the papers, didn't I? Who the eff do you think you are? In Dublin that phrase has a completely different connotation. And it's about not losing the run of yourself, and don't become hubristic and don't start believing what you do is as important as a nurse or a doctor or a fire-man or a teacher.'

Were any other listeners trying to identify whom Duffy sounded like at that moment? The chip on the shoulder, the sullen resent-ment, the stagy common sense … Didn't he remind you of Bertie Ahern?

For a man who doesn't believe in 'losing the run of yourself', though, Duffy can't seem to keep a sentence in check. Asked by Tubridy if he had got a sense of closure as a result of the programme, Duffy said he believed there were other stories unpicked from the family tree, and went on as follows:

'I keep telling my own three – they're thirteen – I keep telling them, my granny, who they knew, they knew, because she only died recently and they had sat with her and gone to see her … She lived in Kilbarrack, in the flats in Kilbarrack, she lived on the fifth floor in a fourteen-storey block and the reason she lived on the fifth floor to the time she died was she had a son who she looked after and she wanted a bigger flat and she wouldn't live in the senior citizen's flat.

'She used to get the Dart into town every Thursday to collect her pension in the GPO and do the shopping in Roches when Roches was Roches, Ryan. That same granny, who my children knew, I saw in the 1960s in a place in Dublin called Keogh Square, which was the Richmond Barracks, 1916, and is now St Michael's Estate …

'I saw her in the 1960s cooking on an open fire in a room with no sanitation, no running water, no heat, no electricity, and our novelty was, Ryan, to go down and do toast on a fork on an open fire.'

All that yakking for a yarn about toast. He should have been a sports commentator.

✦ ✦ ✦

Patrick Freyne

TV reviews

Clown jewels

Bill Cullen embarks on his annual search for Ireland's greatest sycophant.

26 September 2010

If I was producing TV3's *The Apprentice*, each episode would start with a darkened boardroom and an empty spotlight into which 'local boy made good' Bill Cullen would step. 'But where are the clowns?' he'd croon, staring into the camera with his big sad eyes. 'There ought to be clowns,' he'd tunefully assert (Stephen Sondheim's melody adding force to his insatiable desire for clowns). Then the camera would cut to the reception lobby with the pretend secretary and her not-really-plugged-in laptop. 'Quick, send in the clowns ...' Bill would plead desperately through the intercom. 'Don't worry,' the secretary would sing back. 'They're aaallreaaaady heeeeere ...' before turning to this year's apprentices to say, 'Mr Cullen will see you now.'

The appeal of *The Apprentice* is not that it offers an insight into the inner workings of corporate Ireland, but that it is, in fact, a Clown College filled with clown people. Its alumni do not end up working for Goldman Sachs or KPMG, they end up on *Celebrity Salon* or volunteering for medical experiments or selling their underwear on eBay.

The other giveaway is the fact it happens each year. Any jobseeker with a survival instinct would ask: why does Bill need so many apprentices? Obi Wan Kenobi just had the one. What is Bill doing with them? Well, I suspect they end up like childhood pets that Bill forgets to feed. Each new season starts with his other half Jackie

Lavin finding last year's winner stiff as a board under the couch, floating listlessly at the top of Bill's aquarium, or completely vanished save for some bloody fur left in a neglected hutch ('We need to go again,' mutters Jackie down the phone to TV3. 'We think a fox got the last one').

And so this year's specimens gathered like puppies at the pound – the girls all business suits and wasp-chewing scowls and the boys all faux-masculinity, aftershave you can smell through the television, and heavily-greased hair (as the series progresses and Bill's megalomania grows, I assume he'll try sticking them to the ceiling). Bill begins with some cautionary praise. 'What you sixteen have accomplished is no mean feat,' he says. 'You beat off 16,000 other applicants to prove you were the best business brains in Ireland.' (Now, there's an accidentally rude double entendre there which I won't spell out, but if it's true, then it really was a pretty gruelling application process.) Then he sends them off to pick team leaders and to think up team names.

'I was thinking of Team Synergy,' says one lady. 'That sounds like a makey-up word to me,' says another. In the end, the girls' team pick 'Fusion' which also sounds like a makey-up word but isn't. And the boys pick 'Elev8' 'because there's eight of us', forgetting that next week they may have to call themselves 'Elev7'.

Bill seems impressed by the team names, but then decides to shake things up by telling the leader of the boys, Cathal, that he must lead the girls' team, and the leader of the girls, Ciara, that she must head up the boys. 'So Team Elev8 and Team Fusion ... we now have some confusion,' says Bill and the apprentices laugh so hard at this joke I think the whole series might end there and then with Bill saying: 'Congratulations, Apprentices, you have passed the real test. You have all successfully climbed up my arse ... which is paradise and where you may live for eternity.'

But he doesn't. Instead he sends them out to bother/sell-hotel-vouchers-to the general public. As they do so, we're slowly given insights into their lives. 'I think I've been through more at twenty-seven than the other candidates,' muses Ciaran 'Flipper' Walsh, referring, I presume, to his former career as a crime-fighting dolphin. In fact, he's talking about his former career as a professional poker player which he reasonably worries will make people think he's 'a risk-taker and a gambler' (he's literally both!). Team leader Cathal Heapes reveals that, 'I work best in short sharp bursts' which is just as well really, as Bill sends him packing after just one episode. For the most part, while they were all entertainingly ineffectual, none of them had the star quality of last year's breakthrough apprentice, the noble savage Breffny Morgan. While that will probably change in the coming weeks, right now the apprentices are an undifferentiated mass of young people in suits.

Which is also a good description of the front bench of Fine Gael, whose spiritual founder, Michael Collins, was being advocated as *Ireland's Greatest Person* on RTÉ. This was part one of a five-part RTÉ documentary series about the five greatest Irish people, as discerned by an exhaustive poll. Over the coming weeks, luminaries will make the case for Bono, John Hume, James Connolly and Mary Robinson, before RTÉ reveals once and for all who Ireland's greatest is after collating the results of a phone vote.

Now, the notion that you can decide who is the best between Michael Collins and Bono is pretty dubious. That said, it would be fun if it was done right, with Bono, Michael Collins, Mary Robinson, John Hume and James Connolly all competing in Apprentice-style challenges. ('While Michael Collins wasn't great in the writing-and-recording-a-pop-song round, Bono was surprisingly good in the assassinating-members-of-the-British-security-forces round,' I imagine writing in my parallel-universe review). Unfortunately, this isn't an option, and instead we are treated to a straightforward hagiography of Collins from former PD (and even more former Fine Gaeler) Michael McDowell, who, like many before him, has managed to pinpoint the exact moment in history when it became wrong to pursue political ideals by way of terrorist acts (11 July, 1921).

Stylistically it had many of the hyperactive camera effects and strange soundtrack choices (the theme from *Pulp Fiction* was played over a GAA match) that mark much Irish documentary-making, and filming was clearly arranged to coincide with a city break to London (why film McDowell up the London Eye?). There was also the sense that always exists when a politician praises a historical politician, that we were being invited to hear an implied 'like meself' at the end of every sentence: 'Collins was a pragmatist who did whatever Ireland needed whenever it needed it ... (like meself).' 'Collins was covert and calculated, ruthless and efficient ... (like meself).' 'Collins had a price on his head and was on the run ... (like meself!)'

Political hero worship was also the subject of BBC's *The Special Relationship*, which documented the friendship between Bill Clinton (Dennis Quaid) and Tony Blair (Michael Sheen). All other events and relationships were rendered as secondary, as their connection was framed through election campaigns, political scandals (the Lewinsky affair) and humanitarian crises (Kosovo). It was silly.

There was actually footage of Clinton and Blair looking longingly at one another through windows and furtively whispering down the phone line to one another as their wives slept. 'Kiss him, you fool!' I yelled, but the sizzling premier-on-premier action I anticipated never happened.

Still, as a Hays-code-era romantic comedy about a long-distance power couple it worked pretty well. As a compelling drama about political power, however, it failed.

✦   ✦   ✦

America Idle

28 March 2010

G ive me your tired, your poor, your huddled masses yearning to breathe free, and soon I'll have their beer-buzzed, thong-wearing descendants dry-humping one another in a hot-tub on MTV. It's the American dream. It's the better life that tubercular soot-stained Italian immigrants dreamt for their children, as they coughed consumptively, anglicised their names, and prepared to work their fingers to the bone all those years ago. Indeed, I'm pretty sure these brave souls are now in heaven saluting the flag as the remnants of their DNA lap-dance, fist-pump, binge drink and get vomit in their hair-extensions.

Jersey Shore is a fly-on-the-wall reality programme about eight self-identified Italian-American Guidos and Guidettes (this is, apparently, an ethnic slur turned badge-of-honour) living and working together for a summer on the eponymous beach-front party location. It's a world of orange tans, gelled hair, fake breasts, obsessive body building, and self-conscious, brand-aware nicknaming ('I'm known around town as Sammi Sweetheart,' says Sammi Sweetheart, which I interpreted to mean: 'I go around town asking people to call me Sammi Sweetheart because I really want people to call me Sammi Sweetheart.'). Apart from Sammi Sweetheart, there's also J-Wow, Snookie, Pauly D and most impressively, The Situation (there's also Vinnie, Ronnie and Valerie, but they've got boring normal names).

So why is The Situation called The Situation? 'Because of that situation down there,' he says, proudly pointing to his seriously overworked ab muscles. He looks really pleased with himself so the camera crew have to stop themselves from yelling: 'Good lord, man, what have you done to yourself?!' The Situation's abs look like cross-dimensional chaos creatures from a HP Lovecraft horror story, or, as my wife so delightfully put it, a stomach full of tumours. It's not wise to stare directly at The Situation's abs. It's like staring at the sun.

The Situation talks about himself in the third person a lot, like the Incredible Hulk, the Queen or a toddler. 'I hope they're ready for The Situation,' says The Situation. 'The Situation is anxious to get down to *Jersey Shore* with his hot clothes and his tan!' says The Situation. 'The Situation smash puny soldiers! The Situation once owned India! The Situation done a poo-poo!' says The Situation.

Soon enough he's chest-bumping happily and flirting with the seven other bad decision-makers at Jersey Shore, a place which seems to be the mythical spawning ground for a certain type of Italian-American stereotype ('Take your shirt off at Jersey Shore and the girls come to you like a fly comes to shit,' explains muscle-bound Ronnie, cunningly demonstrating both cockiness and low-self-esteem in one sentence).

Like salmon, it seems that the guidos of Jersey Shore are merely migrating in order to mate. It's this realisation that makes me see within *Jersey Shore* the beauty of nature and God's creation (Pauly D's gelled hair, is in this context, magnificent plumage). This sense was heightened for me because I'd watched RTÉ's new (and fascinating) nature programme *Wild Journeys* earlier that same evening. So when The Situation, Pauly D and Vinnie lured three passing ladeez into their hot tub (an essential reality television show prop if nudity is one of your 'themes'), I could still hear the rich voice of *Wild Journeys'* narrator Ruth McCabe saying, 'The males are bursting with excitement! They are competing for access to the spawning grounds (i.e. the Hot Tub) ... areas of clean even gravel washed by fast-flowing well-oxygenated water.' Okay, the bit about gravel doesn't quite make sense; McCabe was talking about salmon. But elsewhere the parallels were also striking.

'Territorial disputes break out all along the river,' says McCabe of salmon on *Wild Journeys*. 'Don't be bringing trashy skanks into my house!' shrieks Valerie on *Jersey Shore* ('Whorebags!' she says for good measure).

'Swimming alongside the female, the dominant male repeatedly woos her with a shimmering dance,' says McCabe on *Wild Journeys*. 'Don't hate the playa, hate the game!' says The Situation to Sammi Sweetheart on *Jersey Shore* while doing a shimmering dance. 'Certainly there wasn't a researcher in the boat who'd seen anything like it!' said Pádraig Whooley on *Wild Journeys*, and although he was talking about something else entirely, I had to agree.

Obviously I hope the parallels between *Jersey Shore* and *Wild Journeys* end there. Salmon travel all the way from Greenland to a stream in the Connemara hills in order to mate and then die. If *Jersey Shore* ends with eight post-coital figures bobbing face-down in the New Jersey water, I'm pretty sure there will be lawsuits. That said, I couldn't promise that it's not going to happen.

On *Cougar Town* someone else could be found injuring herself in an act of love. Jules Cobb (Courteney Cox) is the recently-divorced mother and career woman who has spent her youth being responsible and now wants to party and seduce handsome young men, but, as she discovers in episode two, she's not as flexible as she once was. *Cougar Town* comes with a lot of cultural baggage. Firstly, it's a television vehicle for an ex-*Friends* actor, and so might as well have been built in the Harland & Wolff shipyard circa 1912, so doomed is its voyage. *Joey, Studio 60 on the Sunset Strip, Dirt* – they've all long hit their ratings iceberg. And secondly, the whole media-created notion of the 'cougar' (sexually aggressive older ladies) is really, really annoying, and leads desperate feature writers to write silly, silly articles reducing complex human experiences to farce.

Apparently there was once only two kinds of lady (virgins and whores) and then thanks to *Sex and the City*, there were four kinds of lady (Carries, Samanthas, Mirandas and Charlottes), and now fresh off the production line we have a new kind of lady ... the Cougar. 'Thank God for that!' says you. Having to be one of only four kinds of lady was a terrible amount of pressure for the type of person who needs to be told what type of person they are by television programmes and magazine articles. Having five types to choose from is such an improvement!

Thankfully *Cougar Town* is better and more nuanced than this worldview and its own silly title suggests. It has a good ensemble cast, some original characters (Jules's ne'er-do-well, alimony-seeking ex-husband Bobby is a stand-out), and the type of spiralling in-jokes pioneered by more genre-expanding shows like *30 Rock* and *Scrubs* (*Scrubs*, like this, was also created by Bill Lawrence). Just remember, Courteney Cox isn't representing all single women over the age of forty, nor does she embody a real-life sociological trend. She's playing a character in a television comedy. It's not real. You can tell it's not real because attractive Courteney Cox finds it difficult to attract men, and her character, despite working in the property business, isn't living under a bridge eating rats.

The Situation from *Jersey Shore*, on the other hand, he is real. He should be the spur for a barrage of speculative feature articles. Here's a start: 'The Situation – he represents all men between the ages of twenty-five and forty, he's a lover and a fighter, his stomach looks like a back-road in Cavan, and once he has deposited his milt in a gravelly egg-filled inlet, he will return to the sea to die.'

✦   ✦   ✦

Dolly the Sheep would be more baaaaad ass

12 April 2009

In new cod-science-fiction cop-show drama *Eleventh Hour*, evil illegal cloners discard some human embryos, and top science guy and smouldering hunk Dr Jacob Hood (Rufus Sewell) asks a silly policeman who has questioned his authority, 'Have you heard of Dolly the Sheep?' and I find myself really hoping that the next sentence out of his mouth is going to be '... for she is my sidekick and she will kick your ass!' Instead he goes on to give us an idiot's guide to cloning.

I can't help feeling cheated. A programme about Rufus Sewell and Dolly the Sheep fighting science crime would have been awesome, automatically suggesting several amazing scenes and plots. 'How are you going to stop me, Dolly?' gurns the evil scientist in an evil voice in my evil imagination. 'You are but a humble sheep. Aaagh! Stop eating me! I'm not grass!'

Instead Sewell's sidekick is a generic sexy FBI ice maiden who knows kung fu and is annoyed by, yet attracted to, his eccentricities. 'He's a brilliant biophysicist but he spends most of his time in his head, so I have to watch his back,' she says, and I can't help thinking this sentence would have sounded much better coming from Dolly (although she'd have said, 'I have to watch his baaaaaack').

Anyway, *Eleventh Hour* is a Jerry Bruckheimer remake of an English television programme of the same name, and it's also very similar to *Fringe*, another US export in which a sexy blonde FBI agent helps out a mad old genius. Like *Fringe, Eleventh Hour* is built on the assumption that science is weird and scary and thus needs to be policed by special operatives investigating 'science crimes'.

You see, all that technology they used to make the programme – the cameras, the microphones, the trucks – these all arose naturally out of 'nature' and have nothing to do with 'science' at all. The lights, for example, were simply plucked by the crew from lighting rig trees, much as our hunter-gatherer ancestors might have done, and Rufus Sewell was carried from England to America, not by science-plane, but in Jerry Bruckheimer's jaws, much as a bear might have done with a fish. No, for the purposes of this show, 'science' means big, scary stuff like cloning and nuclear weaponry and 'flu pandemics, and it always involves someone 'trying to play God', a phrase I spent the whole programme waiting for, and which was eventually uttered in the last fifteen minutes as Sewell played mid-wife to a mutant clone and evil Dr Geppetto (that was her name!) made a getaway. Since when was 'playing God' a bad thing anyway? Surely it's only a problem if the answer to the question 'what would Jesus do?' is 'try to illegally clone mutant foetuses'? (Oh hold on, he does that in Mark 3:17).

There's also some stuff in the bible about forgiveness, and this was the subject of *Five Minutes of Heaven*, a drama based on the real-life experiences of Joe Griffin (James Nesbitt), a Lurgan-born Catholic whose life has been changed by witnessing the horrific murder of his brother years ago, and Alastair Little (Liam Neeson), the UVF man who murdered him. And it made for some powerful viewing.

After a documentary-like re-enactment of the crime, it's decades later and a panic-stricken Griffin is going to meet Little for the first time since the murder, for a fictional television programme called *One-to-One*. Nesbitt's wonderfully edgy and frantic performance is counterpointed by the unctuous film crew, and by Neeson's own calm self-possession as the former terrorist who has made a life for himself travelling the world and talking about his experiences. Nesbitt has spent his life being blamed by his mother for his broth-er's death, and delivers rambling, heartbreaking and funny mono-logues to whoever is there to hear them. ('Here you are, pal, a fully signed-up member of the celebrity circuit of life's victims: men in love with donkeys, twins stuck together by their bollocks, elephant women who can't get out of their chairs ... and now you.')

The script (by Guy Hibbert) takes a few hard, well-aimed kicks at the reconciliation industry, the sensation-hungry media, and the mealy-mouthed words of some former terrorists. Neeson's per-formance is also fascinating. There's a great trick played by the scriptwriter, in which Little's seemingly sincere recollection of the murder is chillingly undermined by his own rehearsed repetition of the same words later on. As the film progresses, however, it's clear that he's a man who finds it hard to tell his own guilt from the

eloquent words he's used to express it, and that he needs the meeting with Griffin more than Griffin does.

The problem is, once these dynamics are established, the drama
sort of fizzles out. After a potentially murderous Griffin backs out
of their initial encounter, Little spends the rest of the film trying to
re-engineer a meeting, and it begins to look a bit like this is going
to be, like *Waiting for Godot*, the play in which nothing happens
... twice. Of course, this is television, so instead of nothing happening, the second act climaxes with Griffin and Little smashing
through a second-floor window into a broken-boned embrace on
the footpath below. Which was daft, and whatever it was meant to
symbolise, it just undermined two exceptional performances from
Neeson and Nesbitt, and what had been, until then, a nuanced
drama about how traumatic events and complex emotions can't be
resolved and repackaged into media-friendly sound-bites.

Media-friendly sound-bites are exactly what *Yes We Can! The
Lost Art of Oratory* was all about, despite a lot of claims to the
contrary. The premise was that Barack Obama had brought oratory
back to political discourse, and so Alan Yentob led a pool of aca-
demics, politicians, spin doctors and authors (including the crank-
ily brilliant Gore Vidal) in analysing the history of public speaking
and critiquing what made great speeches so great. It was a 'greatest hits' nostalgia show in which the usual suspects (Winston
Churchill, FDR, Martin Luther King) were all dragged out to stir
the souls, amid some incoherent theorising about the importance
of oratory and a well-modulated voice.

The programme was really about how Alan Yentob finds Barack
Obama 'dreamy', so he didn't even notice how it didn't have a core
argument, and reduced famous speeches to the sound-bites he
claims to distrust ('I have a dream'; 'ask not what your country can
do for you'; 'we will fight them on the beaches'; 'you do the shake
and vac').

Furthermore, Yentob didn't seem particularly worried by the
more troubling side of oratory unearthed in his own programme:
that some classical scholars thought it was a form of dishonest
subterfuge; that a well-crafted speech from Tony Blair tipped his
country into an unnecessary war; or that the insidious oratory of

Adolf Hitler had horrific consequences. No, these things were no match for the fact that Yentob thinks Barack is just brilliant. So the official message of *Yes We Can!* was: 'words are great!', but this was undermined by plenty of evidence that words were cheap, and that Obama's oratorical skills could eventually prove to be as relevant as Brian Cowen's singing voice. In fact, I'd say it's possible to work out how important oratory is to good governance statistically. But I won't, because statistics are a form of science, and as I've learned from *Eleventh Hour*, using science would make me some sort of witch.

✦　✦　✦

Don't check in to RTÉ's lousy no-star hotel

10 August 2008

Panic spreads quickly through the RTÉ canteen. 'They're coming! They're coming!' shrieks Dave Fanning as he pushes and shoves Marian Finucane out of his way and starts a terrified stampede for the door.

'Oh my God! Oh my God!' wails a hyperventilating Kathryn Thomas, standing on the hands of a collapsed Ryan Tubridy, who's groaning a decade of the rosary in a heap with Myles Dungan and Maxi.

'AAAAIGH!' yells Caroline Morahan as she knocks Anne Doyle out of her escape path and bites a piece off Aonghus McAnally's ear.

Then. Suddenly. There's silence. Not a bird can be heard. The air is sucked from the room. Philip Boucher Hayes turns, opens his mouth as if to speak, but simply points to a distant hill. The RTÉ board members have appeared on horseback, in full body armour, silhouetted in the evening sun.

The presenters begin screaming and yelling again.

But the board-members are silent, steely-eyed and carrying nets. They look to their leader for a signal. Cathal Goan, director general of RTÉ, sits straight-backed on his horse. His face is a grim death mask. Almost imperceptibly he nods. Then with a horrific war-cry the entire board of RTÉ ride down into the canteen. Horses snorting, their nets aloft. It's like a scene from *Planet of the Apes* as they cut through the terrified presenters. When the dust settles, two figures are slumped in the nets. The director general raises his right hand. It is enough. It has been a good hunt.

And that, no doubt, is how RTÉ got otherwise dignified people like radio person John Creedon and weather-lady Evelyn Cusack to be on *Fáilte Towers*, a reality TV show in which bottom-rung celebrities try to run a hotel for a couple of weeks.

As for the other 'famous people' on display – glamour model Claire Tully, Eurovision losers Donna and Joe (for the purposes of this show Donna and Joe count as one full human celebrity), yer one from *The Apprentice* (Jennifer Maguire), and that R'n'B singer nobody's heard of (Luke Thomas) – they probably got onto it as part of some sort of Fás course.

As for Brian Dowling? Well, word on the street is that he's been living a sort of Truman Show-type existence since he won *Big Brother*. As far as he's concerned he's just got a new job in a hotel.

Anyway, *Fáilte Towers* isn't so much scraping the bottom of the televisual barrel, as it's finding there was a false bottom on the barrel all along, beneath which there was a secret room filled with poo.

In each episode, three of the celebrities are voted by the public to face the judges, Sammy Leslie of Castle Leslie, chef Derry Clarke and TV personality/hotelier Bibi Baskin. This trio decide who stays and who goes based on their 'work', but because the show is edited by monkeys, thus far they mainly make their decisions based on things we haven't actually seen.

Indeed, *Fáilte Towers* is defiantly, uniquely and impressively badly put together. There's jumpy edits, bizarre sound-level problems, disjointed storytelling, and no coherent narrative.

And there's also loads of repetition. Every dramatic episode is shown at least four times. Whether it's Brian Dowling cleaning a piss-filled urinal, Joe McCaul dropping a tray of potatoes, or Don Baker angrily jabbing his finger at Derry Clarke while repeatedly saying 'are you calling me a liar?', we're shown a flashforward of the event before it happens, then it's shown 'properly', then it's shown again in flashback, and finally it's presented as part of a montage when someone is jettisoned from the hotel.

They also show things bizarrely out of sequence. In Tuesday's episode, for example, Jennifer Maguire refers to cleaning up vomit earlier that day, but the incident seems to happen in the next episode. And unless RTÉ has managed to twist the laws of space and time, that's just plain lazy (who could blame them, sez you, the way they're hunted by those dirty apes in management).

Anyway, thus far the hotel has been visited by hen parties, nudists, room-wrecking wannabe rock-and-rollers, hotel inspectors and people from Kerry. But they're all just distractions. Everyone knows this show is really about self-righteous judges, there-but-for-the-grace-of-God presenters (Baz Ashmawy and Aidan Power), and famous people cleaning up vomit, sniping at one another and crying.

Fáilte Towers is, indeed, poo-tastic. I think Brian Dowling (who's been quite funny throughout) summed it up nicely when he said: 'I think the s.h.i.t. [he spelled it out like that] is going to hit the le big fan. It's going to splatter. I am going to have shit on my face. Michelle is going to have shit on her face. Claire is going to be covered in shit, Donna's going to be covered in shit. So is Evelyn. We are all going to be covered in shit' (I'm sure someone in RTÉ is, as we speak, devising a programme called 'Poo Island' which takes this literally).

Richard Dawkins, the proselytising atheist, author and scientist is presenting a new series *The Genius of Charles Darwin*, and he would have loved *Fáilte Towers*, proving as it does, that intelligent design can't explain everything ('If there is a God then why does he let *Fáilte Towers* happen?' I might have asked my mother as a troubled child, if my life had been edited by the time-bending editors responsible for *Fáilte Towers*).

Anyway, amidst what is otherwise a very well-organised elucidation of the detail and discovery of Darwin's theory of evolution, Dawkins decides to go into an English secondary school to destroy the faith of some religious teenagers. What Dawkins doesn't seem to grasp that it might be possible to believe in evolution and an almighty deity. So the show finished with some poor teens pummelled into admitting that maybe there might be something in this evolution thing, while adding 'I'll still say my prayers though,' as if that was something to apologise for.

Now, Dawkins also talks to geologists, biologists, visits the Galapagos Islands, looks for fossils, and clearly explains how Darwin's big idea changed everything. But he can't stop himself demonstrating a total disinterest in other points of view – saying things like 'no reasonable person could believe otherwise' or 'evolution is a theory of life on earth far more wonderful and more moving than any religious theory of creation'.

I'll keep watching, on the off-chance Dawkins arm-wrestles God into admitting he doesn't exist, or better still, announces what I'm sure he secretly thinks – 'I, Richard Dawkins, created the universe. It was wet that Saturday and Mother told me to go to my room and play with my trains ...'

Stuart Carolan and Barry Murphy's romantic comedy *Little White Lie* wasn't quite fully evolved. Which is a shame, because much about it was really cool – the characterisation, the parodies of Irish TV and radio programmes ('so you found an earlobe in your cornflakes?' says a Joe Duffy-like radio presenter), and some lovely dialogue.

Even the daft setup had potential – a struggling actor (Andrew Scott) pretending to be a psychiatrist to woo a children's television presenter (Elaine Cassidy). But it lacked sexual chemistry, so the will-she-won't-she, will-he-won't-he drama didn't really come off.

It was as if Carolan and Murphy got so involved in creating the detailed little world of their film that they didn't bother colouring in the core relationship.

Still, it was very funny, very watchable, and in its atypical depiction of Dublin and Dubliners, very refreshing. In fact, I'd love to see it expanded out into a fully-fledged drama series where the characters would have more time to develop. Unfortunately, I'm pretty sure that the budget for such things is wrapped up in about ten years of poo-farming at *Fáilte Towers*.

DIARMUID DOYLE

I've been a wild rover for many's a year

A lifelong fan celebrates his love affair with *Corrie* on its fiftieth birthday.

5 December 2010

I remember the date, or I think I do, all these years later. On 23 November 1973, a Friday, I arrived home from school to find an enormous aerial attached to the chimney of our house in Kilkenny. In those days, there was no cable TV outside Dublin, so if you wanted BBC and ITV you had to get your hands on one of these metallic monstrosities and point it towards Wales in the hope that it would trap a stray signal on its way from the valleys. For some reason, this always worked better in winter than summer, when reception regularly disappeared into a noisy fuzz on screen.

To add to the occasional woe, Harlech TV and BBC Wales would often break in with the local news and sport from Llandudno. But to a ten-year-old already getting impatient with the nightly entertainment in one-channel land, the aerial was like a bailout to a zombie bank. The television addiction started around about then, as did a lifelong love affair with the Welsh accent. So, too, a few months after that November day, did my relationship with *Coronation Street*.

The affair was more of a slow-burner than love at first sight. My mother watched it regularly, at 7.30 p.m. on Monday and Wednesdays on HTV, and my initial reaction was that if the adults were watching it, it must be rubbish – a reasonable point of view for any child to take, but wrong in this case. Over time, I found myself sneaking surreptitious glances at the television to see what all the fuss was about. By the time Betty Turpin, Emily Bishop, Hilda Ogden, Rita Fairclough, Mavis Riley and Bet Lynch won a

Spot The Ball competition to go to Majorca in the early summer of 1974 (and actually went and shot some scenes there) I was hooked.

Three of those people are still in the series, and you always feel that Mavis is on the verge of popping over from her home in the Lake District for a cup of tea, a liquid as important to *Coronation Street* as oil was to Dallas. It's a series that values its old characters. Even when it was under ratings pressure in the 1990s to bring in a raft of younger, better-looking residents, it always treasured its oldies, always found decent storylines for them.

Looked at purely as a working environment, it has clearly been a happy place to earn a living. Ken Barlow (forgive me if I refer to these people by their *Street* names; that's how I know them and their real lives are of no interest to me) has been there since the first episode, fifty years ago this Thursday (9 December). Emily Bishop celebrates her half century in January; Betty Turpin (or Williams as she is now, following *Coronation Street*'s practice of making all married female characters take their husbands' names, feminism bedamned) is there forty-one years. Rita Fairclough (now Sullivan after her 1992 marriage to the kindly but fatally haemhorrage-prone Ted) has been around thirty-eight years. So has Deirdre Barlow, daughter of the fantastic Blanche Hunt, who died earlier this year on her holidays in Portugal. She made her first appearance in 1975. Jack Duckworth was there more than thirty-one years before his own recent death, brought about by a tragic combination of non-Hodgkin's lymphoma and a broken heart. He was the 115th *Street* character to die.

So when I'm asked why I love *Coronation Street* so much (and I really do love it, with the unshakeable passion of the perpetually smitten), I usually start with the old characters, with the way the show constructs a community around them, celebrates their importance, instills them with the wisdom of years and uses them as an often humorous sounding board for the madness in their midst. Fourteen of those 115 deaths were murders so Ken and Betty and Emily (whose husband Ernest was one of those gunned down) have clearly seen a lot. And yet they manage to keep going, these wise old heads, living their mostly non-eventful lives, keeping a beady eye on proceedings and giving the whole thing an air of reality, even when the more outlandish doings of some of the younger ones have you wondering whether this is the last days of the Roman empire or a working-class street.

The question of *Coronation Street*'s 'realness' comes up from time to time. Fifty years ago, a tightly knit community on a quiet terraced street with a pub on the end was probably a common enough occurrence in England, or at least common enough to make it believeable. Not so now, goes the argument against the *Street*'s credibility. Such communities don't exist any longer. Even on terraced streets, people don't know many of their neighbours, still less sleep with them, which seems to be Item No. 1 on the *Corrie* residents' association list of things to do. Nobody works across the street from their homes anymore, like Tyrone and Kevin and some of the girls in the knicker factory. Having a pub on the corner is an alcoholic's dream, not a working-class reality.

So what? *Coronation Street* has never made any serious claim for itself as a reflection of wider English society. The recession has had no effect on its storylines whatsoever. The recent change of government has gone almost entirely unnoticed. There hasn't been a word about the Irish bailout. The show exists mostly inside its own little bubble, and is all the better for it.

Where *Coronation Street* does fall down for many people is on the question of race. When it finally brought in a character from what used to be the colonies (Dev Alahan, from India, in 1999) it gave him a corner shop to run. Regular black characters like Fiona Middleton (now departed) or Cheryl, the stripper turned barmaid, or Lloyd in the taxi firm, are lighter-skinned black people than you normally meet around Manchester. The one exception, Shirley Armitage, who was Curly Watt's girlfriend for a while in the late 1980s, was brought in mainly to be a victim of racism. You get the impression that if Ozwald Boateng turned up on the street, he'd be given a job stitching knickers but no meaningful lines to utter. It's as though the *Street*'s producers have concluded or decided that somebody very black might frighten the viewers off. In 2008, that other great soap opera, the United States of America, tried something similar with its president, so *Coronation Street* has set a bit of a trend in that regard.

I suspect that people are making too much of the race thing, however. One reason I like *Coronation Street* is that its producers (and many of its actors, I suspect) are hostile to political correctness and see it as the scourge of creativity. The smoking ban in Britain in recent years was greeted on the *Street* with a veritable army of cigarette-brandishing characters, who seemed to be there for no other reason than to challenge the nanny state.

This distaste for state intrusion into the life of the local community can also be seen in *Coronation Street*'s consistently hostile treatment of policemen and women, a subject worth an entire article in itself. Stereotyping being the enemy of political correctness, *Corrie* has gone out of its way to give us characters – like Sean Tully, as camp a gay man as you could find, or Jim McDonald, the drunken, fightin' Irishman – who have traditionally existed in jokes but not so often in reality. The object is not to be offensive but to make the point that people are entitled to think whatever they like, no matter how much it may annoy liberals.

Which brings us nicely back to Ken Barlow. The only character on the *Street* since that first episode fifty years ago, Ken was also the first person I remember noticing in my early months as a fan. Who knows why? I was a bit young for philandering. In those first episodes, Ken was due to go to college, a journey of discovery he hoped would provide a permanent passport away from *Coronation Street*. For Ken, being a socialist and a liberal did not involve living among the working classes. Fifty years later, however, he is still on the *Street*, still unhappy, still railing against the status quo, which these days involves marriage to Deirdre, the worst-dressed woman in England.

Over the years, that discontent has manifested itself in sex, which has become almost as important to *Coronation Street* as tea. As I write, six characters are involved in infidelity or have notions in that direction. I watch now, a forty-seven-year-old fan, and wonder, not entirely disapprovingly: where do they get the energy? This is especially true when seventy-one-year-old Ken (who's had twenty-five girlfriends, including three wives, over the fifty years) is putting it about which, for once, currently, he isn't. Still, you know if you're a regular viewer that it won't be long before some *Guardian*-reading floozy turns his head again. He is, in many ways, one of the great tragic characters of English popular culture – permanently defeated, frustrated and on the verge of an escape that never happens. And yet, despite it all, he retains a certain nobility and an admirable lack of bitterness. He's my favourite character.

Like I said, it's the old ones who get to me, although it's to *Coronation Street's* great credit that it keeps producing wonderful characters, young and middle-aged, as well as old, of whom very very few rely on the aforementioned stereotypes for their success. I'm a bit of a NIMBY when it comes to *Corrie* and am always uneasy when a new character comes to town. Will they be credible? Funny? Able to blend in? They almost always are. Families like the Battersbys, the Harrises and, more recently, the Windasses, arrive like whirl-winds of disruptive energy and over time are civilised into funny, attractive and sympathetic characters.

If *Coronation Street* were to last fifty more years, you could pick three or four of the current crop – Rosie Webster, Gary Windass, Tyrone Dobbs, Chesney Brown, for example – whom you could imag-ine in much older roles, succeeding the Barlows and Faircloughs and Turpins of today. That ability to regenerate is a phenomenal achievement for any show of any kind in any country.

My dream job would be to write scripts for *Coronation Street*, although I'm aware of at least one journalist from an English news-paper – a very good writer – who penned a few scenes for an article she was doing and had them assessed by one of the show's producers. He savaged them. Putting words into the mouths of such fabulous characters, making them feel real, bringing out their innate humour is a skill not as highly prized as it should be. The recent death of Jack Duckworth, in which he was danced into the afterlife by his dead wife Vera should have been mawkish, sentimental and unforgive-able. Instead, it was beautiful, perfectly pitched, the work of highly skilled actors and an equally accomplished writer. There wasn't a dry eye in my house.

✦ ✦ ✦

OLIVIA DOYLE

Radio review

Alas, no more eruptions from 2FM's resident 'volcano'

9 May 2010

In a week when an understandable pall hung over RTÉ radio, it was a relief to hear a discussion of the latest ash-plosion from Iceland end thus: 'A suggestion from Tom Barrett, "Why not bomb the volcano, have one massive eruption, possibly bleeding off the problem?" read Pat Kenny from an incoming phone text on Wednesday. 'I don't think anyone except yourself, Tom, so far has suggested that.'

In a normal week, Pat's friend and rival for listeners on 2FM might already have been looking for the texter's number so he could give Barrett's big idea the over-the-top treatment it deserved. It was not a normal week.

Gerry Ryan's funeral on Thursday was by turns moving and funny and theatrical, as befitted him, and while its live broadcasting by 2FM may or may not have been over-the-top, it was so in one respect. 'There's nothing that would suggest excess, it's very simple,' said Mark Little to Colm Hayes, as they talked over a beautiful rendition of *Ag Críost An Síol*. Nothing excessive, perhaps, except for Mark Little and Colm Hayes providing a running commentary throughout. Yes, there was a need for some form of introduction to the proceedings but I'm not convinced that the seconds of reflection-friendly silence that occasionally occurred during the ceremony needed to be so comprehensively filled. But that's radio, and you don't go changing it. May he rest in peace.

Some things remain immutable, like Michael O'Leary's ability to get value for money. He might have spent a pretty penny on the 160 pedigree Aberdeen Angus cattle that populate his 200-acre Mullingar farm and stud, but a crew of six have the job of looking after them, as well as tending to 'fifty or sixty National Hunt horses coming home for their holidays'. So, a smaller crew than you'd find on the average Ryanair flight but a bigger crew than you'd find on the average Ryanair customer service desk.

The Squire of Gigginstown was on the always excellent *Countrywide* (RTÉ 1) last Saturday, talking to reporter Brian Lally while at home on the range. The interview had actually been recorded two weeks previously, with presenter Damien O'Reilly revealing that O'Leary 'kept his appointment to talk to us despite being in the middle of the worst aviation crisis in history'. And his secret to staying cool? 'No matter what the problems are, a walk across the fields of Ireland looking at nice Angus cattle and horses, good and fast and slow ones, it clears your head, it's a great way of life,' he said. The horses are 'just a money pit', though.

On BBC Radio 2, Monday saw Graham Norton step into the shoes of the Gerry Ryan-inspired Chris Evans for the week's breakfast slot. Subsequent mornings would hear him flirting with Julie Andrews and Rula Lenska, among other fabulous mystery guests, but his opening chat was with Debbie Reynolds, a genuine Hollywood star who's still hoofing it around the showbiz circuit at the age of seventy-eight, labelling many of her numerous exes 'crooks' and meeting her even more numerous fans. 'People say to me, "You look so good for your age, and up close, you're so lifelike,"' she trilled, before rattling off staggering impressions of, among others, Katharine Hepburn, Barbra Streisand and, yes, Jimmy Stewart.

On hearing of her bad luck with men, a listener recommended that Debbie seek O.I.L. – guys who are 'old, ill and loaded'. So Debbie told Graham that he was 'very cute', even in his unshaven state. 'I am loaded ... not old or ill, though,' said Graham, too charming to mention any other impediment to their union. 'You know, I'm Princess Leia's mother so that makes me a queen,' Debbie continued unabashed, before Graham pressed her on how relations are with her intermittently estranged daughter, Carrie Fisher. 'In order for my daughter to talk to me, I have to lie down in the driveway so she doesn't run over me,' said Debbie. They don't make 'em like that anymore.

And finally, to *Arena*, RTÉ 1's self-proclaimed 'arts and culture programme', where *Garage* director Mark O'Halloran was this week ably standing in for Sean Rocks.

He'd just signed off a lively interview with Cockney Rebel's Steve Harley on Wednesday when, unannounced except by herself, up popped fashion journalist Constance Harris, saying: 'I'm going to talk to you today about Irish women's fear of their legs.' And so began a bizarre riff on Irish dancing, bike cycling, maternal genes and pink skin, with a passing mention of this season's new on-the-knee skirt and the fact that 'Courteney Cox in *Cougar Town* is living in the things' (was this the arts-and-culture bit?).

'The main thing is, girls,' Constance concluded, 'get out of the shadow of the long skirt ... it's desperately ageing. It's not attractive – start flaunting a little bit more flesh.' One can only hope Tom Barrett was listening.

✦ ✦ ✦

SPORTS

ENDA McEVOY

Out On His Own

Cork hurler, Donál Óg Cusack, has shown strength and courage with his revelations about his sexuality.

25 October 2009

Alll men have secrets and here is Donal Óg Cusack's, so let it be known. He doesn't like Kilkenny, he's had it in for them since the 2002 National League final and he reckons they're the sport's equivalent of the Stepford Wives. To most hurling folk, therein lay the real meat of last week's autobiographical revelations. Oh, and he might own one or two more Liza Minnelli albums than the rest of us, but that had been the most public of unuttered public secrets beforehand. What difference does it make?

Listen, this is a man who screwed his courage to the sticking place, stormed the battlements, took on Frank Murphy and his minions in their own fortress and routed them. Twice. After ending the Cork County Board's decades-long undefeated run, coming out to the nation surely amounted to little more than a medium-sized piece of cáca milis.

Look at all the firsts he accounted for in the process. The first prominent hurler to come out publicly. The first GAA player to do so. The first Irish sportsman of note to do so. The first practising sportsman in the northern hemisphere since Justin Fashanu nineteen years ago to do so. It would have to be a Corkman, wouldn't it?

When the *Tribune* listed its 125 most influential people in GAA history last January we ranked Cusack as the fifty-seventh. Update it in five years' time and he'll be in the top twenty, perhaps the top ten. Even within the space of seven days he's already engineered a small change in the semantics surrounding sexuality. On Sunday, Aertel greeted his announcement with the headline, 'Cusack admits he's gay.' By Tuesday it had been amended to the less pejorative 'reveals he's gay'. A declaration of homosexuality does not equate to an 'admission' of homosexuality.

For it to be Cusack who boldly went where none had gone before him is no surprise. 'Moderation,' he declares in the book, 'is for the bland, the apologetic, for the fence-sitters of the world, afraid to take a stand.' With him there are no half-measures. It is everything or nothing.

Had he fought on the Western Front nine decades ago he'd have been the first man over the top the moment the barrage stopped and the whistle shrilled. (And would have taken his company with him into the mouth of the enemy machine guns, many people in Cork will add sourly. But let that lie.)

That he is now a role model for young gay men is undeniable. That there couldn't be a more determined, more articulate, more grown-up role model is equally so. Not some dreary young drag queen. Not whatever amiable nobody emerged from that I-use-the-term-laughingly 'talent contest' to sashay into a glittering new career with the *Xposé* girls. It was apt that Cusack revealed his sexuality the day after the world said goodbye Stephen Gately, a perfectly decent, sweet and inoffensive young man at whose funeral one of the offertory gifts was a bottle of moisturiser.

Gifted, successful and attractive, Sligo-born Dearbhla Walsh, the Emmy-winning director of *Little Dorrit*, represents everything a young gay woman might aspire to. Donal Óg Cusack, a similar high achiever in an adult world, may just be Walsh's male equivalent. What's more, he could if he so wishes become a powerful voice for the gay community on certain issues in future. And if he doesn't wish it, that will be his perogative. Cusack is a hurler who happens to be gay as much as he's a gay person who happens to hurl.

So the sky didn't fall in this past week, just as the roof of Citywest will not collapse if Cusack ever brings a fella with him to the All Stars. Did anyone seriously anticipate otherwise? If there's one encouraging discovery we've made about ourselves as a nation these last few years it's that in some respects we're more mature about sex and sexuality than we might have imagined. Do all that many people

really care about what others are getting up to in the bedroom provided they don't make a song and dance about it?

Exhibit A: the opening last year of a lapdancing club near this
writer's domicile sparked fear, loathing and public protests. When
the venture closed due to lack of interest and reopened as a gay bar,
nobody took a blind bit of notice. As long as they don't do it in the
streets and frighten the horses, etc. Anyway, there are enough GAA
folk of a certain age out there with gay sons or daughters, nieces or
nephews – whether they know it, or choose to know it, or not – for
finger-pointing to represent an uncomfortable exercise.

Two years ago John Amaechi, formerly of the Orlando Magic and
Utah Jazz, came out in his autobiography following retirement. All
was well that ended well for Amaechi; having feared 'the wrath of a
nation' on making his announcement, he was forced to admit a few
months later that he had 'underestimated America'. There's always
one, naturally, in this case the commentator and former player Tim
Hardaway. 'I wouldn't want him on my team,' quoth Hardaway. 'If
he was I'd really distance myself from him because I don't think
that's right and I don't think he should be in the locker room when
we're in the locker room.'

One cannot imagine the inhabitants of the Cork and Cloyne
dressing rooms being quite so precious, and not merely on the
grounds that none of them is likely to be mistaken for George
Clooney any day soon. Any individual seen running for the far end
of the room will be doing so in response to Cusack claiming that
they're not training hard enough and suggesting a 4 a.m. start for
their next session, not out of some adolescent imperative to keep
his back to the wall for fear of homosexual wiles. Are hurlers that
vain as to reckon a teammate fancies them? Scarcely.

The issue of the abuse he can expect from opponents is a different matter. Verbals can be as vicious issuing from the field of play
as from the terraces. The 1990s may have seen a low water mark
in this regard, with players abused by opponents over their colour
(Seán Óg Ó hAilpín), failed marriages (Davy Fitzgerald), the suicide
of a sibling ('Nice day for a hanging …') and alleged Traveller ante-
cedents ('Go home, the caravan's on fire!'). In the event of hearing
Cusack being called a big gay f**ker, or whatever, by the opposition

full-forward, will referees book yer man for using 'abusive or provocative language' under Rule 5.17 or will they turn a deaf ear? No
less relevantly, what will the reader do if standing at a match next
year alongside some troglodyte calling Cusack a big gay f**ker?
Sometimes all it takes for ignorance to flourish is for right-thinking
people to say nothing.

On that point, it is heartening to discover from *Come What May*
that the Semplegate fracas two years ago wasn't sparked by a homo-
phobic slur by a Clare player after all, and it is to Cusack's credit that
he now deplores the silly, self-indulgent statement bemoaning their
hard lot released by him, Diarmuid O'Sullivan and Ó hAilpín following their suspension.

But he doth protest too much about Kilkenny's lack of support
for the GPA in 2002 and thereafter. It wasn't up to Kilkenny, or
anyone else, to march in lockstep with Cork in their struggle with
the County Board; that was their battle and their battle alone. And
the 'Stepford Wives' jibe, taken in conjunction with the 'Our world/
their world' episode about Waterford in Brian Corcoran's autobiography, implies an attitude towards opponents that is both disquiet-
ing and, in view of the Cork panel's constant preaching of the gospel
of respect, surprising. The depiction of Frank Murphy as a far more
warm and engaging person than the Dark Lord of stereotype, however, suggests Cusack has discovered that the spectrum contains
shades of grey between the black and the white.

May Donal Óg live as happy and fulfilled a life as a person can.
And no harm if along the way he discovers that moderation doesn't
always have to be a sign of weakness.

✦ ✦ ✦

Kilkenny champions

The Cats don't have to win five in a row to cement their
place in hurling folklore because they have already done enough.
But this could be the year when they are finally caught.

23 May 2010

*D*e mortuis nil nisi bonum and all of that. Rather than writing their obituary after they've shuffled off this mortal coil, then, let's pay tribute to Brian Cody's Kilkenny – the operative phrase indeed – while they're still alive and well and living among us. One knows not the day nor the hour, but it's coming ever closer.

Seven All-Irelands in a decade. Six All-Irelands in eight years. The first All-Ireland four-in-a-row since the 1940s and the first asterisk-free All-Ireland four-in-a-row in history. Eighteen championship wins on the trot. An All-Ireland final performance that yielded two wides and thirty-three scores from thirty-seven shots. Two All-Ireland/National League doubles, with a couple of ritual springtime Nowlan Park disembowellings of Tipperary (eighteen points) and Cork (twenty-seven points) thrown in for good measure, as if *pour discourager les autres*. Eleven scorers from play in last year's All-Ireland final. The inspiration for the county's quartet of All-Ireland triumphs in 2008. And on and on and on.

For backers of favourites they've been a dream, shattering the spread match after match. They have not so much rewritten the record books as torn them up, set fire to them, thrown away the ashes and sat down to write their own volumes. There has never been a team like them before. There will never be a team like them in our lifetime again.

They have had their detractors and that was understandable too. Various grounds for criticism merit contemplation here and now.

Kilkenny were bad for the game? Nonsense; it's the bad teams who are bad for the game. If Tipperary or Galway win the All-Ireland this year, moreover, it will be largely because they have responded to the standards set by the champions.

They introduced Gaelic football defensive tactics to hurling? To a point. Then again, hurling teams that adopt a new approach to manipulating space are never regarded as prophets within their own sport (think of the horror engendered by Cork's possession game), and the Kilkenny yin of closing off room in their half was complemented by the yang of opening it up in the other crowd's half, defending in depth while unleashing hell down the other end of the field. To the dynamics of colonising space they brought an updated reading.

They were faceless and lacking charisma? Yes. That said, it wasn't their job to teach the world to sing and it's to their enduring credit that they didn't become entangled in hype and hoopla despite all the triumphal processions and civic receptions.

They had it easier doing a four-in-row from Leinster than they would have had starting out in Munster? Yes again, but one reason most of those provincial games turned into turkey shoots is that Kilkenny never took their eye off the ball or treated their opponents with less than respect, a respect that extended to beating them out the gate when they got a run on them. A respect that they would go on to extend to Munster teams.

They overdid the fouling and were sometimes downright gratuitously physical? Perfectly true. Certain moments from the 2007 All-Ireland final, the 2008 Leinster final and – even if Tipp gave as good as they got on the day – last year's National League final do not make for edifying viewing. Yet it seems to have gone unnoticed, or at any rate uncommented on, that the two players sent off for bad pulls in Kilkenny matches last summer were members of the opposition. It may be stating the obvious to add that most consistently successful sides in every sport have had occasional recourse to the knuckleduster and, furthermore, that none of those folk who like to sing 'Hosannas' to the intensity of the Munster championship can possibly condemn Kilkenny for their physicality.

Their manager was unnecessarily petty once or twice? Clearly. There's a line in Cody's autobiography where he grumbles about the team being written off (yawn) at the end of 2005 and adds: 'We'd show them!' It's a sentence, uncharacteristically shrill of the man, that jars on a number of levels. Whatever happened to trying to be successful for its own sake, Brian? Why some managers get worked up about the media rather than accepting them for the necessary evil they are never fails to amaze. Perhaps Cody is so tired of saying the correct and politic thing so often that it's cathartic for him to let loose – at Marty Morrissey, at the *Tribune*, at the All Star selectors – every now and then. If it makes him happy, so be it.

But the biggest gripe the world has with Cody's Kilkenny is that they've been too successful. To say they were respected rather than adored misses the point. For one thing they wouldn't wanna be adored; for another, serial champions never are. The one outfit in the annals of hurling that were truly loved were loved as much for the romance they brought to the game and for their sportsmanship as for their victories. Counties like Kilkenny do not bring romance to the game. Great stories are written about farmhands and, ahem, gamekeepers, not about landed gentry. ('Ah yes, who could have believed that I'd be part of my county's thirty-second All-Ireland victory ...')

One compliment that hasn't been paid to them, and should be, is that they were good and gracious winners. There was no dissing of outclassed opponents, no taunting them with ball tricks when the result was safely in the bag. Kilkenny won four consecutive All-Irelands without making the rest of the country despise them. Not every county could manage the same.

Points, not goals, were their daily bread. The goals helped kill off opponents, the points set them up for the kill in the first place. Time and again Kilkenny reached for and struck a register of ruthlessness like no team before them had. Against Clare in the 2006 All-Ireland semi-final they were a point ahead with ten minutes left and looking edgy; cue a barrage that led to seven points from eight attempts. Against Galway in the quarter-final they'd gone from leading by 1-6 to 0-5 after twenty-three minutes to leading by 2-19 to 0-8 after forty-five minutes. Against the same opponents at the same stage in 2007 they were level eight minutes from time before rattling an unanswered 2-4. Up to last year, Cork in the 2006 All-Ireland final were the only team to get within three points of them in terms of white flags.

But Dublin would hit as many points in last year's Leinster final and Tipperary would hit more in the All-Ireland final, the first occasion Kilkenny had been outpointed in the championship since the 2004 All-Ireland final, twenty-two games earlier. Even in their last championship defeat versus Galway in 2005 – a game that could have been scripted by Raymond Chandler: when in doubt, have a man with a gun in his hand walk through the door – they landed as many points as their opponents. Which is another reason why last

September marked the end of their natural lifespan as a team. After four years on the road, bread alone could no longer feed them.

Among their greatest strengths has been to have one or two others, usually Eoin Larkin with points and Eddie Brennan with goals, supplementing their staple diet of Henry Shefflin scores. Martin Comerford always had his regular-occasional days and Aidan Fogarty chipped in more often than is realised. But Larkin, who has averaged three points per game since 2007, has been wildly out of form this year, Comerford is likely to have to be content with the role of impact sub and Fogarty lacks the craft to magic something out of nothing when Kilkenny are on the back foot. The time has come for TJ Reid and Richie Hogan to step up, not least because this is a team getting old together.

The average age of the side that won the 2006 All-Ireland was bang on twenty-five, with two twenty-one-year-olds and a twenty-year-old therein. The average age of the side that won the 2009 All-Ireland was a little more than twenty-seven, with only one twenty-one-year-old therein. And that does matter and will matter, for it was experience and nothing else – it was categorically not the vigour of youth – that saw them through against Galway and Tipp last year. The line that separates experience from old age is a fine one, and Kilkenny are no longer the right side of it. The lion in winter, or at any rate in late autumn.

A couple of years back asymmetric warfare appeared to be the only way to discomfit them. Some rabbit from the tactical hat à la Galway's three-man midfield in 1986, some ploy designed not simply to keep the score down but to actively ask questions of them. That will not happen now. There is no longer cause for it. Tipperary twice took Kilkenny on in pitched battle last year and twice very nearly defeated them. An extra match this summer – not so much an All-Ireland quarter-final as a semi-final coming on top of a quarter-final – may be the game that pushes them over the edge. And Cody has to be lucky, or at any rate not unlucky, every time. His opponents, as the formerly loquacious P O'Neill might have put it, only have to be lucky once. Someday one of them will be.

Who, when and how? Pat Treacy of KCLR 96FM, one of the shrewdest hurling men on Noreside, identifies mental tiredness as the biggest danger. Think of Eddie Brennan and Michael Kavanagh, both with time and space to spare, missing simple pickups in the second half last September. Nobody will be able to say they hadn't seen the writing on the wall, the Kilkenny management included first and foremost, which is why Treacy lauds their approach to the National League. 'I think they identified the staleness themselves and tried to take every precaution against it by resting players during the league.' If Kilkenny are to be beaten, he believes, it won't be because they were caught on the hop by Galway in a Leinster final. 'They'll be waiting for that if both teams get that far. But an All-Ireland semi-final, well ...'

Nor will the champions fail for lack of enthusiasm, argues Eddie Keher. 'I've no doubt they'll have the same drive as they've had for the past number of years. But the other teams have all upped their game and have come very close to them. In the end they'll be beaten by a better team on the day.' As against that, Keher points out, a successful return by Noel Hickey would liberate JJ Delaney and provide a tailwind. 'Last year their options were curtailed by injuries. If they have better luck in that regard this year they'll take some beating.'

The team that sees them off will be younger, fresher and hungrier. They'll also be as accurate as Kilkenny, or as near to it as makes no difference. Unsurprisingly, over the course of the four-in-a-row Cody's side have become more and more deadly with their shooting. Seven wides in the past two All-Ireland finals tells its own story.

Twice in 2009 they had to hurl for their lives, initially against Galway in the provincial semi-final when, five points down ten minutes into the second half, they mustered twelve scoring attempts during the next twenty-five minutes. The first one Brennan, attempting to place the sliotar in the top corner, swung narrowly wide. The second, a long-distance Shefflin free, failed too. But each of the next ten found the target, not one of them despatched from Hail Mary distance. Instead Kilkenny poked and prodded away until they'd worked an opening. No haste, no hurry, no overplaying. Their decision-making was deep-chilled, their accuracy laser-guided. Galway had three scoring chances during the same period and put two of them wide.

Clinging on by their fingertips in the second half of the All-Ireland final, the holders' need to make every shot count was more acute still. To a large extent the match turned on a three-minute spell around the hour mark. With Tipp leading 0-19 to 0-17 Shane McGrath, Pat Kerwick, Seamus Callanan and Noel McGrath all had chances for a point. Callanan obliged; the other three missed, the first two because they went for broke rather than playing the percentages and dropping the ball short. While all of this was happening Kilkenny had one chance, an effort from TJ Reid that just about crawled inside the near upright at the Railway End. The real wonder was not the champions' subsequent double-barrelled blast but the fact that they were still alive to pull the trigger.

In much the same way that Kerry did not need to win a fifth in a row in order to seal their fame (if anything, come to that, Seamus Darby burnished rather than tarnished their legend), Kilkenny do not require five. Winning three was history-making. By winning four and beating Tipperary in the process they finished the decade the way they'd begun it, thundering home in an All-Ireland final they dared not contemplate losing. Their testament is already hewn in stone. What need to embark on the *Mona Lisa* when you've painted the *Last Supper*? Those Kilkenny folk who insist that half of the team of the 1970s would have walked onto the current XV are forgetting that the reverse also applies. Either way, they may steel themselves for a change of diet. Not that a few years of puddin' suppers will do them any harm after an epoch of lobster and foie gras.

Nobody knows, least of all the man himself, when Cody will ride off into the sunset. Make it five and he may be tempted. Come up short and, knowing him, the temptation will be to stick around and do an Alex Ferguson by building yet another new model. Whenever he does go, the announcement will come as a shock but no surprise.

In their talent, in their resolve, in their power, in their fearsome focus and in their modesty, Brian Cody's Kilkenny have been a cause for celebration. And when at last they succumb to a better team, that will be a cause for celebration too.

Ewan McKenna

The White man's burden

An unfulfilled snooker genius, Jimmy White has battled through
booze, bankruptcy and cancer but still considers himself lucky.

22 February 2009

Being Jimmy White – an existence spent scuttling between the seldom-used backrooms of dank, dreary bars, midday promotions in village bookies and cubicles with just enough room to slide the cue all the way back. On Friday it's a hidden-away qualifier for the World Championships, an event that earned him the title of peoples' champion but never more. Here and now it's an exhibition in the function room of an Athy hotel, a town that lost its own snooker hall a decade ago when it became too dangerous. Both games involve scratching and scraping at the past, trying to hopelessly claw it into the present.

White wanders in, takes a quick look at the freshly-laid table, the five rows of seats that have been brought from the dining room and starts remembering wilder days in Ireland. The time he bumped into UB40, who were over playing a gig and ended up with them and Phil Lynott for seventeen consecutive nights. The more common week-long benders with Alex Higgins that always seemed to start in the Gresham. Given his former lifestyle it's little wonder his ghost-writer spent her advance in six weeks, following White out on boozy evenings while trying to catch up on a past that seemed the far side of hazy.

He's due to play Higgins in a couple of hours but most of the early-day commotion has surrounded trying to get the Northern Irishman out of a pub. When Higgins does arrive there's a suspicious looking bottle peaking from his pocket and by the end of the night he's threatened to stab someone in the chest, to smash a digital camera, turned on a ten-year-old boy and had the referee stand over his shoulder on every shot for fear he'd lash out. Had White not changed his ways it would have been easy to draw parallels and point to where his own future lay. You enquire if he ever feared ending up that way.

'Many times I looked myself in the mirror and said I've got to stop this. But when you are involved with drinking it's not that simple. You can go weeks without it and think you are fine and then you go somewhere and have a couple and you are back on it again.'

So are you an alcoholic?

'I've been doing bits of programmes with Ronnie Wood, he's not drinking either at the moment. My last drink was 27 December and apart from that, the week of the 14-21 December I went to see my nephew, and prior to that I hadn't a drink for seventy-three days. So I can take or leave drink. Really, it's not my baby. I can go out now and have a coffee and have a good time, makes no difference. But I come from a family of drink. Unfortunately. So I'm always aware. But sometimes you are brought up in an environment like that.'

The family he speaks of is his father. A builder in the east end of London, he spent his Fridays cutting into the pay cheque in a bar near work. Young James White would sit in the car as the clock ticked into the evening and beyond. Aged eleven, he was finally allowed in and started to play pool. Aged thirteen he'd made a century break on the snooker table. Before long his natural habitat had become the Pot Black Club near Clapham and the principal of Ernest Bevin Comprehensive tried to cut him a deal – if he came to school in the morning nothing would be said about him disappearing back to the club after lunch.

But it was too late. Within a couple of years he was earning big bucks from hustling, giving the majority to his mother and gambling away the rest, and at eighteen became the youngest winner of the World Amateur Championship. Yet despite six final appearances, the professional equivalent never followed for the most gifted kid of them all.

'I was a bad boy. I used to like the gargle and that cost me a couple of those finals. I was always up late the night before and when you are young you think you can recover. Then you suddenly wake up one day and you are thirty-five; you've got a headache. I was up playing cards, drinking. And I've got no one to blame but myself. I had people around me and even if they went to bed I was always going to be my own worst enemy.

'That was then and in a couple of the finals I twitched on the black, like you would at golf. And I was 14-8 up in one of them and I started thanking God and all the people I wanted to and I wrote the speech in my mind. That's why I told Ronnie O'Sullivan that these discos will always be there when it's all over. It's my only regret, the one thing I'd change. I'd go to bed early and go out after these games instead of before them.'

✦

Cancer. It was 1995 and White was in the shower one morning. He reached down only to find a hard lump on one of his testicles and quickly realised something was wrong. He dried himself and let the thought pass but it wouldn't go away. He didn't want to but deep down he knew. His GP knew as well. 'Listen you are going to the hospital this afternoon.' 'What?' inquired White. 'I don't like the look of this at all, Jimmy. You've got to go.'

'I went to the hospital and they said we've got to take that out tomorrow. I went to see the doctor at two in the afternoon and by seven in the evening I'd got a gown on signing these consent forms. I thought I was going to die. I had to build up the courage to ring my wife and tell her. We do a campaign for testicular cancer and every male, there's a stigma there just not to say to their mum or dad that they've got to check this. Sometimes these things harden up within weeks and it's something you have got to get done. There was a bit of that with me. Thankfully I was alright.'

Others close to him weren't. Within a couple of years his mother had passed away as did his brother, Martin, who died of lung cancer at fifty-three. The latter crippled him. 'It was a horrible time. He was a hard working man, got struck down and died within six months.' But you are more curious about his own health at that time. The night before the funeral he put five grand behind a bar and started to drink. Within a few hours he had taken his brother's corpse and brought it out on the town.

'My sister just started drinking and crying more and more. The funeral parlour was only across the road so I said let's go and f**king see him. We went over and as true as we sit here, there was this big chain with this big padlock and I just kicked it and the door opened. Swung right open as easy as that. So we went through. We'd seen him in the day, and he was dressed, so we just put his hat on, put him in the car, took him to my brother's, then to my house and so on.'

Is that comic or tragic, you ask?

'Both.'

Doesn't it scare you that you were in a place in your head where you could do that?

'It was such devastation. I was at a stage where I didn't really know who I was.'

Without making light of it Jimmy, others have lost people to cancer and don't do their own version of *Weekend at Bernie's*.

'You have to understand what nowhere really means I guess. Me and my sister and my other two brothers ended up finding ourselves nowhere if that makes any sense. Just nowhere in our minds. It was very weird. It was angry as well as weird. It was all screaming and crying and laughing. It was all over the place. I was all over the place. The taxi driver said your friend doesn't look too well and it was quite hilarious actually; we all got a good laugh out of that. But we put him back the same night and then all the police came the next day and they were going to arrest us. But they saw there was no damage done and let us off and I didn't get arrested for breaking and entering. But I was still nowhere.'

✦

How do you get to nowhere? Too much, too soon? Loneliness? Depression? Tragedy? Bad advice? No advice? White's case might tick all of those boxes but it's still impossible to overlook an addictive personality. There are the cigarettes ('I may have a packet of cigarettes for a week now but I do hate cigarettes, I absolutely detest them'). There's the drink he reckons he's blown at least half a million on since people started to see him as a success. There's been the gambling too, which saw him blow well over a million in that time ('It can be very addictive but I'm not addicted'). And while the rumours he blew his 1994 world runner-up cheque of £128,000 the next day in the bookies are untrue, it's little wonder that despite ten tournament wins and over £4.5 million in career earnings, he was declared bankrupt and his wife Maureen left him after twenty-two years.

'For me all that stuff became quite a normal life. Obviously coming from a working-class background it's not easy, because all of a sudden you are surrounded by rock stars and women find you attractive. You know it's all plastic but try and resist it. You pretend it's real even if you know deep down, and you go with it, and suddenly where are you? I've been in too many positions looking back and I find it hard to believe some of the places I've been in. With drink I remember too many times waking up and thinking, 'F**king hell, how have I ended up here?'

'So all that money disappearing, some of it was down to me, but there was bad management too. You put faith in people to look after your finances and find two or three years later you've been robbed. It's really the children's money that they are robbing because you want to leave your kids secure. As they say, I drank a lot of it, gambled a lot of it and blew the rest. But I'm not complaining.'

Since going bankrupt, he's been putting his life back together, brick by brick, although some have continued to fall off. He was cautioned after cocaine was found at a hotel bar but says he was in a group and it was pinned on him. He tried to change his name to James Brown by deed poll following a sponsorship approach from HP Sauce only to have the application rejected. He had a hair transplant but when he took a look in the mirror his eyes were black and his chin had dropped more than a few centimetres. He even had his dog kidnapped.

'I put a poster on all the trees saying I lost my dog and there was a £300 reward. Then I found him but these posters were still up and suddenly he goes missing again. I had gone in the police station and this kid beside me had said his coat was gone and that he left it at a fair. I knew then it was gypsies that took it. I phoned a few people, found out where the fair had gone, got in touch with the top guy and arranged to meet Johnny Francome at the clock tower at Epsom. I knew Johnny when he was a boxer and he actually did *Snatch*; he was the one who taught Brad Pitt how to talk. He said he didn't know it was my dog. You know my dog is the only Staffordshire Bull Terrier to have a coloured picture on the front page of *The Times*. I've learned to laugh at these things. Can't do nothing about the past.'

And that's what makes White so likeable. Despite being beaten on the river nearly every time, he's never complained about his hand in life. He lost his snooker club but now has a stake in another one. He went to see Paul McKenna about his game and ended up being hypnotised for each of his flaws from drink and drugs to gambling and women, although reckons he wasn't fully committed and hypnosis alone won't fix him. As for his career? He's made moves this season, making round one of the Welsh Open last week and jumping eighteen places in the rankings to forty-seven but the whirlwind of former decades has become just a strong breeze even if he won't admit it.

'I'm pretty tuned in at the minute. I've had lots of practice, put in lots of hard work. But it's been a hard road just to get myself to tournaments but now my "A" game can win any tournament. I've put all that other stuff behind me and I'm just enjoying playing. Not that all that other stuff wasn't fun, don't get me wrong. I loved every minute of it. Please don't go making this sound like him moaning.'

So, being Jimmy White – what's it really like? 'I've survived cancer, I'm still playing the game I love, I've got five healthy children.' There's only one word for it he says. Lucky.

✦   ✦   ✦

Fighting his corner

Olympic glory, suicidal thoughts, Buddhism and now working behind bars: it's been a strange life for Nicholas Cruz Hernandez since defecting from Cuba, but he's still managed to keep on smiling.

7 January 2010

Some days the gym was filled with the swish of leather on leather. Others, when Nicholas Cruz Hernandez would invite some Cuban acquaintances over to waste away the hours with recollections of their homeland, the clunk of dominos would reverberate around the place. But most of the time there was just the silence that tortured him. It was then he could hear his thoughts and they had no reason to be kind.

Just four years earlier, the coach was a national celebrity. He had been the mysterious, gangly figure people called Black Paddy and was behind the national treasures brought back from the Barcelona Olympics. He was warm and friendly and successful and everyone wanted a piece of him. But everyone quickly forgot and by 1996 he was living in a makeshift quarters at the back of the gym on the South Circular Road with little more than a temporary bed and cooker. He could handle the mild poverty but couldn't cope without what he left behind for this lonely life.

One night he picked up a rope he found lying next to one of the rings. He wandered out to the door, took a look at the trees and picked out the biggest branch. 'I thought in my mind what it was going to be like when they saw me hanging from it. Then I was thinking will I leave something in writing, telling them not to blame anyone, that it was my own decision. I wanted to look inside myself and see if this was more than talk in my head. And it was. It was in my heart to do it. I had absolutely nothing left. This was it. The end.'

✦

Nicholas Cruz Hernandez first stepped off the plane on 4 May 1988 and expected the worst and the best from Ireland. Instead he got the best and the worst. After the Irish Amateur Boxing Association had asked for help, Cuba answered and sent the head of their Higher

Institute for Physical Education. He awaited racism and tiptoed his way onto Dame Street but slowly gained confidence, wandered over O'Connell Bridge and ended up in a bar chattering away to the locals. He was overwhelmed by the friendliness but later stunned by the sporting rubble he found instead of the top-class facilities he had grown up with.

His task was to help prepare the team for the Seoul Games early that autumn. At one stage he took them to Kerry for a training camp but found nothing but a ring on the ground floor of the hotel. In the end he borrowed a sledgehammer and tyre from a nearby yard and used them for cardio and strength work; he smashed rocks and used the smaller pieces as dumbbells; he used trees for chin-ups; and, long before Ger Loughnane, he had his team doing squats up and down the dunes on a nearby beach. Then he went looking for a masseuse to the amusement of higher powers.

'The boxers were great. So proud. The fighting Irish. But I sat with the president of the association, Felix Jones, Lord rest him, and I asked him about vitamins and he was looking at me as if to say, 'What are you talking about?' In the end Cuba boycotted the Games and they didn't want me to go and that was hard because I'd built up such a bond with the guys. They believed in me.'

Four years later he finally got his chance, even if it very nearly slipped away. When the team were staying in the Olympic Village in Barcelona, the boxers found a window above the door to the Irish area and started throwing water at the athletes coming in and out. Sonia O'Sullivan was first. A while later Michelle Smith came out and ran for cover but slipped and cut her leg. Pat Hickey, head of the Olympic Council of Ireland, called the fighters and Hernandez in for a meeting and warned them if there was another incident, they'd be sent home before a punch was thrown.

'They were just bored, but after that meeting I took the lads upstairs and said there's no way we are going to throw this away. There was a place where all the boxers trained but everyone was there so we set up an area on the ground floor of where we were staying. I was getting our boys up at six to train and I had a lot of complaints from the equestrian team saying they couldn't sleep. It was funny because by the end of it there was no one left competing but the boxers. All these people that were complaining were watching us training and wouldn't give us any space. We were the guys.'

When Hernandez returned to Cuba shortly after helping Wayne McCullough to silver and Michael Carruth to gold, even Castro was talking about him. His family presumed he was a millionaire after he made news across continents and asked how much he had received. He told them he got a few hugs and plenty of satisfaction. They laughed and asked him to be serious. He was. Felix Jones had promised him money but he never saw a single penny. Yet for some reason, when Ireland came calling again, he left everything behind.

It was 7 March 1996 and Hernandez was giving a seminar to coaches and boxers in Puerto Rico. He had done too good a job in Barcelona and his bosses were happier to send him to a fighting wasteland rather than these shores. Before he'd left for the nearby Caribbean islands he'd told his wife if he didn't come back he'd be in Ireland. She cried. He still doesn't know why he muttered those words because he had no plans to defect.

'On the last day of classes there, I went too early. I was the only one there and I remembered I had a number in my pocket of one of the secretaries in the institute. I called and she said a fax came. She gave me the phone number on it. It was from Ireland so I called and it was the IABA who asked could I prepare the Irish for the Atlanta Olympics. The president of the Cuban federation was in Puerto Rico for a meeting and I told him, asked for my passport. He said no. I knew that meant if I went back to Cuba my travelling was over.

'So I went looking for the bags and I said to the other coach, would you stand as a witness, that I haven't taken anything else. He knew what I was doing and said there's no chance I'd find the passport. When I stuck my hands in one of the side pockets I found a brown envelope with three passports. He couldn't believe it. There was a bit of a drama because the top guy wanted it back. He warned me I was defecting and that was five years' of a ban. I knew that but I didn't believe it. It didn't seem true.'

The next day he was in Ireland. He had been married for ten years to Maria Christina. His daughter Laura was seven. His son Nicholas Jnr was one. Most days here he'd walk to a local post office with a letter in his hand, knowing that it would be intercepted before it ever reached them. Every night he'd be woken by nightmares. By 1998 he had grown into a dark shadow of his former self. A member of the IABA noticed, took Cruz to his house and told him to try and call his wife again. Finally he got through.

'Nicholas, your sister has been ringing here with messages for you,' she alerted him.

'What is it?' he asked.

'Your father, he died. He was in hospital for six days.'

'He was ninety-six and they were the only six days he spent in hospital. He had to leave the tobacco farm and live in the city and that killed him. I started applying for a visa to go over there and bury him but the reply came back that I had abandoned the mission and therefore couldn't come back. I never found myself in a situation that I thought I was going to take my life but I had that rope ready and was looking at those two trees.'

✦

Cruz is sitting in a pub in Phibsboro, his trademark smile slapped across his face and a thick Irish accent sneaking out with certain words. He's just finished for the night in Mountjoy, teaching prisoners yoga and stress management through boxing. Before, he did it in Spike Island, St Patrick's Institution and Portlaoise Prison. In all of them he used to tell inmates his story and how, while he could walk out the door, he was just like them, in an open prison. They listened and understood.

By 2001 he took on the role with the prison service full-time when his days came to an end with the Irish boxing team. It was that year he finally saw his ban from entering Cuba end but couldn't get there on the salary the IABA were offering him. A young Bernard Dunne asked him one day just how much he made in the role and was taken aback by the answer of €15,000.

His road to mental recovery began soon after his father's funeral. He met a Shaolin monk in Dublin who had little English and was here all alone. He decided the monk was in a far more difficult situation than him and it was time he stopped feeling sorry for himself. The connection between the two went further. Cruz had bought a Buddha some years before for fun but the monk showed him the spiritual side and it helped him in his time of need.

'The prison work helped me too. I connected with people and felt like I had a purpose. In Portlaoise I met Dessie O'Hare. An amazing man, we did a lot of work together and became great friends. He was such a disciplined man, with that vow of silence. Nearly four years. I couldn't believe. Great charisma. He studied a lot, learned a lot, superbly mastered yoga. I heard from people about things he did and I never asked him and was never concerned about that. I take people in the present time; I don't judge anyone. Maybe he wants to change and needs help to change and I can be there. I feed on that.

'If I do something for someone and they are happy and I can bring a smile, then I feel great. They called him names, the 'Border Fox'. I wasn't interested. It was the same in St Patrick's, I realised the help a lot of young people need. They need a friend and I know what that can be like having gone through so much here myself. There were times when I needed someone but I got through it, and I realise there is a plan for me. I used to bring the rope I thought about killing myself with to places like that. I split it and made it longer and used it to help guys learn to bob and weave and it was a reminder to me of where I had been.'

More recently, he lost the rope but there are other reminders. He still has the Buddha and in 2007, fifteen years after helping Ireland feel so proud of itself in Barcelona, he got together enough money to buy a house in Portlaoise. Sometimes he walks around and feels the walls, making sure this is real and this is his. Other times he sits there in the quiet with a smile on his face.

He's learned to deal with the silence. Just as he's learned to accept the difficult path he's chosen in life.

✦   ✦   ✦

Liam Hayes

We should thank the Meath team for making the big call that the GAA studiously avoided

18 July 2010

The lowest and most ridiculous point reached in the days immediately following last Sunday's Leinster final was when the lads on the Meath football team were asked publicly if they would offer Louth a replay. Luckily, the whole sorry, ugly episode was immediately grabbed by its collar at that exact same point, and Nigel Crawford and the lads should be congratulated for answering with honesty and courage, and with a very definitive no thank you. It did appear to be more of a 'No thank you – now feck off!' The Meath team was in no mood to leave anyone in doubt about what was in their heads.

Everyone else, it appeared, was running around in circles, in quite a dither. Half the GAA community was in an idiotic frenzy. The other half was speechless. And, in between, there seemed to be a large gathering of GAA officials, at national level and Leinster council level, who were making it quite clear that they needed a few good nights of sleep before getting their heads around what had to be done. Thankfully, the Meath team was quite clearcut about where they stood! And, in my mind at least, they had three very good reasons for deciding that they wanted to hold onto the trophy that they had just received.

1. Some of the lads on the Meath team had been punched and kicked after the final whistle.

2. The Meath team, according to the officials on the field, had won the game and therefore the Leinster Championship, fairly and squarely during the full course of the game.

3. This bunch of footballers who make up the Meath team have

spent the larger part of their adult lives, to date, working their backsides off to reach a Leinster final and actually win a Leinster title.

They've fought long and hard all those years, most of which ended
in failure, and massive frustration in losing so often to Dublin. Ten
years, in Meath's case, may not seem very long when compared to
Louth's wait of over fifty years, but over half of the footballers on the
Meath team had dedicated each of those years to winning a Leinster
title. In comparison, Louth football teams, in decades past, and
over the last ten years, have mostly been talking and dreaming of a
Leinster title and not a whole lot more than that. It would be foolish
to conclude that Meath's ten years' wait should, for one second, be
left second in line to Louth's fifty years' wait.

The honest verdict of the Meath team brought everyone to their
senses, and directed the controversial and damning episode to a fast-
enough conclusion. There's no doubt about it, this group of Meath
footballers are worthy Leinster champions.

Now, about Louth! They would have been even worthier
Leinster champions, sure they would. They were extremely plucky
for short periods of last Sunday's game, and they also played some
brilliant football for short periods of time. JP Rooney's goal was
breathtaking, and it truly deserved to be the crowning moment on
a hugely historic day for every last man, woman and child living in
Louth.

Before Rooney's goal, Louth should already have had the Leinster
title fully wrapped up. Their defence, individually and collectively,
had performed at a higher level than anyone had expected, and the
manner in which O'Rourke, Ward, Bray and Sheridan were effectively shut down was exceptional for a group of defenders who also
had to contend with the almighty pressure of their first Leinster
final.

Equally, in the middle of the field, after a poor enough opening twenty minutes, Louth settled and took control thereafter. The
defensive and midfield platform, therefore, was in place for Louth
to win. They should have won. They should have been well out of
sight, once Rooney side-footed his goal from the edge of the large
square. That was indeed the goal of the last decade, and if Brian
White had taken even 50 per cent of the easy chances that came his

way from play and free-kicks in that second-half before Rooney's goal, then that magnificent shot would have had Louth five or six points in front with the finish line well in sight.

There was never going to be a replay. And the very question of a replay should have been shot down by the Leinster Council by late last Sunday evening. The opening of that door and the granting of a replay to Louth in such a high-profile game would have turned every disputed game in the future, at club and county level, into ridiculous tug-of-war contests which ultimately might be uncontrollable for the association.

In the great frenzy, in the days immediately following the game, people were forgetting themselves completely. All sorts of foolish arguments were presented on behalf of the Louth team. One of the dumbest of all was the call for the CCC to get stuck into the Leinster final and rule on what happened in the same manner as they would retrospectively rule on foul acts by individual players during games. The CCC operates itself in order to stop individual players getting away with blue murder in games. That body is there to nail down filthy acts of play, in particular, or actions which amount to cheating in extreme cases. The only person the CCC could have called up to explain himself, after this Leinster final, was the poor referee.

The CCC could never have said 'boo' to the Meath team or any member of the team, and any question of Joe Sheridan acting in a malicious or disgraceful manner by scoring the winning goal would be laughed out of the GAA's court or any other court in the land. Sheridan acted spontaneously and instinctively, and properly for a forward, and should never have to explain himself or his actions to anyone.

And, if there had been a replay?

Who'd have won it? That is an insensitive question to ask but let's ask it all the same.

In a replay, in my opinion, the odds would have swung back heavily in Meath's favour. They had vastly underperformed in winning and they would have fully realised that they needed to make a giant-sized statement in the replay. Would this Louth team have been able to stand up to the massive pressure of a replay and a pumped-up, more intent Meath team? I don't think so.

✦

Any other county in Ireland wondering why they can never win any-thing, should look at the work in Monaghan and Sligo as very helpful on their road maps to success. Sligo's greatest danger this afternoon against Roscommon is that one or two of their players might be thinking that with all of the hardest work done – in beating Mayo and Galway – that the county's name is already on the Connacht trophy. But Kevin Walsh will be reminding everyone in his dressing-room that any Sunday of the year Sligo would have trouble defeating Roscommon.

Everyone wants to see Sligo coming to Croke Park as Connacht champions, and if they can do so and play with the same stylish and aggressive manner in which they have performed for the last two months, then they will be a threat to anyone.

Seamus McEnaney's Monaghan are also real, live contenders for the All-Ireland title this year, but it remains to be seen what sort of condition the team will be in, mentally and physically, at the finish of this afternoon's Ulster final against Tyrone. If Monaghan keep a calm head, and play their own game, they can win the Ulster title.

Tyrone have not really broken sweat so far this summer. Despite the team's normal run of unfortunate injuries, which continues today with the omission of Stephen O'Neill from the starting fifteen, it's all been smooth enough sailing for Mickey Harte and his back-room team. Tyrone, on the surface of it, look the smartest of co-favourites, with Kerry, for the All-Ireland title.

The big question that might be answered between now and then, however, and the question that McEnaney will be willing his team to deliver this afternoon, is have Tyrone the hunger left in them if they're backed up against a wall?

The answer will decide whether Monaghan are Ulster champions this evening.

✦ ✦ ✦

Will Kerry folk now admit this team was good but not great?

28 September 2008

The madness has ended, thankfully. I even became infected myself these past few weeks, and at one stage this column was seriously contemplating Kerry winning the 2008 All-Ireland final by anything between five and ten points. I honestly felt that after throwing themselves into the championship in a disorganized and unruly but fiercely powerful manner that Pat O'Shea and the more elderly gentlemen around him would calm their team and help extract one complete, almost error-free performance from the defending champions.

Genuinely, I felt that after getting so many things wrong in so many games all through the summer, this Kerry team would have the guts and the balls – and most especially the headspace – to not only take Tyrone but to take them in a commanding enough stride.

But, hey, this Kerry team just continues to disappoint me. For the last twelve months I have been explaining that this bunch of Kerry footballers should not be mentioned in the same breath as the Kerry football team of the late 1970s and does not even stand up in serious comparison to the Kerry football team of the early 1980s. They are on a par with Kerry teams of the 1990s, which means they are mediocre-to-good by their own county's rich standards.

Last Sunday, Kerry came agonisingly close to claiming a hat-trick of All-Ireland titles. If Declan O'Sullivan's late shot had zipped beneath Pascal McConnell, or if the ball had ricocheted or spun inside the post, Tyrone would have had trouble even trying to make a draw of it. Let's make that clear. Kerry's performance was almost good enough on the day.

And, if they had, all of the journalists I know – friends, young fools, the more senile members of the press gang – would have been throwing bigger and fancier bouquets than in seasons past upon their latest victory. Same as they are all getting carried away right now with Tyrone's very exciting performance. The country's GAA journalists continue to disappoint me too, I've got to admit.

What we got last Sunday was Gaelic football's greatest living coach beating Pat O'Shea by – let's use a Ryder Cup singles score-card, for the day that was in it – something like seven and six, or eight and seven. And, on the field, we got a Tyrone team sensibly, calmly, ferociously, going about their business in a daringly confident manner, and still only barely edging their way to victory over a leaderless Kerry team, which was also critically short of guts and balls and other necessary items for most of the second-half.

Tyrone deserved their victory. Harte, more than any Tyrone man, fully deserved his third All-Ireland title of the decade. The manager and his team should not have had to endure the ridiculous line of questioning about their verbal taunting of their opponents. Neither should Harte and his heroic players have had to listen to nonsense about their sensitivity, and sometimes blatant over-reaction, to the slightest sign of Kerry aggression.

When any team performs so close to 100 per cent of its ability, on the biggest stage of all, on the final day of the season, all we should say is 'Thank you'. What a treat it was. The verbals and the play-acting, while they're not all that nice to watch, have been ingrained in Gaelic football since I first got up onto my two feet and made my way to the nearest GAA field.

Tyrone are All-Ireland champs and Tyrone are a nice, ordinary enough team. The team's specialness is really apparent in two individuals, Brian Dooher and Seán Cavanagh – and, to the latter, I would like to officially say that I will never, ever, ever again ask when is Seán Cavanagh going to formally start the second-half of his career. Cavanagh's ball-winning ability, movement and speed, and his incredible scoring power, has single-handedly made this championship memorable and, perhaps, has also spelled the end for this ever-so-wasteful figary of putting in a beanpole or a basketball player at full-forward on every second county team. We had Jack O'Connor's desperation of three years ago to thank for that blight on the game which, thankfully, might now come to an immediate end thanks to Harte's more creative instinct to place the most all-round talented footballer he has available to him in the number fourteen jersey.

Now that the All-Ireland final has, definitively, put an end to my little dispute with Kerry folk about the general health of the county, I am not looking to commence an angry discussion with the people of Tyrone. But just because they are champions does not mean they are a brilliant team. Also, with one summer still to go this decade, it's a little premature to name them as the Team of the Decade – Kerry are still one title ahead since the commencement of the new millennium, with one championship still to be contested.

Tyrone went from average to good to superb this summer. But now, seven days after their great victory, we just know that they will have to struggle and battle and doggedly find their way out of the pack of teams which go to the start line for the 2009 All-Ireland Championship. In their own way, that makes them magical.

Although we know that Cavanagh, Dooher and Conor Gormley will be every bit as strong and consistent over the next twelve months, there's no sure thing that we will see the two McMahon boys forming a breathtaking pairing in the full-back line ever again. Philip Jordan and Davy Harte will remain in the wing-back roles – and remain compulsive viewing in doing so – but up front, all around Cavanagh, nobody has any idea who will play where, or what Mickey Harte will even be thinking. It's mad really, and it's amazing. If Tyrone were dumped, fast and unceremoniously in 2009, we wouldn't be at all terribly surprised either.

Seán Cavanagh will win Footballer of the Year, that's for sure, although personally I'd give it to Dooher. He made mistakes last Sunday, he looked slow and ponderous at times, got dispossessed or lost possession several times, but not one Tyrone footballer ever took their eyes off their captain, and their captain never once looked over his shoulder. Dooher led. Cavanagh and the others followed. The only adequate thank you from the Tyrone team and from the country to Brian Dooher is this one final, great reward.

Meanwhile, this time last year, I warned Kerry folk, as they were still running around the place making a lot of noise, that in years to come they would look back on the All-Ireland victories in 2004, and 2006 and 2007, and that they would in hindsight consider those finals to be somewhat unsatisfactory, if not quite hollow.

Twelve months later, how are Kerry folk feeling now?

✦   ✦   ✦

MIGUEL DELANEY

Only by winning in style will Spain be seen as the true masters of the beautiful game

11 July 2010

Stroll around Spain's training camp in Potchefstroom, as surprisingly relaxed security allows you to do, and you certainly wouldn't get the feeling a World Cup final is at stake. For a start, despite the money the players earn, the Fanni Du Toit centre – about 100 km and a 100-million-Rand investment away from Soccer City – isn't too much of a step-up from a school sports ground.

The grass is yellowed and dried from the sun, the brown 1970s-decor walls only missing lesson timetables. And, appropriately, it's filled with children. Some screaming as Sergio Ramos ambles by, some attempting to high-five Carles Puyol. Over one fence then, left-back Joan Capdevila tells a group of reporters he's relaxing by watching DVD box-sets like *Fringe* and joking that his son is named Gerard … 'after his father'. Over another, David Villa absent-mindedly asks who it was that asked for a photo.

Such ease is a long way from the anxiety that seemed to afflict the squad during and after the defeat to Switzerland. That Spain can become the first team to win the World Cup having lost their opening game is testament to their mental resilience and evolution throughout this tournament. But not necessarily, according to a growing argument, their ability to exhilarate. It was a related point that led that air of relaxation to be broken by a hint of genuine rage during the week.

'What did people think?' Xavi asked *El Pais*'s interviewer in frustration. 'That we were going to win every game 3-0? I can't believe what I am hearing sometimes. Do you not realise how hard it is? Teams aren't stupid. We're European champions, they all pressure us like wolves. There isn't a single metre, not a second on the pitch. Always ten men behind the ball putting pressure on.'

It was an answer to a question over why Spain had struggled for fluidity throughout the World Cup – something they subsequently found
in fairly definitive fashion against Germany. But it may well have been
a response to the increasing voices that claim victory for Spain is no
longer a victory for truly free football. That they're exceptional without being exciting, closing out teams rather than really killing them,
despite their undoubted quality. That, in short, their games are dull.
Pass, pass, pass until someone passes out.

That very debate, however, has brought a very bitter split among
World Cup watchers in South Africa and beyond. The most common
argument back is that anyone who says Spain games are dull simply
doesn't understand football. A number of commentators and coaches
have rowed in on this side. But the most common counter-argument
is that it's not about understanding, it's about visceral enjoyment.

Hoping the numbers don't lie, both sides have turned to stats. Not
that you can stand either argument up too well on them. Spain have,
predictably, played more passes per game – an average of 617 – than
any side at a modern World Cup. But, remarkably, they've scored
fewer goals – seven in six – than any previous finalist in history. That's
not what people expect from potential champions with such an array
of attacking talent. They expect Brazil 1958, Brazil 1970, France 1984,
or, of course, Spain 2008.

Because, although the argument claiming Spain no longer excite
isn't one completely without credence, it does require quite a lot of
context. Two years ago, in terms of capturing the imagination, Spain
were the Germany 2010 of Euro 2008. They didn't just control teams
but caroused through them, scoring two a game and opening up
opposition with some astoundingly sleek interchanges. The semi-final
rout of Russia and final victory over Germany were two convincingly
complete international displays.

One of the factors, however, that helped forge such a watershed
win was that Spain effectively caught sides by surprise. They had actually been just as exquisite two years beforehand in the 2006 World
Cup. But the fact they were still growing as a group meant the more
experienced French side exposed a few remaining flaws. By Euro
2008 and the benefit of an extra two years together, they had a level of

club-like fluidity few opposition sides expected. That so many players were brought up together at Barcelona undoubtedly eased that evolution. And, with Spain then on a high after claiming Euro 2008, they carried such form into that relentless winning run. In the qualifiers for the World Cup, it shouldn't be forgotten, they won all ten games and scored twenty-eight goals.

Passage to the World Cup, however, also brought six months to prepare and pore over videos for everyone else. As Xavi explained and his club side Barcelona have also found, the vast majority concluded that the only way to counter such a team and stand any chance of success was simply to cut out all space near goal and deny them the opportunity to make any kind of angled interchanges in behind a bank of ten. Indeed, it's a credit to Spain that Germany simply wouldn't break with their usual abandon on Wednesday because they were too wary of leaving entire areas unpatrolled. All any team, no matter how talented, can do against such an approach is probe and probe and probe until an opening eventually presents itself. Even Brazil 1970. Still held as the high priests of attacking football, when re-watching their magnum opus on ESPN Classic recently it beggared belief just how much space that Italian team – themselves regarded as the culmination of catenaccio – offered up. Thanks to much greater physical and mental preparation, football today is much more regimented and militaristic in approach. Yet one man who successfully bridged the eras as captain then coach has defended Spain to the point of almost defying his nationality.

'Spain's football against a powerful Germany,' Johan Cruyff argued during the week, 'demonstrates their quality. They are a copy of Barcelona, the best advertisement of football. They play well, wanting to please and champion an offensive style. I am Dutch but I will always defend the football Spain play. The fact is that if you try to outplay them, they will kill you.'

Cruyff's defence of Spain goes even deeper though. His Ajax and Netherlands teams were acclaimed as the next step in attacking-football after Brazil, yet Total Football was above all about total control. Of the ball and space. Many mostly remember the Cruyff turn, his flying volley against Argentina or the flowing attack against West Germany. Few recall the fact that – just like David Villa's solo strike against Honduras or Andres Iniesta's piercing run to break Paraguay – these were isolated instances of inspiration amid long periods of passing and patience. Just as Spain forced Germany to chase for an average of 1.2 km more than they did and wore them out to the point Miroslav Klose complained, 'When we did eventually win the ball we were so exhausted we couldn't do anything with it.' Both Ajax and the Netherlands broke teams through possession. Neither side had particularly spectacular scoring stats at the top level – less than two a game in the European and World Cups – and Ajax's peak probably came in a 1-0 European Cup final win over Juventus that was only narrow in scoreline. Having commanded the same kind of lead in the 1974 World Cup final though, Cruyff's international side went too far. Rather than simply beat West Germany, the Netherlands were so convinced of their own superiority they sought the chance to completely humiliate their wartime oppressors and instead lost everything.

Ironically, it's the opposite of such an attitude that gives the argument against Spain most credibility. Rather than finish with a flourish, as they often – but not always – did at Euro 2008, they have attempted to close out games with relative caution. Late 1-0 leads against Portugal, Paraguay and Germany led to a lot of sideways passing but few surges. That, however, was down to insecurity rather than arrogance.

As Capdevila admitted at their camp on Friday, 'The fact we'd never been to a World Cup semi-final and all that expectation of us had an effect. Against Paraguay it definitely interrupted us.' Iniesta's brilliant break in that game and their edge survival thereafter – think Iker Casillas's save from Roque Santa Cruz – calmed nerves to the point they produced their most complete display since the Euro 2008 final against Germany, but a slight element returned in the final minutes. Possession but with a few tell-tale signs of panic.

Into uncharted ground now, there wasn't even a hint of it at Potchefstroom on Friday though. Xavi – perhaps paradoxically – spoke of his 'determination to enjoy the final', Xabi Alonso (or 'big Xavi' as the press officer calls him) that he 'simply feels' the best is yet to come and the team's most beautiful moment will arrive in Soccer City tonight. A lot of arguments would end if it did.

✦ ✦ ✦

Agents provocateur

Alex Ferguson hates them even though they make the football world keep turning. In a special investigation, the *Tribune* looks at the roles and wrongs of agents.

31 October 2010

I t's time for a mid-level Premier League player to renegotiate his contract. He expects a wage-rise or maybe a specific clause to hold up negotiations. Neither does. There is one significant sticking point though. The club's manager has been speaking to his own representative. The boss then goes back to the player.

'If you want a new contract with this club, then you've got to sign with my agent. That's the only way you're going to progress.'

Elsewhere, a group of businessmen take over a decently supported British side. They conclude the deal with the bank's money – investing none of their own – and then take salaries from the club. Throughout all the negotiations, they only deal with one favoured agent. Eagerly sitting on the cash merry-go-round, that representative is paid a huge figure in agent's fees only to then give the businessmen a backhander.

There are names attached to each of these individuals. Some well-known. Their identities can't be revealed for legal reasons but that's almost irrelevant due to the fact that the examples fit a number of different situations that are happening across the breadth of British football.

It's a convenient out, at the moment, for many managers and officials to blame the 'agent culture'. And, as one agent working extensively in Britain told the *Sunday Tribune*, the generally negative image of his profession is 'completely justified in a lot of cases'.

It's an image that also came into harsher light this week, however, with Alex Ferguson's comments in the aftermath of Wayne Rooney's contract saga. 'You have to deal with the agents of this world today, which is difficult. The players are no problem ... some agents are difficult.'

Rooney's representative, Paul Stretford, was – whether rightly or wrongly – highlighted as an Iago figure, manipulating events to his own ends. That image was muddied further by some of the whispers that have appeared in the media over that time. One indicated that the timing of Rooney's disenchantment was interesting given that, only last season, Stretford received a half-million-pound bonus because Rooney had stayed at Old Trafford for five years. Another pointed out that FIFA plan to reduce a licensed agent's total commission from any deal to 3 per cent in 2011, meaning a representative might want to maximise his earnings under the current regulations. Then there's the financial magic Mino Raiola worked in Zlatan Ibrahimovic's convoluted move from the San Siro to Barcelona and back again.

With such stories, it becomes easy to apportion blame for football's river of greed. But, just as the Rooney situation had much more to it than the player supposedly nodding his head to each of Stretford's suggestions, the sport's very relationship with agents is a great deal more complicated than that. For a start, Ferguson himself was as selective with the truth when it came to his view of agents as he was with his view of the Rooney situation. He may not think much of Stretford but he didn't mention the manner in which other agents have helped him build his Old Trafford empire.

The spotless – in every sense – Jorge Mendes advised United on Cristiano Ronaldo, Nani, Anderson and Bebe. Much earlier, the more notorious Rune Hauge provided valued opinion on Peter Schmeichel, Andrei Kanchelskis and Ole Gunnar Solskjaer.

While it should be said that none of these transfers were suspicious or irregular, each of them illustrate how ingrained agents are in the infrastructure of the game. While many are indeed the parasites Ferguson indicates, some are simply products of the system.

And, when it comes to actual corruption in football, agents aren't exactly the cause many would otherwise claim. Instead, a very different impression emerges from those prepared to talk candidly.

There is definitely a space for agents in the sport, as shown by the many who go about their job ethically and the decent football people they deal with. The problem, however, is that the very nature of the job attracts opportunists. And their numbers are disproportionately boosted by the area of the job. As a number of individuals – from ex-players and agents to those currently involved – insisted to the *Sunday Tribune*, 'The industry is rotten at many levels from top to bottom.' In essence then, it's not just certain agents that are crooked. They only represent the crookedness of many areas of the game.

A series of stories illustrate this. One source said that managers have often told them, 'Yes, I'll sign your player but, when we pay you an agent's fee of a 100 grand, you pay some of that back to me.'

The *United We Stand* fanzine recently printed an anecdote – corroborated elsewhere – of a Premier League manager turning to his bench towards the end of a game: 'Right, which one of you is on the biggest appearance fee? OK, you go on so long as x percentage comes back to me.'

A different company was approached by an agent saying that he was in partnership with a Premier League manager. If the company gave him £10,000, the lone agent could provide any young players they put forward with a contract at the manager's club. The teenager would then be moved on at a profit because his CV had been greatly enhanced.

As one former player explained, 'If you were to ask supporters who they think is on the take, they'd come out with the same names, "Oh, he looks dodgy," this idea that there's only a few. There's a lot at it.'

Indeed, it shouldn't be forgotten that only four years ago Steve McLaren's agent Colin Gordon expressly stated that 'English football is totally corrupt'.

'We're not talking about the old brown-paper envelopes. We're talking about millions upon millions. It is a very, very sophisticated business. Are agents corrupt? Not all – but the majority. It's accepted abroad … the English game is considered the "dirty man of Europe".'

Back then, Gordon also claimed the system is so sophisticated that investigators will never trap the agents and managers who avail of it. But there's another reason, as a British-based agent told the *Sunday Tribune*. 'There are a lot of dodgy agents and unethical people in football, but the only way you can do an unethical deal is if there are two parties to it. And it will never be flushed out of football, because it will be like turkeys voting for Christmas.'

'Even when they go and carry out a review, they'll go through that system for six months and, by the end, they'll very rarely nail someone. The reason is because, right from top to bottom, there are people who are prepared to compromise their ethics because there's so much involved. If they have to break the rules to get a player, they'll break the rules.'

◆

Perhaps fittingly, it was football's own greed that created the space and necessity for agents in the first place. As the professional game began to expand, the maximum wage was introduced in 1900. Added to it, however, was the unjustifiable restraint of trade – as the British High Court ruled in 1963 – that was the 'retain and transfer' system. This allowed the clubs undue control of contracts and wages, right down to the penny. At that stage, football was more about serfdom than stardom. In such a climate, agents disappeared from the game other than isolated instances like when Denis Compton signed a deal with Brylcreem or the more liberally-regulated Italian clubs began to sign players such as Denis Law and John Charles.

It was around this time, in the late 1950s and early 1960s, that the situation in Britain reached breaking point. Most notoriously, Manchester United – with the significant aid of Matt Busby – greatly exploited its players. It was one of the reasons John Giles left for Leeds. Along the same lines, George Eastham refused to sign a new contract with Newcastle in 1959 and requested a transfer, which the club refused. Eastham refused to play for the club again and – as the retain-and-transfer system dictated – left the game to find alternative employment. Although Newcastle eventually sanctioned Eastham's move to Arsenal in October 1960, the player brought proceedings against the club with the backing of the increasingly influential PFA. The 'retain' elements of the system were shattered.

From there, a new world was opened up. But slowly at first. It wasn't until the explosion of commercialisation in football in the mid-1970s – largely thanks to Joao Havelange's control of FIFA and the influence of sports promotion pioneer Horst Dassler – that agents began to really flex their muscles. By the late 1980s, almost a decade before the Pandora's Box that was the Bosman ruling, the

English FA were already looking to curb their power.

In many instances, agents were merely former players exacting revenge on the system that for so long exploited them. To a certain degree, that still remains the case.

As part of this article, the *Sunday Tribune* attempted to survey each of the twenty agents licensed to work in Ireland. Of the thirteen that responded, their backgrounds cover a broad spectrum. Despite those differences, the majority adhere to a broad ideal of what an agent should be and do.

Fundamentally, an agent handles a player's negotiations with clubs as well as any outside business interests such as sponsorship and image rights in order to prevent him getting exploited. Eamon McLoughlin – a former League of Ireland player for UCD who also studied sports business before getting a job in Platinum One – explains this is where many players are happy to leave it.

'Some will negotiate their contract and just go, "Grand, see you again in two and a half years." Other guys want to speak every day about how training's going. It mightn't be so much a job they want you to do, they just want you to stay in touch … sometimes a younger guy, you'll get a text, "I've had a fight with my girlfriend, please ring me."'

Andrew Cousins, another former League of Ireland player, has seen the benefit of doing so with his client, Birmingham's Jay O'Shea.

'The day-to-day is speaking to him, speaking to his coaches. Making sure he's going well, and Jay, like a lot of Irish lads, has a great attitude. Although I think a big thing is not to get too involved – only when they want you. Sometimes what might seem the pettiest thing to an average person can really affect players. Like if you're suddenly told you're training with the reserves instead of the first team. When you are in that bubble, that can be the worst thing that can possibly happen to you. You can be depressed, lonely. That side of things comes with the day-to-day.'

Gbolahan Balogun is a trainee lawyer as well as an ex-player. One of five Nigerians among Ireland's twenty licensed agents, he has been in the country for eleven years and 'wanted to keep his passion for the game'. Balogun represents clients across a diverse range of countries and leagues – from Britain's lower divisions to North Africa and the Middle East.

'My day involves trying to get in touch with clubs and a lot of telephone work. I speak with scouts in a lot of different countries. For players you represent, you are almost their personal manager. I think a lot of that is overlooked. You can also go a whole year without signing any player or getting any movement and people don't hear about that. A player might have to go to Dubai but still not get a move at the end … You also have to take out indemnity insurance, which is very expensive.'

William McSorley represents a number of players in the top divisions either side of the border as well as a goalkeeper in League One. He explains, though, that a lot of his work consists of agents from abroad ringing for advice or to consult. In other words, lubricating transfers.

It was that side of the industry Gary Neville appeared critical of when he called for 'the removal of agents from the game' in 2007, claiming that players didn't 'need people taking hundreds of thousands of pounds off them, just good advice from a solicitor or an accountant'.

That is exactly why there is now a licensing exam, however. As Balogun explains, 'It is not something that you just go and pass. It is everything about football; there are a lot of legal issues and technical questions. Of sixty going, maybe only two pass.'

Not that the exam is flawless. Peter Auf der Heyde is a South African living in Cork who sat the exam in order to help the career of a talented fifteen-year-old compatriot who stayed with his family. Although he passed the exam, he noticed a discrepancy when one of his answers was marked wrong. The question regarded a complicated issue regarding the selection of a Saudi player in Australia. 'I phoned FIFA and pointed out why they were wrong. The exam hadn't taken into consideration that Australia and Saudi Arabia were now part of the same confederation. Although they said I could have the marks, they still didn't have the courage to inform the national associations of this. And that's an indication.'

Auf der Heyde feels this minor matter is just the tip of an iceberg when it comes to the general laxness in policing either agents or corruption in football. As the football consultant and scout Tor-Kristian Karlsen recently told the BBC, 'The agent business is like the Wild West. It's messy and too time-consuming for FIFA to police and too bureaucratic.' Indeed, the world body is currently debating whether to de-regulate agents again, since an estimated 70 per cent of international transfers are completed with unlicensed agents. In some cases this is relatively innocent. Many representatives are family members. In other instances, McLoughlin explains, 'A lot of people develop a relationship with a player and suddenly realise they can make money off the back of him. They fall into it and think it's simple, that there's no skill-set – if that is the right phrase.'

Neither the actual skills required nor the exam can prepare agents for some player requests though. An English agent tells the story of a colleague attempting to sign up a middle-tier Premier League player. The clincher, however, was odd.

'Will you do me Tesco's?'

'Sorry?'

'You know, me shopping?'

'We've had that before,' McLoughlin admits. 'There was one high-profile Irish player. He turned around and said, "Will you go and get me tickets for a concert?" We told him to go and jump. We don't do that. A lot of players just want a yes-man. Or they just want someone who's going to be their best friend. And I found out the hard way, players will say they're your best friend, and then somebody will come along with a better offer.'

Often, there's a lot of exaggeration behind better offers. Indeed, for certain members of the profession, their entire career is one long game of brinkmanship. That's what many enjoy. The very best agents – the super-agents – legitimately have the contacts. The very worst – in the truest sense of the word – invent them. That's something Cousins has found to be the case both in his old life as a young player and his new life as an agent.

'When I was young and naïve and let go by Leeds, lots of agents wouldn't answer my call when I really needed one. They string you along. Then one agent told me he had a club lined up for me for the 2 January. He never said who. I went back over straight after Christmas, training every day on my own. So 2 January came, no phonecall. Never heard from him again. That stuff happens a lot.

'Another time I was over at a Premier League game and there were six or seven fellas lined up outside the manager's office. It was like a competition to see who had the loudest suit. I started laughing. But maybe they were laughing at me. I'm not in it for that. I think that's a lot of it, people will pretend to be more than what they are. I mean, I can spin a story saying me and Alex McLeish are great friends. When really, I could ring him, but we'd only speak about Jay. That's the long and short of it. But often I've seen agents tell a player they know someone in the game well ... then the player sees them introduce themselves to that same person for the first time.'

It's that alternative element of brinkmanship that can also bring those into the game who are merely after a fast buck. 'There's a lot of people that do live up to the image, that people would say are parasites,' McLoughlin says. 'They might view the player as an asset and work with him for one year rather than develop something over the course of his career as we would try to do.'

With reference to the Rooney situation, the question was put to the agents interviewed: would you actually agitate your client for a transfer? Cousins said no, that he would only take into account the players' happiness.

Here, however, Balogun adopts a much more dispassionate view. 'A player is a marketable commodity. Your job is to look after their interest. People don't understand this. If I feel my player can have better options elsewhere it is my responsibility to look for the best deal and tell them. Also, you cannot tell a player what to do. Most are over eighteen. An agent is like a lawyer. You merely tell your client what all the options are. It would be irresponsible to not do that.'

McLoughlin, to a certain extent, can see that viewpoint. 'We don't really know the ins and outs of the Stretford-Rooney situation, or what his strategy was so it's impossible to comment. The thing about it is though, the only person Stretford has to answer to is his client and not the 100 million Man United fans.'

It's perhaps a reflection of the inherent problems football faces that so many more people will get self-righteously angry about that acceptable side of agency work, rather than the corruption that's rife elsewhere in the business.

KIERAN SHANNON

Triumph over adversity

The loss of a brother, cousin and best friend have only emboldened Noel O'Leary to approach football as life – with fearless resolve.

19 August 2007

For a moment Noel O'Leary was sure he'd got away with it. It was down in Tralee on a shitty wet Saturday night, Kerry had just beaten them, and towards the end he'd snapped. The Kerry boys had been winding him up all night and then Tomás Ó Sé kicked the ball at him and O'Leary had gone and eyeballed him, lashed out, and picked up his second yellow card for his troubles. As he was walking into the dressing room tunnel, Billy Morgan tapped him on the back and half-grinned, 'Well done, Noel!' At that, inwardly, O'Leary smiled too. Someone understood. If anyone could, it was Billy. The sight of that green and gold jersey, the passion, the fury; sure he knew all about it himself.

And then? Well then when they were inside, Morgan closed the door and proceeded to give his wing back, as O'Leary so eloquently puts it, 'an unmerciful fecking'. In front of everyone. He shakes his head and grimaces bashfully at the memory, thought and accusation. Too fiery and volatile – even by Morgan standards. 'But he was dead right too,' says O'Leary. 'I was a bit mad that night. A rush of blood to the head.'

Admit it. It's how you know him, perceive him. There mightn't be a better attacking wing-back left in this year's Championship or anyone on the Cork team more adept at playing that ball into Michael Cussen, but to you, he's that serial yellow-carder who keeps getting into scrapes. He'll probably take up Geraghty today and, well, it's hard to see both of them lasting the distance. But, as

Dan might say, if you don't know him, don't judge him.

He's from a place called Cill na Martra, the second smallest parish in the biggest county in Ireland, a few miles outside Macroom, off the road to Ballyvourney, but as a kid he developed a passion for West Cork football and West Cork footballers more than fifty miles down the road. There was Castlehaven and Tompkins and Cahalane. And even though they were junior, there was Urhan and Ciaran O'Sullivan too. He remembers going with his father Donal as a twelve-year-old to see them play Midleton in a county junior championship replay in 1992 in Ballingeary.

'I'll never forget it. The first day Ciaran was awesome. The second day he was having a brilliant game again when one of the Midleton lads turned round and made shit of his nose. Ciaran was down for three or four minutes, blood pissing out of his nose. Next thing, he gets up, the ball comes in and Ciaran grabs it underneath his own goalpost, goes straight up the centre of the field and shoes the ball straight on the 45 and splits the posts.

'My father turns round to me and says, "That man will be playing for Cork next year."' And at that, his son vowed that's how he'd play for Cork too. Like Cahalane, like Ciaran. Blood and bandages, boy.

And that's how he played for them as a minor. With passion. Raw passion at times, but passion, and when the Cork senior hurlers were presented with their 2000 Munster medals the same night as O'Leary and his colleagues were presented with their All-Ireland minor football medals, Diarmuid O'Sullivan, a two-time All Star even then, made a point of going over to O'Leary to tell him how much he loved the way he played the game.

A year later they were teammates winning an All-Ireland junior medal together, and a year later, on the senior panel, winning a Munster football championship together. O'Leary had to wait until he was twenty-one to break onto the starting fifteen though. When he did, he did with intent.

'I thought, "Feck it, a tougher attitude to this set-up would be no harm at all. We'll try not to take any prisoners if we can." I suppose I went a bit bald-headed into it though. Did a lot of stupid things.'

Whatever about doing anything stupid, O'Leary managed to do something unique in that 2003 league campaign, picking up a yellow card in each of Cork's seven league games, and just for good measure, picking up two in the last game against Tyrone. But over the years he'd like to think he's tempered down that temper. He's no longer the wild buck of 2003, though, he'll admit, some sort of red mist does seem to descend upon him when he encounters that green and gold. And on days like that, he's reminded it's only a game, that there's more to life. And he'll agree. Yeah, it's a game, there's more to life, but what you must understand it's that game that has helped him get through the life he's had.

The first to go was Mark. They were cousins but more like twins; the same age, the same humour who'd 'more or less lived with each other; him living up in our place or me down in theirs'. Then, in January of 1999, Mark and his girlfriend broke up and all of a sudden he was dead. Suicide.

'It was an awful shock at the time. Because nothing like that had ever happened to us before. But that was my first year with the Cork minors and the football was a great thing to have. It gave me something to turn back to.'

O'Leary and Cork would win that year's Munster final, inspired by a magical display from another dynamic wing back called Tom Kenny, but a few weeks before the following year's Munster final, tragedy struck again. This time it was Benny, his best friend.

'Benny,' he smiles, 'Benny was a gas man. Strange, he had no interest in football but we had a bit of an old business going there. We bought a quad-bike between us, spraying weeds and spreading manure on farms for farmers. A couple of weeks before we played Kerry, there were about thirteen or fourteen of us out the back at home. Benny was spinning around on the bike. And feck it, it was a case of the two of us getting too used to that bike; we'd wear no helmets or anything like that, you know. And sure, whatever way he went across this little slope in the field, didn't the bike turn and fall on top of him.

'At the start we were saying to ourselves, "This man is going to hop up now any second," because he was a bit of a joker, like. But we went over, and Jesus, when we looked at him he had gone blue in the face. Myself and my brother Ciaran tried to clear his mouth but it was no good.' By the time the ambulance had hit Macroom, Benny was gone.

Again, football offered some measure of solace and that summer Cork went on to claim Munster and then the All Ireland. O'Leary's eyes light up at the memory of it and old teammates. Some of them you've heard of: Masters and McMahon, the latter of whom will play with him in Croke Park today; Conrad Murphy, who was the best of the lot of them; Kieran 'Hero' Murphy from Erin's Own. But then there were others who you mightn't have heard of. Paul Deane, Dinny O'Hare; 'Maybe not the most skilful, but hard men and great lads as well.' Only in the last year or two with the seniors, has he experienced a team chemistry and bond like the boys of that summer enjoyed. It was the time of their lives and should have been the year of their lives, but before 2000 was out it had been the worst of O'Leary's.

He'll never forget the game that was on the box that day: Glenflesk and Nemo in the Munster club final, and himself and the father watching Moynihan and Johnny Crowley trying to win it nearly on their own. But as the day and game went on, his mother was becoming increasingly anxious. Ciaran, Noel's seventeen-year-old brother, had yet to come home. There was no word from him or of him. Noel and his younger brother, Donal Óg, told her to relax, reminding her that it wouldn't be the first time he'd have stayed over at a friend's. After the game was over though, there was still no word. They'd phoned Ciaran's girlfriend who he'd visited the previous night and she'd said he'd gone home.

'The father was saying then, "God, maybe he was drunk coming home and fell somewhere. Donal Óg, go into the shed and get our wellingtons and we'll go to the fields and look for him." Donal Óg went into the shed only to find Ciaran already there. Same story as Mark. Seventeen. Just finished with the girlfriend. Gone.

'Definitely what happened to Benny was a big part of it. Ciaran was there when it happened and he used to get upset about it. He'd always be on about it at home. But in saying that, you wouldn't have taken much notice of it. I mean, it was natural enough he was upset about it.

'I think it was a pure spur-of-the-moment thing. It and drink. In most of these cases that's what it is; a spur-of-the-moment decision brought on by the drink. Looking back, Ciaran wouldn't have been the best to take drink. He was only seventeen, a bit of a wild lad but a good lad, but you could see that he used to get upset after drink.'

That's why he'd tell anyone: know the people who don't react well to it. Be there to tell them the one that's one too many, especially when that one might be the first. Be there to say hang on, everybody hurts, but it passes. It's maybe not the normal message or cause advocated by a GAA player, but O'Leary feels strongly about this. So do his younger brothers, who hardly drink at all.

'A lot of people mightn't like talking about this, shy away from talking about it, but it's happening every day in other homes. People might learn from it. I have no problem talking whatsoever about it. Or Benny or Mark. It was an unbelievable run for us at the time, but it happened. It's a big part of who I am.'

There's little O'Leary isn't upfront about. At times he might sound all bashful like Páidi Ó Sé just like he plays like a young Páidi Ó Sé but the 'Yerrah' response is not for him. There is a refreshing honesty as well as affability about him. In the tree surgery business he set up a few years ago, beating around the bush is kept to a minimum. It's the same in conversation. He cuts through the bullshit.

The Cork under-21 team management during what he now calls the lost years, for instance. 'It was the worst set-up I've ever seen. Selectors turning up late; poor locations, no tactics before games, no buzz in the camp. For them three years we didn't even threaten to win an All Ireland when we had the players to do it. In 2003 we ended up losing to Waterford. Rightly so. That was the game they parachuted Setanta [Ó hAilpín] and [John] Gardiner in for before the [senior All-Ireland] hurling final. No disrespect to the two lads but they never trained with us that year while they were taking the places of fellas who'd trained all year. Sure that's not a team.'

He'll accept his discipline could be better too. Okay, he doesn't think he should have been suspended for the Louth game this year, because as he showed the guys in Croke Park, that time in the Munster final Paul Galvin was holding and twisting his ankle …

'I'm not saying he was doing it intentionally' … and O'Leary was only trying to wriggle his way free. Then you push him on it.

'That was all though, Noel. You were just trying to get him off you?'

'That's right.'

'Genuinely, Noel.'

He smiles. 'Well, maybe there was a slight bit of a kick-out too.'

He'll be straight up about the support of the current senior team as well, or lack of it, to be precise. Last week Waterford lost their fourth All-Ireland semi-final in the Justin McCarthy era and a country, let alone, county, nearly went into mourning.

Lose today and the Cork footballers will likewise have lost four semi-finals in six years, and yet the masses on Leeside will be indifferent to their plight. O'Leary is close friends with some of the hurlers, especially O'Sullivan, but as much as he wishes them well, at times he can't help but be envious of them.

'It's unbelievably disappointing, our support, even if we're long over it now. The hurlers get caught in a sticky situation and are down three points and the crowd roars them on, which is a huge help to a team. We go three down and people just turn their asses to us. That's when we need them.

There's absolutely no doubt about it, if we win this All Ireland, it'll be for this panel of players and management team. I honestly think there's only about two or three hundred genuine Cork football supporters out there.'

He'd love to win it for Morgan ('His head for the game is unbelievable. And his passion. Even watching him giving speeches and seeing the veins start to pop; you'd be proud to play for a man like him'). For old teammates like Ciaran O'Sullivan who was probably as good as Moynihan but was never seen as such because he never won that Celtic Cross. But as he says, mostly for the men around him each night in training. That's what it's about.

Right now, they're near and yet so far. They're only one game away from a final but the way they've been playing they seem a lot further away than that. Maybe the hurling snobs have a point; the team hasn't played with any flair; it's yet to cast off its inhibitions.

He'll admit that. But the 2000 minors should have lost in the first round to Clare. They went on and won the All Ireland. That team and this team have a lot in common. This crowd could go all the way too.

'Look, there's no doubt that if we play like we did the last day against Sligo there's no hope for us against Meath. They're playing a nice brand of football and seem to be able to find space all the time, while we seem to be getting clogged up an awful lot. But we know the football we're capable of and the football we've played. It's going to come out some time again, hopefully on Sunday. [James] Masters is going to be a loss alright but the man himself, pure gentleman, said it openly in the papers that his injury gives lads like [Daniel] Goulding a chance and they might burn up Croke Park.'

He'll feel for Masters today. This is about the only year O'Leary himself has been free of injury. A week after his championship debut against Limerick in 2003, his old buddy Diarmuid O'Sullivan gave him a clatter in a county championship game. O'Leary played on but he had taken the Ciaran O'Sullivan spirit to extremes ... his ribs had been cracked, something that kept him out of the qualifier defeat to Roscommon. The following year in Killarney his medial ligament gave way; the following year against the old enemy in Croke Park, he and Conor McCarthy collided and he had to be taken off, and then last year, a viral infection from a very costly half hour of sunbathing in La Manga kept him out of the starting line-up for the summer.

But he kept coming back, kept bouncing back up, kept walking on.

He knows no other way.

✦   ✦   ✦

Upfront fury

Frustrated by failure to play to his potential, Owen Mulligan almost quit the Tyrone panel earlier this summer, but his zealous need to succeed drove him on.

25 September 2005

'**A**gainst Monaghan I saw Martin Penrose warming up on the sideline. In years gone by, I'd be, "That's for some other boy." That day I was looking over, saying, "That's for me." It was too. I looked over again against Dublin. Peter was warming up. I said, "He's coming on for me." It was actually for Ryan Mellon but then I saw a few more boys warming up. I said, "I need to do something very fast here or I'm going off. I'm definitely going off."

'So I did that.'

THAT.

You know that well by now; the TV guys rightly show it every chance they can. The turn, the first dummy, the second, the rocket. You know that it was the moment that turned and ignited his season, Tyrone's season, the season itself. That it must have been some weight off his shoulders. Just how big a relief, you 'have no f**king idea'.

You don't know that only two weeks earlier he told Mickey Harte he was on the verge of quitting the panel. That if that ball had sailed past Stephen Cluxton's post, not just Tyrone's 2005 All-Ireland dream would have been over but possibly his inter-county career. That during that Monaghan game, Heather Mulligan had to turn round to another woman in the crowd and say, 'For the last half-hour I've sat here and heard you abuse Owen Mulligan. Owen Mulligan is my son.'

You don't know – not even Owen Mulligan himself knows – that one of his sisters avoided games this summer because of the vitriol directed at her brother during the Ulster final. You don't know that, instead of just pumping his fist after that goal, he wanted to 'rip off [his] top and stick the fingers up at all the wankers that had been mouthing'.

Or, at least you didn't know.

Not to worry. Let's put you in those shoes. You are Owen Mulligan. And first, it's the distant past. Your first hero is a local hero and future friend, Stephen Conway. You go to the 1989 Ulster final with your father Eugene and Scotchy points a last-minute 45 to force a replay. You later pluck up the nerve to go into the club dressing room in Cookstown and ask Stephen to sign your uncle's Silk Cut cigarette box.

After Scotchy comes another hero. Peter Canavan. Soon he's a local one too, teaching you leisure and tourism in Holy Trinity. Well, maybe he doesn't teach you much because you don't listen much but you're all ears when it comes to football. He tells you not to be holding onto that ball in midfield, to hit this pass and that. You try his way and find it always comes off. You look over at him, he doesn't even look at you and you think to yourself, 'Jesus, you're right.'

You win a schools All Ireland under him but miss another with the county vocational team after breaking your arm. You cry your eyes out, fearing you'll never play in Croke Park. It's actually a blessing in disguise. Because you've become a bit hesitant going up for the high ball, you're moved into the forwards. You win an All-Ireland final in Croke Park the next year. You also learn from it.

Shortly after that minor final win, the club seniors are training. You go drinking instead. That drives some players mad, then the management too. But you say, 'F**k youse so.' It will be one of the biggest regrets of your life. You miss a holiday to Canada. The boys come home, all saying, 'Mugsy, you should have seen that trip.'

After that you swear that never again must your natural confidence cross over into arrogance.

The silverware and lessons keep coming. In 2001 you win your second under-21 All-Ireland medal and your first senior Ulster one but about your only contribution to that latter triumph is scoring a goal off Ger Reid fifteen seconds into your debut; the rest of that summer you spend 'getting involved with men pulling your jersey and starting fights'. In 2002 you're even more peripheral. It's not just your form, it's your attitude. 'Though it's a bad thing to say, on the bench you kind of lose interest and start thinking, "I don't have to do that extra run, I don't have to train."' Then Mickey Harte is appointed senior coach. You know he values tackling and work rate so you tackle and work harder than ever before.

Soon the whole country is talking about the master and student combo of yourself and Canavan and the bleach you've in your hair.

You first tried it when you were a minor for a bet. This year it's for a woman, your granny; when you had allowed your hair go its natural brown, she said, 'Will you get that hair back to the way it was? I can't make you out anymore on the TV.' Now everyone can't but notice you, the way you're playing.

The next thing it's September and Canavan is telling you to practice your frees because he mightn't be playing. You do, every day on the club pitch. Canavan actually plays but goes off again and though you've been foolishly exchanging pushes with Francie Bellew all day, you sense it's time you take a bit of responsibility. You land two massive frees.

Then suddenly you're on your knees, Francie is shaking your hand, a clubman, John Brennan, has you in a headlock and Cookstown shoulders you to the foot of the Hogan Stand. You look down and Croke Park is a mass of white and red. Next evening, so is Aughnacloy, then Omagh. You pick out an old boy from Cookstown, one of the Glackin twins, and with tears streaming down his face, he's looking up, saying, 'Thanks, young Mulligan. Thanks.' And it hits you.

'What the f**k have we just done here? What the f**k have we just done?'

2004. You're drinking 7-Up in a bar, watching a rugby international on the big screen, not knowing another customer is phoning his manager. 'I have money on Tyrone to win Ulster again this year yet I'm here watching Owen Mulligan drinking.' You later tell Mickey the truth and he understands; while the world's become yours, you've become the world's. You know, though, that there have been many other times when you've been drinking more than 7-Up. You've been living it up.

Women want to say they shared a moment with you. Fellas want to say they had a pint with you. But other fellas want a pop at you. You know you should walk away but before you know it, you're in another bout of fisticuffs. But hey, you've got your All Ireland and sometimes you've got to fight for your right to party.

Then at quarter to seven on a Tuesday morning, just as you're heading off to work as a joiner, your mobile rings. Ger Cavlan tells you to sit down. Cormac McAnallen is dead. You start laughing.

'Cavo, were you out again last night?' He tells you he's dead serious. 'Cavo,' you say, 'if you're telling me lies, I'll bloody break you.' But he's not; you call Canavan and he's already up with the McAnallens. You feel distraught. You feel guilty. Why him? McAnallen was easily the fittest man on the panel. He didn't drink. All you've done since the All Ireland is drink.

Thank God for Kevin Hughes. When the coffin comes out, Hub is there beside you, for you. After the funeral meal in Paudge Quinn's, he stands up and says, 'Boys, I lost my brother in a car crash. I lost my sister in another. But I moved on. You're going to think I'm mad here but you've just got to move on.'

At first you can't. You keep going out. Maybe Cormac's the reason, maybe he's just an excuse. The week before the championship, you're injured when a car bumps into the back of yours but the simple reason you're dropped is because you're playing crap.

You realise Hub is right. You have to move on. You're Tyrone's best forward against Fermanagh, Galway and Laois. The next day out against Mayo, it doesn't happen. It's almost a relief. 2005 will be a new start. You'll be fresh. Or so you think.

2005. It's late February again when you phone Mickey Harte to tell him you're going to miss training ... again. 'Sorry, Mickey, but work here's mad busy.' You're lying, of course. You're not at work. You're at home, on your couch, exhausted.

You started the year, the day, with the best of intentions, getting up at six o'clock to take Bob, the boxer you got as a present, for a run.

And you genuinely are flat out from work where nearly every customer wants to know when you'll have the job finished. You've settled down; yourself and Tina are going to share a house. Still, you're just after scoring a goal against Dublin in the league and you're down to start in the McKenna Cup final.

Then in that game against Derry, you get a hit below your knee. The physio tells you not to play against Offaly the following week but you do. Twenty minutes into that game and your league is effectively

over. Yet come the first round of the championship, you're starting against Down. You can't believe it. You also get the nod against
Cavan.

You stink Clones out. The Wednesday before the replay, you
leave your phone in the van. When you head off for training, you see
three missed calls from Mickey Harte. You know why he's phoning.
You pull into the car park and Mickey is there waiting for you. You've
been dropped.

You're furious with yourself. You just know it's going to be a complete stuffing match after the treatment Sean Cavanagh got in the
drawn game and know you're not going to get back in for the Ulster
final. But you think, 'Maybe this is the kick in the ass you need.'

You keep getting up at six to run with Bob. You start going to
train early, working hard on the left foot Mickey told you to develop.
You start leading the way in the sprints. You train with the club on
the nights the county aren't out. You're constantly in the gym in the
Glenavon. The desire, the fitness, is back. But the form isn't.

You're brought on in the Ulster final. You nearly feel like an
impostor. Whereas in 2003, everything used go through you and
Canavan, now everything goes through Stevie O'Neill. Hours before
the replay, Mickey tells you Peter won't be starting. Neither will you;
instead he's going with Ryan Mellon. You nod. But inside, you're
reeling.

With twenty minutes to go, yourself and Canavan are brought
on. Then Canavan is sent off, then Stevie too. You think, 'This is
a chance is to grab the headlines, to grab the winning point.' But
you don't. Oisin McConville does. That day it seriously crosses your
mind to pull the pin.

You've always said that if you're not good enough to be starting,
you won't be sticking around taking the panel spot of some young
fella and having the crowd shout, 'Get that stupid prick back off!'
For the last few weeks you've had friends say, 'Pull the pin, Mugsy.
You should be on that team. Look at the forwards today. Bloody
crap.' And you're thinking, 'Maybe they're right. This is getting too
frustrating. Maybe I will hang them up.'

For some reason, though, you go to the next training session.
And for some even stranger reason, Mickey Harte tells you you're

starting against Monaghan. Again you struggle; setting up a goal for Stephen O'Neill is all you do.

Your mother hears the 'supporters'. You can too. Last year apparently you were a drug dealer and riding men's wives; this year, the discussion boards say you're good mates with Wayne Rooney. Yourself and Tina laugh that one off but you can't laugh off what your mother and father are having to put up with. Right now they're both prayed out.

Their last hope is Frank McGuigan. They ask him to call up to the house. Frank asks how everything outside football is. 'One hundred per cent,' you assure him. He assures you your football will come good too. You're trying too hard. 'Don't be afraid to make a mistake. There's less chance you'll make one that way. You can't become a bad footballer overnight, Mugsy.'

You can become a brilliant one again though.

A few Tyrone subs are warming up. You know it's fight or f**kin' flight. So you fight for a ball played in by Stephen O'Neill. And after that, it all just happens. The ball seems to stick to you when before it was bouncing off you. You sell a dummy. You think, 'Why are you boys falling for that dummy?' But you throw another, and again they buy it.

Then you let fly. You intend for it to go to Stephen Cluxton's right, but it flies past his left. Croke Park explodes. And with it, so does the tension within. Afterwards, you phone the parents and you can sense the relief in their voices. The next day, the replay, you're sure your first shot is sailing wide and shout out 'S**t' but it turns inside the post.

You can now do no wrong. You score a goal with the left foot Mickey had you working on and stare out the Hill. That's 1-5 now from play. After the game, you applaud that Hill. It applauds you. You're no longer a 'poof' to them. You're a player.

The next day out, Francie again makes life tough for you. Again you do your bit. And again, poor Francie ends up having to congratulate you. It's a big scalp. Before the game, you wanted to beat Armagh more than you wanted to beat them in 2003. But now it's not enough. You want what you experienced on 28 September 2003.

'People talk about it being like a drug, about getting that same trip over and over again. You want to get that feeling again, that feeling of winning and being carried off the field and going up the steps.

'But the whole thing is a drug. You'll have people begrudging you but at the end of the day, travelling down on the bus, listening to Mickey give a team talk, running out in front of 80,000.' You are Owen Mulligan. Or at least today you'd like to be.

✦   ✦   ✦

Malachy Clerkin

Dedicating followers to his fashion

Australia, Lebanon, France and Italy all feature strongly in the nomadic life story of Leinster coach Michael Cheika, but it is his dalliance with the world of haute couture that may raise eyebrows.

16 April 2006

I t starts with a note he's not supposed to see in an office he's probably not supposed to be in and a phone number he's definitely not supposed to ring. Or maybe it doesn't. Maybe it starts further back than that, with a twenty-year-old Lebanese woman visiting her sister in Sydney in the 1950s and just deciding not to go home. Or then again, maybe it doesn't. Maybe it starts – really starts – a fortnight ago in Toulouse with his team deep in their own 22, with his out-half doing what no Irish coach would dream of telling him he's supposed to do, with his team running the length of the pitch for the kind of try no Irish team is supposed to score. Wherever it starts, wherever it ends, Michael Cheika's story isn't exactly the most linear one you'll ever hear. The best ones never are.

Just for kicks, we'll start with the note. Cheika joined Randwick Rugby Club in the Sydney suburb of Coogee when he left school, although even an apparently straight-forward sentence like that needs a little qualification. He'd never played the game. He'd liked it, watched it, regularly went down to the Randwick Oval on a Saturday to shout at those involved in it. But never played it. The reason was simple: A working class kid, he went to a working class school and working class schools in Sydney played league. So he played league.

Within two years of joining up, though, he was in the Australian under-21 squad. Just like that. These were the dying days of amateurism, though, and systems and structures weren't what they would become. In a different era, given different circumstances, maybe he'd have gone on and made a name for himself as a player. As it was, he found himself a crack and slipped through it. Which is where the note comes in.

'One day, I was in the coach's office and I found a little note on his desk,' he says. 'There was this guy from a club in France who'd written to him looking for players. He was just looking for any random players our coach could send him. Now, I knew the kind of guy our coach was and there's no way he would have told anyone about that note in a million years. So I lifted it off his desk and stuck it in my pocket and rang the guy myself. I ended up going to France and playing there for a few years and in Italy for a few more.'

In all, he did Europe for seven years. Well, sort of. He got into a routine of playing through the calendar – winter in Europe followed by one at home and then back again in time for the start of the next one. They say Richie Benaud hasn't felt a winter chill on his face for over forty years; Cheika barely saw a summer throughout the 1990s. It's not a gripe, though. Not remotely.

With amateurism on life support, clubs had no shortage of backers prepared to throw the switch. Cheika trousered what was on offer and happily staved off the day when he'd have to get a proper job. When he wasn't playing rugby, he was travelling goggle-eyed throughout Europe, taking in everything from Portuguese sunsets to Russian trains journeys, from Dublin bars to Tuscan villas.

'There's so much culture and history on this continent to immerse yourself in. Maybe Europeans don't appreciate it as much because they've been here all their lives but for someone coming from a pretty rough-edged part of Sydney or wherever, you're talking absolute worlds apart. I really got to love the European lifestyle, the fact that everywhere has a proper history. The fact that there's a historical relevance to two tribes facing off against each other or to two countries that are next door to each other. I suppose as well, I was lucky to get to learn a few languages. It made up a bit for not pursuing a tertiary education at home.'

There comes a time, though. It's all very well being a multilingual gadabout thousands of miles from home winking at the haughty girl behind the counter at the boulangerie. But one day you wake up and all of a sudden you're twenty-eight. Shit.

So he went home and decided to get a job. He just hadn't a clue as what. Some cousins of his were involved in fashion, ran retail stores. To pick up a few bucks here and there, he went in and helped out. 'I used to do the occasional shift for them. It was good way to meet girls, if nothing else. I mean, where else can you go and get paid to tell girls they look beautiful? So I used to go there and hang out more than anything. But I picked up a few things about the business along the way.'

Now, to most people, 'picking up a few things about the business' would mean learning to spot when one of the delivery men is trying to scam you out of a few hundred quid and the like. Not Cheika. He saw an ad in the paper one day that said that Collette Dinnigan was looking for a business manager.

These being the sports pages, the *Tribune* is going to take a punt here and guess that you, dear reader, haven't a rashers who Collette Dinnigan is. Turns out she's far and away the biggest fashion designer in Australia. She dresses people for the Oscars. When Halle Berry attended the world premiere of *Die Another Day* in 2002, she wore a Dinnigan creation. Cate Blanchett, Nicole Kidman, Kylie Minogue? Clothes-horses for this woman.

And having done not an awful lot more than a few shifts winkling phone numbers out of surfer chicks by telling them their bums didn't look big in this skirt or those jeans, Cheika reckoned he would have a go at running this mutli-millionaire's worldwide fashion empire for her. Told you his story wasn't exactly linear.

'Collette wanted someone who could speak French and Italian, which I could do, and I sort of made up most of the rest. I didn't think for a second I'd get the job and I basically went there with a hand-written foolscap page in an envelope which I slipped under the door. And I don't know, she must have been really desperate or something because she called me back and I met with her three times in three days and ended up working for her. So that's what properly kicked off my interest in the fashion side of things.

'Working for her was such an amazing experience, the complexity involved in bringing her creativity to production really appealed to me. It was taking the ideas and creations she had and converting them into the reality of pieces in stores. Being part of that was great and it gave me a lot of international experience from a fashion point of view that helped me when it came to setting up my own business later on.'

(Meanwhile, in a galaxy far, far away, a quiet Cork school teacher called Declan Kidney was instilling in two of his pupils – an out-half called Ronan O'Gara and a scrum-half called Peter Stringer – the basics of the skills that will attempt to ruin the afternoon of Collette Dinnigan's former business manager next Sunday. Mad world.)

He was still playing with Randwick and by this stage, not only was he the sharpest dresser at the club, he was also the captain. The complete separation between the two segments of his life suited him down to the ground. Nobody at work talked rugby, nobody at Randwick talked sequins. Not to his face, anyway.

Still, he was restless. He set up a business of his own, dealing in all sorts – fashion, property, a restaurant even. And, even then, it wasn't enough. When the call came from David Campese (a Randwick alumnus) saying that there was this club in Italy looking for a coach, the idea intrigued him more than anything. He'd never dreamt of being a coach and even now he isn't all that certain why he decided to go.

'I left a few unhappy people behind me, not to mention my business partners. Collette was very good about it, even though it was clear that the few months I was taking off from her was going to turn into for ever. I think my reasoning was that if I go there and make a balls of it, then at least I've had a go and at least I've done it in an area that's as testing as possible. Because I didn't have any comforts to fall back on, you know what I mean? I was there by myself, just me and a load of people I didn't know. So I suppose it was as much to see if I could do it as anything.'

He did okay. Some things he found difficult, others not so much. Not having friends or family to come home to helped in a perverse way because it left him with nothing to concentrate on but this new way of life he'd gotten himself into. And preserving distance between himself and players didn't pose any problems either since he'd never really been one for the piss-up and the sing-song anyway. Padova came sixth at the end of his season in charge.

'I enjoyed it. I wouldn't have kept at it if I hadn't liked it. The challenge really got me going. But there was so much I had to learn. As a coach you've got to have a totally different set of personal skills with regard to players. You've got to be nice to them, for a start. You have to think about the collective in everything you do. It was a good experience.'

He couldn't stay, though. Life got in the way.

✦

When World War II ended, whole countries emerged blinking into the sunlight with no immediate idea about what to do with themselves. Australia had more going for it than most places – a land abounding in nature's gifts of beauty rich and fair, like the song said. What it didn't have was people. Or to be more clinical about it, workers. All these natural resources but nowhere near enough hands to cultivate them.

So the government went trawling. Out went the nets and up went the call. Australia is open for business. Come one, come all. Cheika remembers his father telling him stories about the advertisements that were posted all over Lebanon. A new life, a new hope.

'There was very little going on in Lebanon. It's a poor country, no real resources, no big industry. It was colonised by the French after World War I and became a more intellectual place than it might otherwise have. There are a lot of universities there and it's a bit more European than a lot of countries in that region.'

His father was twenty when he followed a whole generation out of Lebanon. Ten years later, on a visit to Sydney to stay with her sister who had similarly decamped, his mother met and fell in love with him. Instead of going back home as she'd planned, she stayed, reared a family and indeed lives there to this day. She does so without her husband, though, his failing health the reason for Cheika's return from Padova. He made it home in time for the last chapter of his father's life.

The year in Italy had been a small dose, like a vaccine for coaching almost. But it didn't take. He was laid low with all the symptoms by now and he knew he'd never shake them. Within a year of his return, he'd taken over the Randwick team he'd previously captained, his former teammate David Knox by his side. In three seasons under them, Randwick finished third, second and first in their division, going through his final year there unbeaten. It made him hot property and he applied for the head coach's job at the new Super 14 franchise Perth. When offered the assistant's role, he declined and put the feelers out for a top job somewhere else. Alan Gaffney – his first coach all those years ago at Randwick – saw Leinster in need of a coach, Cheika in need of a blank canvas and indulged himself in a subtle piece of matchmaking. The rest is as they say ...

'In the beginning, it was a matter of meeting everyone, getting to know the people. You can't just come in and make sweeping changes, you have to assess what's happening in a place, respect everyone's space, understand the history of the place. Like, I understood pretty quickly that there was a lot of scepticism around because this was the fourth coach in four years and also because I wouldn't have been the most high-profile applicant around. I knew there'd be a lot of, you know, "Who is this bloke?" So the first thing that I needed to do was get to know guys and start the respect-building process.'

He knew bits and pieces about Leinster through Gaffney and Gary Ella, and the rest, well, folk weren't long filling him in on the rest. Or at least, what they considered the rest to be.

'When we started off, everyone wanted to tell us something about the team. I went to a few dinners with people I'd met who didn't know I was the new coach of Leinster and they'd be telling me this and that. Every stereotype you've ever heard of about Leinster, I'd managed to pick up on in the first few weeks. As it turned out, the reality of it couldn't have been more different. These players just took to it with a keenness and an eagerness that made our lives so much easier than all these stories said it was going to be.'

So the stereotype thing bugs him even if, as the only man in the place who can properly be said to be a fashion expert, he will admit that there are plenty of the Leinster squad who have firm opinions on their appearance. 'The scarf brigade is pretty strong,' he says mentioning nobody in particular. Well, a certain Triple-Crown-sealing try-scorer's name does crop up.

Mostly, though, he falls over himself talking up his players, the ones putting into action the thoughts and ideas he and Knox come up with. And we're back at the start, back with the try Irish teams aren't supposed to score, back with the verve, the imagination, the balls to decline the safe kick to touch in favour of the length-of-the-field bonanza that came instead.

'At the end of the day, the players know the game is theirs because they play it. Everything that happens is a decision. When to go, when to stay, when to risk it, when to tighten it up. Those decisions are all made on the field and they're made by the players. And I really do think that the coach's role is overrated. I'm not just saying that. We give them what guidance we can. But I've never won a game as a coach – the teams have won them.'

The future is his to do with what he pleases. A couple more years at Leinster and then home, you'd have thought. And it's not especially difficult to see him in charge of an international side some day. Then again, he could ditch it all and take over the world with his fashion empire. With Cheika, he rarely knows himself what's next, so there's no chance of you knowing either.

✦ ✦ ✦

McDowell on a voyage of discovery in Open waters

12 July 2009

Larne Harbour, Co Antrim
Conditions: Calm, mild, slightly overcast

Midday Monday at Larne Port and the breakfast rush is over at Pinky Moon's Pitstop. Which, of course, doesn't for a minute mean that breakfast is over. Not bloody likely, hi. This part of the north Antrim coast was built on the Ulster fry (£6.95) and the filled soda (£3.75) and the tea (£1.40) and the buttered bread (£0.90) and nobody checks their watch before ordering. But the lunchtime sailing to Cairnryan doesn't have the footfall of the early morning crossings so the place is quieter now and the chap selling the plastic leprechauns and Irish coffee mugs in the newsagents across the hall doesn't have to look up from his *Telegraph* very often.

Graeme McDowell does this every year in early July. Not the fry bit, just the ferry bit. The week of the Scottish Open, he loads up the Range Rover on the Monday, drives the hour from Portrush to Larne, rolls onto P&O's finest for an hour and hey presto – he has his own car in the drive for a fortnight. He has his clubs in the boot so he doesn't have to spend an hour and a couple of hundred quid dragging them through an airport – even twenty-nine-year-old multi-millionaires resent lining the anti-golfer pockets of Ryanair and Easyjet at this point – and better yet, he can live out the next two weeks without being a slave to the rhythms of the tour. Logistics become a whole lot simpler when you're not relying on a courtesy car timetable.

Today, he has Ricky Elliott riding shotgun. Now, Ricky Elliott has a lot to answer for. He and McDowell more or less grew up together and were by a distance the two best young golfers in Portrush. When McDowell won the Ulster Boys' title in 1996, it was Elliott's title from the previous year that he assumed. When McDowell ignored the advice of the GUI and set about chasing golf scholarships at American colleges in 1999, it was because Elliott was emailing him from the University of Toldeo in Ohio, telling him to get on a plane.

And when McDowell was looking for an American base in which to settle down for the half the year every year, it was Elliott who fixed him up with contacts in Lake Nona in Florida, home now to more pro golfers than a Learjet sales convention.

But most of all and worst of all, McDowell blames Elliott for the accent. The tortured Lough Neagh/South Beach/All Points In Between hybrid that he long ago gave up trying to shake. Meanwhile Elliott, who's lived in the US for over a decade now, still sounds like he should be racing in the North West 200. McDowell reckons his mate cheated because he spent the first few years over there living in a house with Irish lads while McDowell got stuck down in Alabama and found himself crashing face first into a language barrier.

'I remember the first day I was there,' he says, 'I just couldn't get over the accent. It was so Deep South, real 'Y'awll come back now, y'hear?' stuff. The very first day, I went into Subway and tried to order a sandwich from this old coloured lady, a real southerner. And she just didn't have a clue what I was saying. So I basically said to myself that something was going to have to change or else I'd be repeating myself for the rest of my life. I guess that's what happened and it's stuck ever since. I came home after my first year there with a mid-Atlantic twang. It's terrible, absolutely terrible. I get a lot of abuse for it and rightly so. But you know, if that's the worst thing I get abuse about I can live with it.'

Elliott didn't manage as stellar a college career as his young friend – then again, nobody else in America did either as, in his final year at UAB, McDowell beat Lucas Glover, Camillo Villegas, Oliver Wilson and Hunter Mahan to the Golfer of the Year award – but he makes a very respectable living now at the golf facility out in Lake Nona. Come summertime though, it's too hot to play golf in Florida so for the next three weeks he'll caddie for the Dutch player Maarten LaFaber. Once we reach Cairnryan, he and McDowell are off up the road to Turnberry on a recce. Buddies hitting balls, friends on a mission.

Irish Sea, Larne to Cairnryan shipping lane
Conditions: Perfect, still, sunny

If this all seems very loose and free and easy, it's only because

McDowell has worked so diligently to make it so. He tells the story of his first ever British Open now just to hear out loud how absurd it all was. It was 2004 and it was Troon and as they say up around where he's from, he didn't know what end of him was up. He didn't want to leave anything to chance so he had his whole team there. Swing coach, mind coach, fitness coach, agent, girlfriend, family, girlfriend's family, mates, mates of mates and caddie. So many people, he forgot himself. Rented a three-bedroomed house and had eight people living in it for the week.

'I was running around like an eejit. It was just chaos. Missed the cut comfortably. I remember walking away from that week just kicking myself for getting so caught up in everything. I didn't get my head around it at all.'

Bet you don't regret it now though?

'No, not at all. It was my first major and it was so exciting. The golf course didn't suit me because my technique wasn't very good back then at all. The first nine holes went all the way out to the ocean and were very much left-to-right orientated, with the wind hard off the right. I was definitely a drawer of the golf ball and couldn't spell fade back then, never mind hit one. So it was a very difficult week, along with the circus that surrounded it. But I learned so much from it.'

From there to here in just five years. He's finished in the top twenty at each of the last four majors; Phil Mickelson is the only other player in the world who can say that. He was a revelation at the Ryder Cup last September, a weekend he'd thought about and worked towards every day for the previous eighteen months. He's earned well over €5 million here and in the States, won four times on tour and is long established inside the world's top fifty. The life he's carved out for himself is all he could hope for, lacking only the adornment now of a career week. He'll have the family there alright and the Horizon Sports reps who've made such a difference to him over the past two years but that'll be about it.

'Tee to green, I know I'm good enough to win a major,' he says. 'I know that. But my short game needs to constantly improve. My putting has got better and now the short irons have to come along as well. Inside 100 yards, I have to be getting up and down most of the time instead of some of the time. Look at Mickelson, look at Tiger, look at Harrington. Inside 100 yards, bang – down in two. The thing with majors is that most of the time – Bethpage was a bit of an exception because of how soft it became with the rain – but most of the time, the greens are just so hard to hit. The greens are firm and fiddly and you're scrambling all the time.

'What the majors do is simplify where your weaknesses are. For me over the past few majors, it's been my short game. No question. At Oakmont last year, I was there or thereabouts going into the last two rounds and when I sat down and reflected on Sunday night I knew that my short game just wasn't good enough. As the greens got firmer, faster and tougher, I wasn't able to scramble well enough. Same with Birkdale last year, where I shot an eighty on the Saturday to take myself completely out of the picture after leading on the Thursday night.'

Four top-twenties in a row but not one top-ten. Launchpad or glass ceiling? That is the question.

Cairnryan Port, Dumfries and Galloway, Scotland
Conditions: Cloudy, light wind, rain on the way

'Sorry Graeme, could I trouble you for an autograph?' interjects one of the P&O staff. As he's doing the needful, the chap mentions that Rory McIlroy was on the crossing this morning.

'Some motor he has, eh?' says P&O guy.

'Why, which one was he driving? He didn't take the Porsche did he?' asks McDowell with a smile.

'Nah, the Audi. What are you driving yourself?' asks P&O guy.

'Ah, just the Range Rover,' says McDowell. P&O guy almost shrugs as he walks away.

He can't remember when he first heard McIlroy's name but he has no trouble pinpointing the first time he did a double take. It would have been this week five years ago and he was in Loch Lomond when somebody told him that this McIlroy kid had shot 61 around Royal Portrush, a course McDowell could draw with his eyes closed. 'I remember it clearly,' he says. 'I went, 'Hang on, *what?* He shot what?"'

It was a couple of years before they played together for the first time, in a practice round before the Dunhill Links in 2007. McIlroy had him beaten by the fifteenth. Now they eat together, play together, travel together when they can. They slag each other constantly and rely on each other to find a way to see whatever United match is on, wherever they are in the world. McDowell is fascinated to watch his young friend grow up and even now is constantly amazed at what he can do. It's not a big-brother-little-brother thing though, at least not any more.

'Maybe a year ago I would have felt a bit like that, a bit protective of him you know? But there's no need any more. He knows the ropes better than me at this stage. I'm ten years older than him but that means nothing. I have nothing to teach him either on or off the golf course. We're very close friends now.

'He's after going on a bit of a spending spree with property and cars over the past while and yet you just know from talking to him that he's such a well-grounded kid. But I think that's an Irish thing too. Nobody lets you get too carried away with yourself here and it's one of the things I love about home more than anything. We don't lose the run of ourselves. When I'm in Portrush, I get treated the same now as when I was fifteen years old.'

He'll go back there on Tuesday to watch his brother Gary play in the North of Ireland. He'll stick the clubs in the boot and head off across the water again and when he's done, he'll probably fit in nine holes just to keep his eye in. Then he'll be ready for whatever Turnberry has for him, wind, rain, whatever.

'Patience is a huge part of it when it comes to majors. You have to learn to reset yourself and realise very early on the twenty-under-par isn't going to win, or rather that twenty-under-par will win by fifteen shots if you shoot it. You're back to par being a good score and that's tough to get used to when you're coming off normal tour events where you're expecting to shoot in the mid-sixties a couple of rounds a week. So you have to hit the reset button and not panic when you drop a shot or even when you drop two back-to-back. I think I've learned how to do that now. I know I have.'

And with that, the tannoy tells us we're coming into dock so he and Elliott get up and head below deck. Happy the man whose ship is about to come in.

CIARAN CRONIN

Following in the shoes of a fisherman

Eddie O'Sullivan got paid for what he caught in his uncles' fishing business as a kid. How times have changed as he gets a four-year contract as a net gain for his empty World Cup trawl.

7 October 2007

I n an interview about a year ago, Eddie O'Sullivan told of his youth down in West Cork and the fish business his uncles used to run in that part of the world. There he'd be during the summer holidays, young Eddie, out fishing at all hours of the day and night in order to earn a few bob. 'You got paid for what you caught,' he stated. 'If you caught nothing, you got paid nothing.' How times have changed.

From a job, albeit a summer one, where he would have, at times, toiled hard and not picked up a penny, he now enjoys a role where his post-World Cup net is completely bare and he still gets rewarded handsomely. If during those summers down in Youghal, O'Sullivan felt that Mother Nature was treating him a touch unfairly, then there's no doubt that the stars have re-aligned themselves in such a way as to make up for her unpredictability. Ridiculously so. The more you write about it, or read it, the more absurd it gets. The man who has led Ireland to their worst Rugby World Cup performance in the history of the competition is being rewarded for his many incompetencies over the past few months with a new four-year contract and a significant pay rise to boot. For those of us out there who possess some sense of natural justice – that good deeds should be rewarded and bad deeds punished – our moral compass has been completely skewed.

What makes this even worse is the stunning arrogance with

which the coach and the IRFU have gone about their business over
the past week. It all started minutes after another inadequate effort
against Argentina at the Parc des Princes last Sunday. In a touchline
interview, Sinéad Kissane, the TV3 reporter, asked Eddie O'Sullivan
would he be reconsidering his position now that the World Cup was
over, a wholly legitimate question that the vast majority of the rugby
nation wanted an answer to. O'Sullivan feigned not to hear and
when she asked it again he replied with the words, 'No. Absolutely
not. Absolutely not.'

Kissane then asked another question and O'Sullivan's voice was
still audibly quivering with shock at what he had been asked thirty
seconds previous. Did he not foresee the question coming? Or did
he not think he should have been asked it? Clearly not, because as he
bade farewell to Kissane with the nastiest of looks at the end of the
interview, he walked over to IRFU media manager Karl Richardson
and whispered something in his ear. Richardson then fixed his gaze
on Kissane, motioned her towards him with his index finger and
proceeded to verbally admonish her for a good ten seconds. We're
still puzzled as to why.

How on earth either O'Sullivan or Richardson thought the question was either unexpected or inappropriate is anyone's guess. And
the way in which Kissane was treated by O'Sullivan's withering look
and Richardson's dressing down was unedifying to say the least.

To be fair, the behaviour was out of character for the normally
affable Irish media manager but it might just be a sign of the you're-
either-with-us-or-against-us mentality that seems to be pervading
the IRFU right now.

The media circus rolled on. On Monday, Philip Browne, a highly
paid chief executive, was wheeled out on RTÉ News to tell the
nation that the IRFU were going to stick with O'Sullivan. Just like
the press conference announcing the coach's four-year extension
before the World Cup, Browne spoke little sense and appeared to
entirely misjudge the mood of rugby supporters out there. He spoke
of how 'three bad matches' – we make it eight in a row now – hadn't
changed what O'Sullivan had achieved over the past four to five
years and that he didn't want a situation like in Wales, who were
looking for their thirteenth coach in twenty years.

He's right on that count. Why on earth would the IRFU want to be like the Welsh, an international side whose stylish Grand Slam win in 2005 eclipses anything O'Sullivan has ever done with Ireland? No, he's right. It's better to go out of the World Cup with a whimper having scored just eight tries than to go out having played a full part in the game of this World Cup, or possibly any World Cup, having amassed twenty-three tries. No, no, we don't want to be like Wales.

That kind of talk makes us extremely worried about the upcoming review into Ireland's World Cup performance. As far as we understand it, and it's not that straight-forward, it will work a little something like this. All the different people in charge of the many elements of Team Ireland – rugby, medical, logistics, fitness, communications and so – will each write a report on their respective areas of responsibility and those files will be sent to Lansdowne Road for the relevant committees to peruse at their leisure. As we understand it, Eddie O'Sullivan will not have to stand in front of anybody and explain himself. He'll only have to appear in person and open his mouth if the people reading his particular report, the appointments committee as far as we know, need some more answers. We bet they won't need them. So to sum up, we're going to have O'Sullivan justifying himself on paper to three people – Neilly Jackson, Pat Whelan and Noel Murphy – who'll be willing to accept any kind of waffle to justify their own decision to award him a four-year contract extension. As far as interrogation goes, it won't exactly be Guantanamo Bay. It's going to be a complete whitewash.

And after that? Rumours have been going about the place these past few weeks that the rest of the Irish management team were unhappy with the fact that O'Sullivan looked after himself in the contract stakes and left the rest of his colleagues in limbo. Rumours? How could the rest of the management team be anything but unhappy at the contract situation?

It's funny that O'Sullivan has claimed the consistency of the past few years as his own achievement but the moment things go askew it's someone else's fault. For example, after the French game the coach blamed discipline on the pitch (the players' responsibility) and Ireland's creaky line-out (Niall O'Donovan's job) for the defeat.

Surely a strong character like O'Donovan, and others on the

coaching staff, must be thinking of walking away from it all now. Not only have they not received any recognition from the union for what this regime is supposed to have achieved over the past few years, they're constantly dumped upon by their most senior colleague when things go wrong. However, it's only by thinking about the situation they're in that you understand why they haven't rocked the boat. If any of them resigned their posts, they'd be blacklisted by the IRFU and would struggle to get a job in any of the provincial set-ups. The whole system is farcical. It's like communist China out there.

Piss-off the authorities, the IRFU in this case, and you could be blacklisted and put under house arrest for the rest of your career.

Meanwhile, the big boss gets away scot free. Not once during, or after, this World Cup has O'Sullivan held his hands up and taken responsibility for anything. At Sunday's post-match press conference, the coach, still a little rattled by the surprise of being asked if he was going to reconsider his position, finally admitted that he felt his players might have been short of rugby going into the tournament.

It was the coach's eureka moment. Finally, after four weeks of attempting to put his finger on what was going on with his off-colour side, he came up with some sort of explanation, but he still didn't exactly claim it was his fault. There's been a stunning lack of accountability from the coach throughout the whole competition and while Brian O'Driscoll did the decent thing on Sunday and claimed that the players were responsible for everything that went wrong, the guy sitting beside him kept his mouth shut and allowed his captain's words to drift into the air without any company. Yet another example of poor man-management.

So what should be done? If they weren't so far up their own backsides, the IRFU would now be looking for a new head coach, one with southern hemisphere coaching experience if possible. As we mentioned last week, every team that has performed to any degree so far at this World Cup has employed a coaching team rich in cross-hemisphere coaching experience. It's only the unions who struggle to see past their own noses, the RFU and IRFU in particular, who believe that they simply have to appoint a native as national coach.

Again, we stress the fact that there's nothing wrong whatsoever with having an Irish coach of the Irish team but by the same logic, there's nothing wrong with having a foreign coach of our national side either. It's about picking the right man for the job and right now it appears as though our mentally weary players could do with the influence of somebody who's experienced rugby somewhere other than Ireland or Britain.

Instead of considering this kind of option, however, the IRFU seem intent on doing the best ostrich impersonation they can manage, and hope that by the time they spit the last of the sand from their mouths, everything will be okay.

In the meantime, the WRU will be headhunting the best available, or soon to be available, coach in the world to succeed Gareth Jenkins. Warren Gatland's name has been mentioned and it would appear from his comments this week that the former Irish and Wasps coach is up for the job. Jake White, another technically excellent coach, might also come into contention if he, as predicted, quits the Springboks after the World Cup. Nick Mallett might have been another contender only for the fact that Italy signed him up first.

What will be interesting to observe during the 2008 Six Nations is how the rapid-fire decision-makers out there, Wales and Italy, fare in comparison to Ireland. If O'Sullivan's side can't beat both of these sides at Croke Park, serious questions will have to be asked. In truth, if Ireland can't produce at least four out of five victories next spring, as he has done over the past two Six Nations campaigns, then the logical thing for the IRFU will be to hand him his cards.

Then again, no decision they make ever again can surprise us. Even if O'Sullivan catches nothing, he'll probably still be retained.

✦ ✦ ✦

Lost legacy

Clive Woodward's credibility as a coach is in serious doubt after the Lions' 38-19 defeat to New Zealand closes a disastrous tour.

10 July 2005

As the series trophy presentation took place in front of the Main Stand at Eden Park yesterday, Clive Woodward strolled around shaking hands with his defeated players. For a lot of them, it was probably for the first time and that's not an exaggeration. A number of squad members have been commenting in recent days about how little they've spoken to the Lions coach over the course of the past six weeks.

With the tour at an end and Woodward's credibility as a rugby coach in serious doubt, they're probably thanking their lucky stars that they haven't had their minds filled with the doublespeak and nonsense that routinely emerges from his mouth. There was yet more of it after the game when Woodward declared that his squad are 'better people, better players' at the end of this six-week tour but perhaps the New Zealand inflection of his statement – they pronounce 'e' as 'i' in this part of the world – gives a more accurate reflection as to what state of mind the Lions travel home in today.

Because no matter how much the squad have enjoyed their stay in the land of the long white cloud, they can't be happy with the direction the test series has taken and yesterday's 38-19 defeat in Auckland can only have served to emphasise this point further.

There have been so many glaringly obvious tactical errors from Woodward over the past few weeks, the squad have surely lost whatever faith they ever had in their frontman.

The post-series statistics tell us everything we need to know about the gulf in tactical ambition and class between the two sides and, indeed, the two sets of coaching teams. If the three games are totted up in aggregate fashion, the All Blacks would have won 107-40, a tally that we know could have been a lot more had the heavens not opened up during the first test in Christchurch. It's a similar story with the try count after the three tests, the All Blacks scoring four times as many tries as their visitors, 12-3 the figure confirmed by the tallymen. 'I'm not sure what the final try count was in this one; I've lost count,' said Graham Henry as he reminded the assembled media that his much-maligned Lions side of 2001 shared fourteen tries with Australia over the course of the test series.

So the All Blacks collected their Waterford Crystal trophy – the glass, not the horse – although the Lions supporters would have been forgiven for wondering whether the thoroughbreds in the New Zealand line-up had needed their urine looking at in the past few months. Take Tana Umaga for one. The captain has been immense all series, as a battering ram, as a tackler, as an evasive runner, as a leader – as everything you could ever desire from a rugby player.

Yesterday he scored two tries from close range and it was strange that when he spent time in the sin bin early in the game, his side actually appeared to get better, scoring tries through Conrad Smith and Ali Williams to swing the tide. And that was the story of the game really.

Beforehand, there was a lovely balance to the Lions side with five players from each of England, Ireland and Wales in the starting line-up, and the test team truly became the power of four when Gordon Bulloch took to the paddock with one minute of normal time on the clock. But while yesterday's side never let themselves down as individuals, the team effort was much less than the sum of its parts.

They appeared tired and disjointed as the game wore on but to their immense credit, they never folded to fully allow a youthful All Blacks side, in which debutant out-half Luke McAlister contributed magnificently, to truly run riot.

Before it all, there was an impeccably observed minute's silence for the victims of the London bombings, an event that has had an undeniable effect on the mood of the masses of Lions supporters in Auckland these past few days. However, they still had enough left to get behind their team with the same ferocity and passion as they have since the tour's opening game. In all truth, they've been the only positive contribution from Britain and Ireland to this test series.

Graham Henry praised the supporters' efforts after the game and he even managed to fit in a bit of canvassing for the New Zealand bid for the 2011 World Cup. But the last word of a bizarre tour had to go to Woodward, and the head coach proved that he wasn't all out of crazy just yet. 'If I was brutally honest I'd bring more players on a tour like this and I'd play more games. When I say more games, I'd try to play on Tuesday, Thursday and Saturday and I'd try to make the Lions bigger and better.'

And with that the men in the white coats came in to wheel him away. Well, not really but it wouldn't have looked at all out of place.

Best of luck Southampton FC.

Ger Siggins

Cricket World Cup murder

The murder of Pakistan cricket coach Bob Woolmer, strangled
in his hotel room, was a shocking end to a glittering life.

25 March 2007

The turbulent city of Kingston is still awash with incredible
rumours about the Cricket World Cup murder. The stran-
gling of Pakistan coach Bob Woolmer – hours after Ireland
had knocked his team out of the competition – has shocked the
world and brought the issue of the purity of professional sport into
question once more.

On Thursday night, four-and-a-half days after his body was found
by a hotel chambermaid, the Jamaican police finally announced that
Woolmer had been asphyxiated by manual strangulation.

At a press conference in front of hundreds of reporters, ex-
Scotland Yard detective Mark Shields told how a person or persons
unknown had gained access to Woolmer's room on the twelfth floor
and killed him with such force that a bone was broken in his neck.
Woolmer was a big man, 6 ft 1" and over 18 stone. It wouldn't have
been easy to kill him. The police are following several lines of inquiry
but have yet to detain a suspect.

They believe the coach knew his killer and say that 'those associated with or having access to Mr Woolmer may have vital information that would assist us with our inquiry'.

Kingston has had an unwanted reputation for many years. From
the seventeenth-century buccaneers to modern-day Yardie drug
gangs, it is a city where violent death is common. One-hundred-and-
forty people were murdered in January alone, in a city with a population of 660,000.

The Pegasus in New Kingston is a busy international hotel. The flags of the competing nations fly in the lobby, which has been converted to a cricket theme for the fortnight that the city hosts six World Cup matches. But the prosperous and comfortable facade cannot hide the fact that the violence of the city outside has found its way inside the hotel's doors. Two years ago an American air steward was murdered in his room at the hotel.

After the game last Saturday, Woolmer and his team pulled up in their team bus outside the Pegasus just as a bus taking Irish supporters and media to an out-of-town party drove away. It was 7.30 p.m.

Woolmer went to the bar just off the lobby and had two bottles of the local beer, Red Stripe. At 8.30 p.m. he retired for the evening. It had been a long and stressful day ... the team bus had left for the ground at 7 a.m. that morning for the 9.30 a.m. match against Ireland. It is not known what he did in his room but he logged onto the internet and sent an email to his wife Gill at 3.12 a.m. She said he was fine, albeit upset about the loss to Ireland. The last email he sent was to his ghostwriter Ivo Tennant. It read:

'We might have to do this from afar. I don't know what is going to happen next. We will first play our game against Zimbabwe and then fly back to Pakistan. This will give me more time to work on my book on coaching.

The articles will have to be more general from now on.

Thanks Bob

PS: What a miserable day it has been.

Almost as bad as Edgbaston, 1999! [In 1999, South Africa lost the World Cup semi-final to Australia off the last ball of the game.]'

Whatever happened in room 374 over the next few hours is now under intense scrutiny by Jamaican police. What is known is there were no signs of forcible entry and nothing was stolen from the room. Woolmer's body was discovered by a chambermaid at 10.45 a.m. He was rushed to hospital and declared dead thirty minutes later.

The Pakistan team's media manager, PJ Mir, told reporters that Woolmer was naked and there was blood, vomit and faeces on his body.

Rooms on the twelfth floor are larger than those in the rest of the hotel and were thus allocated to senior members of each squad and those requiring extra space, such as physiotherapists. Four of the Irish party were billeted there: captain Trent Johnston, coach Adrian Birrell, his assistant Matt Dwyer and physio Iain Knox, although all four were absent that night.

The hotel's security was lax before the killing. I visited batsman Jeremy Bray in his room the night before the Ireland v Pakistan match and was able to do so without any scrutiny.

Since Woolmer's death, there have been uniformed guards stationed at each of the three lifts, who travel upwards with guests, who must show a pass key.

It was a shocking end to a glittering life spent travelling the world playing and coaching the game in a way that brought him great respect and affection. Bob Woolmer was a global figure, a man whose innovative techniques brought him to the top jobs at South Africa and Pakistan – he may have been in line to coach England – and who had homes in all three countries.

Two nights before he died, Bob Woolmer was in good spirits. A big, jolly character with one of those odd accents beaten into shape by a career that took him all round the world – he was born in India and educated in England. He was holding court.

The Belisario Suite of the Pegasus Hotel was the venue for a reception hosted by the Pakistan team for the international media.

Woolmer had not been having an easy ride from the Pakistani media and his team was the most controversial in the game. Two star fast bowlers, Shoaib Akhtar and Mohammed Asif, failed drug tests last year and both dropped out of the World Cup squad on the same day, shortly before the competition. Injury was cited as the reason but no one believed that story.

Their captain, Inzamam ul-Haq, was the man who caused a test match to be abandoned in England last summer when he refused to accept an umpire's ruling that he had cheated by altering the condition of the ball.

When I arrived at the press reception it was winding down but it was still disconcerting to see the room divided into brown and white factions. The Asian pressmen stuck to themselves, lined up along one wall while Woolmer talked to the Irish and UK press at the other.

He sucked on his bottle of beer and was very entertaining in the short time I spoke with him. He gave a passable impression of an Irish accent in imitation of a fellow reporter, so I dared him to do the impression at the post-match conference the following day. He laughed and suggested he might say, 'I tought tree-tree-tree for tree was a good enough score.' The following day his team got nowhere near 333, being bowled out by Ireland for 132. I was tempted to throw his joke back at him but thought better of it.

He talked about the book he was working on, and the analysis he had done on the great players of the past. Woolmer's work with computers revolutionised cricket coaching over the last decade and he talked about this too.

He also told the Irish reporters how he knew he was out of a job once this competition was over. His contract was up on 30 June but he revealed that he had gone to his office in Lahore shortly before leaving for Jamaica to discover that it had been given to someone else.

That was so typical of cricket in that exciting but exasperating land. It was to Pakistani President Pervez Musharraf, the patron of the Pakistan cricket board, that the board's chairman Naseem Ashraf announced his resignation last week as the team were eliminated.

The sport of cricket is huge there, far bigger than any other; the route to vast millions for businessmen and enormous influence for politicians. It is also a rare way for the nation to show off on the world sporting stage. Arguably the greatest moment in Pakistan's history since independence was when the team led by Imran Khan beat England in the 1992 World Cup final.

Khan launched a political career shortly afterwards but has been thwarted in his attempts to gain even a modicum of power.

The growing strength of the economies of south Asia, especially India, means the region is now the breadbasket of world cricket. Television rights for this event brought in $2 billion to the ICC, mostly from India. Such riches are in contrast to the modest sums paid to Asian players until relatively recently. Add to that a rapidly increased number of meaningless competitions – to satisfy TV companies – and the temptation for players to play at a level short of their best is clear.

Cricket has been in thrall to Asian gambling syndicates for many years. Millions of dollars change hands every time India or Pakistan play and it doesn't take much to subvert the result. The notorious Cronjegate scandal saw three of the nine captains of the test countries banned for life for taking bribes to fix matches. Players from well-paid sides, too, such as Australia and England, were dragged into the scandal.

And now cricket has a murder on its hands. The fifteen members of the Pakistan squad who spoke movingly about their shock at Woolmer's death at a memorial service on Wednesday night awoke to hour-long police interviews and compulsory fingerprinting on Thursday. It was a final humiliation for a demoralised side.

The Ireland team continued with their preparations for the second phase, upset at the death of a fellow sportsman and bemused at the atmosphere that built up all week. The entire Irish party was away from the hotel on the night of the murder, having travelled to the resort of Ocho Rios where their families and Irish supporters were staying.

Woolmer was a great and generous friend to Ireland, lobbying for extra opportunities for junior members of cricket's family. Ireland coach Adrian Birrell, a South African who knew him well from his days coaching in that country, recalled their last meeting on Saturday night.

'He was very humble. His last words to me were that "the toss didn't matter. You would have won anyway."'

✦　✦　✦